WAITING FOR AN ECHO

ALSO BY CHRISTINE MONTROSS

Body of Work

Falling into the Fire

WAITING FOR AN ECHO

THE MADNESS
OF AMERICAN
INCARCERATION

Christine Montross, M.D.

PENGUIN PRESS ||| NEW YORK ||| 2020

PENGUIN PRESS
An imprint of Penguin Random House LLC
penguinrandomhouse.com

Epigraph from *Black Boy* by Richard Wright. Copyright, 1937, 1942, 1944, 1945
by Richard Wright; renewed © 1973 by Ellen Wright. Used by permission of
HarperCollins Publishers.

Some material from this book first appeared in "Hard Time or Hospital Treatment?
Mental Illness and the Criminal Justice System" by Christine Montross, *New England
Journal of Medicine*, October 2016 © Massachusetts Medical Society.

LIBRARY OF CONGRESS CATALOGING-IN-PUBLICATION DATA
Names: Montross, Christine, author.
Title: Waiting for an echo : the madness of American incarceration / Christine Montross, M.D.
Description: New York : Penguin Press, 2020. | Includes bibliographical references and index.
Identifiers: LCCN 2020004470 (print) | LCCN 2020004471 (ebook) |
ISBN 9781594205972 (hardcover) | ISBN 9780698152762 (ebook)
Subjects: LCSH: Prison psychology—United States. | Imprisonment—United
States—Psychological aspects. | Mentally ill—Effect of imprisonment on—United States.
Classification: LCC HV6089 .M66 2020 (print) | LCC HV6089 (ebook) |
DDC 365/.608740973—dc23
LC record available at https://lccn.loc.gov/2020004470
LC ebook record available at https://lccn.loc.gov/2020004471

Printed in the United States of America
1   3   5   7   9   10   8   6   4   2

BOOK DESIGN BY LUCIA BERNARD

Names and identifying details of patients and incarcerated individuals have been
changed to protect their privacy.

For the 2.2 million adults and children incarcerated in America, with hope.

And for Deborah and my children, with love.

I would hurl words into this darkness and wait for an echo, and if an echo sounded, no matter how faintly, I would send other words to tell, to march, to fight, to create a sense of the hunger for life that gnaws in us all. —RICHARD WRIGHT

CONTENTS

A NOTE ON NAMES

All patients and detainees in this book are real people. Their names are pseudonyms and identifying details have been changed to protect their privacy.

In my practice and in this book, I refer to my patients by their first names. I also address the incarcerated men and women I evaluate by their first names if they give me permission to do so.

The custom in most prisons is to refer to detainees by their last names. When writing about incarcerated men and women who are referred to in this way by others, I have preserved this approach in the text to accurately reflect that custom.

WAITING FOR AN ECHO

INTRODUCTION

Sonia and I are sitting in the lactation room of the prison where she is incarcerated. Neither of us needs the room for its designated purpose, but it's a room with a door. So it is one of the only places where I can conduct an evaluation without her answers being overheard by guards or other inmates. I arrange my papers, click open my pen, and ready myself to ask the questions that will help me determine whether Sonia has psychiatric symptoms severe enough to interfere with her ability to understand her charges and how the legal system works, or to prevent her from working constructively with her attorney to assist in her own defense.

Sonia is fifty years old. Her black hair is streaked with gray and pulled back into a tidy bun. She is neatly dressed in this prison's standard attire—loose denim pants with an elastic waistband, a maroon T-shirt, an oversize gray crewneck sweatshirt, and white slip-on canvas shoes. On my way to this room, I passed women ranging in age from their early twenties to their seventies, each wearing this same combination. All the clothes are identical, and none of them look new.

I open my mouth to begin the evaluation, but when I do, Sonia closes her eyes and inhales deeply through her nose. She opens her eyes, looks at me, and smiles politely. Then she inhales deeply again. And then a third time.

"Sorry, Doctor," she says sheepishly. "You smell like shampoo or something. It smells like heaven." I wonder where she's headed with this—is it a symptom or a provocation?—and then she apologizes again and looks a little embarrassed. "I hope I didn't make you uncomfortable. It's just that this is the first time I've smelled something good in seven months."

The lactation room is attached to the prison's visiting area, which looks like a combination of a high school cafeteria, with its long tables set up in parallel rows, and a day-care center. Seventy percent of America's incarcerated women are mothers of minor children, and the ratio in this facility is on par with that number. I come to this particular prison once or twice a month, and nearly every time there are children in the visiting room or waiting in the lobby for permission to enter. This morning a woman with a state Department of Children and Families badge waited behind me to pass through the metal detector, cradling a tiny infant.

"How old?" I asked her as I dropped my pen and wristwatch into a container and slid off my shoes.

"Two and a half weeks," she responded. "Mom's inside."

Adjacent to the rows of tables in the visiting room, a bright green area rug printed with cartoon figures and the letters of the alphabet covers part of the floor. *Ant . . . Boat . . . Frog. Octopus . . . Penguin . . . Zebra.* A dilapidated toy kitchen leans against one of the walls. Shelves stocked with worn picture books stand next to a wooden changing table—books that I read to my own children as they sat in my lap when they were young. *Owl Moon, Olivia,* and *Amelia Bedelia.*

This morning a woman in the denim pants and maroon shirt was sitting cross-legged on the alphabet rug. She held a nine-month-old boy in her lap and leaned intently toward another—her twins. I'd seen these babies visiting their mother here since they were three months old, and now, in jeans and little fleece jackets, they crawled and cooed at her. She laughed and clapped with them as she blinked back tears.

I HAD NEVER BEEN in jail before I became a doctor. I had an academic understanding of the many systemic challenges that face incarcerated people, but I could not have pictured this room or imagined this scenario. I had no real sense of what correctional facilities were truly like.

As a young physician finishing my training in psychiatry, I met with the director of my residency program to discuss my career. I knew there was an ongoing shortage of psychiatrists in America and that there were countless people who needed mental-health treatment across the country, let alone in my community. In the meeting, I shared with the director the job options I was weighing: an outpatient position in a program specializing in group therapy or a role on a locked inpatient unit as an attending psychiatrist for the most seriously ill patients in the hospital. I wanted a career that would be both meaningful and rewarding but also intellectually engaging. Which did she think I should choose?

"What about the prisons?" she asked me, ignoring the options I had laid out for her. "I feel like all of the most interesting doctors I know work in the prisons."

I gave little thought to her comment at the time. Why would I want to work in the prisons? Why devote my time and attention to people who had committed crimes when there were so many innocent people who needed care?

And so I chose, accepting a position as an attending psychiatrist on the Intensive Treatment Unit of a freestanding psychiatric hospital in Rhode Island. It is a job that I have loved and one that I still hold—and love—today.

The Intensive Treatment Unit is the psychiatric version of the ICU. The patients I treat are psychotic, plagued by voices or visions or paranoid delusions. Or they are in the throes of mania. Or they are actively trying to harm themselves or others. Their lives are replete with hardship. Many of my patients are homeless. Some are drug addicted. Nearly all have been victims of significant trauma. They have few safe havens, and the illnesses that besiege their minds wage a relentless war on their stability, their happiness, their safety.

It turns out that many of them also serve time in jail and prison. Sometimes patients are admitted to my care in the hospital days or even hours after being released from jail. Other times the nurses or I notice that we haven't seen one of our patients in an unusually long time and we check the Rhode Island court database only to learn that he or she has been arrested and is serving time.

Frequently the offenses that my patients recount to me after their release, or that I read about in court documentation, are indistinguishable from the behaviors that precipitate their hospital admissions. They shout in Starbucks or they linger outside stores asking for change. They steal food or subsistence items like deodorant or tampons off convenience-store shelves. They are found with drug paraphernalia. They call 911 with paranoid complaints. If in these moments the police are called, the criminal legal process begins.

Our cultural belief about mentally ill people is that they are more apt to commit crimes than are people who are mentally well. This is not the case. People with psychiatric illnesses are far more likely to be victims of crimes than they are to be perpetrators. Rarely are intersections between our mentally ill citizens and police gravely serious, involving real threats or significant violence. There are chilling exceptions, of course— Andrea Yates drowning her five children, James Holmes killing twelve in a Colorado movie theater—but these incidents, thankfully, are few and far between.

Much more often the acts for which my patients are incarcerated are neither dangerous nor violent. My patients are arrested most frequently for transgressions rooted more in their psychiatric symptomatology and poverty than in criminal intent. The distinction I once imagined between hospital and prison populations exists only faintly, when it exists at all.

My relationships with my patients—who show fortitude in the face of unfathomable challenges—have substantially complicated the binary view I once held: the view that there were people who committed crimes and then there were innocent people, and that only one of those groups was deserving of my compassion and care. Nearly a decade after my residency-training director's suggestion, I found myself compelled to learn more about how the legal system responded to—and interacted with—mentally ill citizens who became involved with police.

I wanted to better understand how—and at what points—decisions and outcomes branched for mentally ill people in the legal system. So I began performing competency-to-stand-trial evaluations in jails, situating myself on the front lines of the confluence of psychiatric illness and law enforcement. And I became a student of the system. I visited prisons and jails in America and abroad. I read stacks of books on law and on punishment. I interviewed experts in the field of corrections. And I listened to the voices of people who had served time in our nation's correctional facilities. In so doing, I began to see how poorly suited the American prison system is for those with mental illness and how the system's general practices indiscriminately shift large numbers of people who belong in therapeutic environments into punitive ones.

I also came to recognize that as a society we have decided to mitigate nearly all forms of loss—from theft and trespass to assault and murder—with incarceration. To repay harm with time. And only some of the people who are locked in our nation's correctional facilities are there by virtue of their guilt. Many others languish within prisons and jails because of their poverty, their race, their addiction, or their mental illnesses. Our aggressive carceral practices have meant that we relegate our convicted citizens to a system of imprisonment that is overcrowded, underregulated, and too often unjust.

My medical expertise is in mental health—specifically in acute cases of danger and distress. And what I found once I began working in the prisons was a system that runs counter to every principle of human flourishing that I know. Our correctional practices prioritize vengeance and suffering over justice and rehabilitation. Incarceration in America routinely makes mentally ill people worse. And just as routinely it renders stable people psychiatrically unwell. Our system is quite literally maddening—a truth that categorically undermines our stated goals of safe and secure communities.

The trajectory of my patients' lives veers sharply when law enforcement is involved. The consequences of these interactions are unpredictable. If psychiatrically ill people are sick enough or afraid enough to be potentially assaultive, the earliest decision by police as to whether they belong in jail or the hospital—a decision often made in the moment of the police encounter—may shape the course of the next many years of their lives. When the outcome is hospitalization or access to treatment, the result can be stability and safety. But when mentally unwell, dysregulated people are taken to jail, the result can be sheer disaster.

As an example, some years ago I evaluated a man named Henry in the visiting area of a men's jail. Henry was thin and disheveled, and he looked at me with guarded suspicion when the correctional officer (CO) brought him into the room where I was already seated. He was wearing a khaki prison jumpsuit with a white T-shirt underneath—and he smelled as if he had not showered in many days. I immediately noticed that Henry's mouth was in constant motion with the involuntary movements of *tardive dyskinesia*, a rare but permanent side effect that can be caused by long-term use of antipsychotic medications.

Henry had been paranoid at the time of his arrest, and his paranoia had not abated in jail. He was refusing to speak to his attorney, prompting the judge to order a competency evaluation.

According to the police report, Henry's legal involvement began when he did not leave the premises of a convenience store after the manager instructed him to. Henry hid behind the store's dumpster, refusing to come out when approached by police, and shouting paranoid statements about interrogation tactics and torture and the Connecticut militia. When he finally emerged, Henry was taken to jail. His charges—criminal trespass and resisting arrest—carried a maximum combined sentence of two years in prison.

But Henry's situation, like that of many psychotic detainees, became far more dire. Henry was prescribed an antipsychotic medication in jail but refused to take it. He might have been paranoid about the pills' safety or might not have had insight into the fact that he needed treatment. At some point shortly after his arrest, he would not come out of his cell when asked to do so. He was then forced out by COs—a procedure called a "cell extraction." Still paranoid, but now with no dumpster to hide behind, Henry resisted this time by fighting back.

In our nation's correctional facilities, detainees who become assaultive are typically sent to administrative segregation—a punitive form of solitary confinement known to exacerbate symptoms of mental illness. Worse still, assaulting a correctional officer is a felony charge, which in Henry's state carries a maximum sentence of fifteen years in prison and a fifteen-thousand-dollar penalty. If convicted, Henry would spend years in prison, where mentally ill people face a disproportionate risk of being victimized. He would eventually leave prison on probation, with legal requirements that would be difficult for him to manage if his symptoms returned—setting him up to incur additional time behind bars.

Compare Henry's situation to that of Robert, a psychotic man who caused a similar disturbance in the community. Robert, too, was plagued by paranoid delusions. He had come into contact with police while yelling loudly in the streets of his neighborhood that he was an unwitting experimental subject in a secret government program. But unlike Henry, Robert was admitted to my inpatient unit after police decided to bring him to the hospital rather than to jail.

Robert was a large, muscular man in his late fifties with a lumbering gait and erratically mussed white hair. He sat on the periphery of the unit and regarded everyone around him with suspicion. Once he was hospitalized, Robert's paranoia became rooted in a fervent belief that the hospital environment was a front and that he was, in fact, being held in a covert government facility where he was awaiting execution. Like Henry, he refused to take prescribed antipsychotic medication. As a result, his paranoid symptoms had improved little since admission.

One night new personnel were being trained on the hospital ward.

Robert was in the kitchen when a staff member began demonstrating how, in case of an emergency, electronic safety blinds could be activated to cover the wall of windows that separated the kitchen from the rest of the unit. Robert became terrified by the movement of the security blinds and, in the throes of his paranoia, interpreted their closure as a signal. He believed that the unit staff was cordoning off the kitchen in preparation to execute the patients held within.

Robert ran out of the kitchen, screaming to the other patients, "Tonight's the night they're going to kill us all!" In what he believed was self-defense in a moment of mortal peril, he began attacking the staff. In less than a minute, he assaulted and injured numerous staff members. Two female mental-health workers suffered concussions, one of them hit so hard by Robert that her supervisor later said that "she flew off her feet like a rag doll." A male staff member who intervened and tried to subdue Robert was brought to the floor by him, kicked in the head, and eventually required knee surgery for injuries sustained in the altercation.

Despite the severity of the attack, none of the injured workers felt that it was appropriate to press charges. They each offered the same explanation: Robert was clearly ill and had been acting out of his illness. He inflicted an enormous amount of damage, but no one perceived him to have done so with malicious intent. As the unit's nursing supervisor said to me in describing Robert's aggression, "He was in pure terror. He thought he was fighting for his life."

Robert eventually began taking appropriate medications, and his paranoia diminished. After fifteen days he was discharged home with outpatient treatment arranged by the hospital team.

Henry, in contrast, remained incarcerated, facing the prospect of spending the next decade and a half of his life in prison.

Henry's story is not an aberration. I have seen countless detainees who faced significant time in prison in just these sorts of circumstances. A man who spent six months in jail for tearing up toilet paper in a shopping mall and shouting profanities at passersby. A woman who spent thirty-eight days in jail after being arrested for sleeping on the floor of a city hospital that, when she was booked for the crime, she listed as her home address.

If these mentally ill detainees become assaultive or are unable to follow police instructions or jail rules, the manifestations of their symptoms lead to harsher punishment, longer periods of incarceration, and lost years of their lives. In precisely this way, our overcrowded correctional facilities become inundated with the psychiatrically ill, straining our prison system and draining money from state coffers.

The first part of this book, then, is about how people wind up in prison. It is not what we have assumed.

No matter how a person has come to be imprisoned, however, everyone behind bars is treated the same. Correctional facilities in our country operate under the absolute—if erroneous—belief that all who are incarcerated have done wrong and that those who have done wrong deserve punishment.

And so the second part of this book is an honest examination of how we treat people in prison: how our approach affects them *and* how it affects us. The outcome is not what we have intended.

I once toured Manson Youth Institution, a high-security prison in Connecticut for fourteen- to twenty-year-old boys. On the tour I was led through one of the prison housing units, which, despite looking like typical cellblocks, are euphemistically referred to as "cottages."

As we walked through the hallways, we passed one cell in which a boy was alone, standing on his toilet, neck craned, stretching his face toward the ceiling and talking out loud at full speed. I said nothing, assuming that the boy was mentally ill. After all, I frequently see actively hallucinating patients who are in conversation with visions that no one else can see or voices that no one else can hear. "Responding to internal stimuli" is the notation I make in the chart to record that my patient remains tethered to these perceptual abnormalities of psychosis.

Down the hallway we then passed another boy in another cell in the exact same position, doing the exact same thing, at which point I knew that the conclusion I had come to was wrong. Though I've seen an incalculable number of patients in the throes of psychosis, I have never seen the symptoms of mental illness manifest themselves identically in different people.

"Why are they standing on their toilets?" I asked the CO.

"It's a big problem," he said. "They figured out that they can talk to each other through the vents. It's loud in here, and also they get in trouble if they're shouting out their cell doors, so that's the only way they've got to talk to each other. They climb on their toilets to get up near the vents, and then they have whole conversations that way."

More than any other scenario that I've encountered in my career as a psychiatrist, this moment has stood out for me as incontrovertible evidence of the fundamental need for connection within us all. These boys on their toilets embodied the lengths of discomfort and risk and innovation that human beings will go to in order to reach out to another. To hear from another. To be heard by another. To wait for an echo. These are children in a critical period of neurodevelopment, in extraordinary circumstances, trying desperately not to go through it all alone.

It is disingenuous for us to imagine that the harsh environments in which we house imprisoned men, women, and children do not damage them. And it is unwise for us to ignore that damaging our imprisoned citizens undermines our communities more broadly.

Ninety-five percent of all inmates in America are eventually released from prison and return to our communities. Yet we willfully ignore the ramifications of releasing people into our neighborhoods directly from correctional environments that are designed for maximum punishment and control. Some people are released directly from solitary confinement to the streets. Some from *years* spent in solitary to the streets.

Five Mualimm-Ak is a prison activist who served nearly twelve years on weapons possession charges. Five of those years were spent in solitary confinement in New York State. Since his release he has worked with numerous human rights organizations, including the Campaign to End the New Jim Crow and the New York Campaign for Alternatives to Isolated Confinement, to protest the continued use of isolation in our nation's prisons.

"I was in Upstate, a supermax prison way up by the Canadian border," Mualimm-Ak writes of the day of his release. "I was in solitary confinement when a guard came to my cell one morning and said, 'No breakfast today. You're getting out.' I was handcuffed and searched, and then brought to the gate, where I was uncuffed, asked to sign a paper, and given a bag of my property and $40. Then I was outside, by myself. It was 7:00 a.m. I just stood there for a long time until a van came to take me to the bus station. It was like a dream. They gave me a ticket and I climbed onto the bus, and I was so overwhelmed that I slept for nine hours. When I woke up I was in the [New York City] Port Authority Bus Terminal, which has to be one of the most crowded, crazy places in the world. I remember folding up right there in the bus station. I didn't know it at the time, but I was having my first panic attack. I was sweating, and I could feel my heart beating in my chest and my eyes darting back and forth. I just slid down to the floor in a corner."

My profession has allowed me to witness that there are forces that determine mental health that we can control and other forces that we cannot. There is suffering brought about by brutal diseases that we do not yet know how to conquer or cure—schizophrenia, with its hallucinations, delusions, and functional decline, is one of the foremost examples.

And then there is suffering brought about by preventable causes—by social ills, by racial and economic disparities, by injustice. There is suffering that we intentionally inflict upon one another. These are all wounds that can be studied, fought against, and rectified. Some can even be prevented altogether. After years of pain and broken reform, the question is whether, as a society, we truly want to work at diminishing this suffering.

Many important books and a great deal of meticulous journalistic coverage have established unequivocally that our legal system distributes justice with prejudice and without uniformity. These are truths. They are facts of the world.

This book maintains a focus on mental health and mental illness: my areas of expertise. However, my examination of our legal system is at all times held within a framework of understanding that people of color are disproportionately overrepresented in correctional populations, African American men exponentially so. Michelle Alexander's incontrovertible analysis of the racial injustice at the core of mass incarceration, *The New Jim Crow*, is required reading on this subject.

The aim of this book—its only aim—is to look closely at the psychiatric effects of American punishment and ask whether the results we yield align with the societal standards to which we hold ourselves and with the goals we set out to achieve. This is a question with enormous stakes for all of us—free and imprisoned alike.

We say that we incarcerate people in America because we want safer communities and justice, yet our current practices provide neither. Our practices are antithetical to these aims. My years of study of the human mind underscore this fact: when we condemn our citizens to the punitive conditions of our jails and prisons, we sentence those men and women and children not only to time but to a life in which they are less able to engage productively with society and less likely to demonstrate accountability for their actions. As a nation we say we want safety and justice, but our methods of punishment actively obstruct these very goals. And yet we double down on our current practices. *Why?*

The third part of this book, therefore, is about the choices that face us. If we look objectively at our prisoners and our prisons and determine that our current practices are failing us, then what are we to do about it?

The plain fact that I have learned in writing this book, as a Swedish prison worker once told me, is that prison is sometimes good but it is always bad. Bad for the mentally ill, without question, but also bad for human beings in general and even bad for the very communities that prisons are ostensibly designed to protect.

Before I began working in our nation's jails, I did not understand this. I believe that we as a society do not understand this. Even those in charge of our justice system—the very lawyers and judges who send people to prison for years—do not understand this.

"In law school, I never heard about corrections," the former Supreme Court justice Anthony Kennedy said in a 2015 congressional hearing. "Lawyers are fascinated with the guilt/innocence adjudication process. Once [it] is over, we have no interest in corrections. Doctors and psychiatrists know more about the corrections system than we do."

Justice Kennedy was right that it will take mental-health professionals, whose vocation it is to help those in acute distress, to find a way through the maddening system we have created. Corrections, as we have currently and historically enacted them, are a profoundly broken enterprise. This is not news. But we haven't fully comprehended what our jail and prison system is doing to the mental health of *all* incarcerated people, what it is doing to our fellow citizens, and what it is doing to our society. The pound of flesh we require is not just time. It is the sanity of all involved.

This book shares what I have come to know, as a psychiatrist, about our nation's corrections system. "The degree of civilization in a society can be judged by entering its prisons," Fyodor Dostoyevsky wrote more than a century ago. This book is about the choices we make in our society about safety and justice. It is about how we mistreat those who run afoul of our laws and how, in doing so, we violate our own standards of humanity. It is also about hope, and vision, and trust that once a problem is faced—truly faced—then perhaps it can be solved.

PART I

Our Prisoners

1.

THREE HOTS AND A COT

Frank was a fifty-three-year-old man with a long history of psychosis. He had been charged with two misdemeanors—breach of peace and assault in the third degree—after going off his psychiatric medications and getting into an argument with his eighty-seven-year-old father. According to the police report, the father had been sitting out in the yard when Frank began "yelling and screaming about religion." Frank had come outside, wearing only a towel, waving an American flag attached to a wooden stick. Hearing the commotion, a neighbor looked out the window and saw Frank strike his father and then throw the flag at him. She immediately called the police. Frank's father was bleeding when the officers arrived. When the police tried to speak to Frank, he told them that they should go ahead and shoot him, because ISIS had been trying to track him down in order to behead him and he'd grown tired of being on the run.

When there are concerns about a criminal defendant's ability to comprehend and participate in his legal proceedings, the court orders a competency-to-stand-trial evaluation to be performed by a mental-health clinician. These concerns might arise in the setting of intellectual disability or cognitive impairment, as when a defendant's IQ is low enough to render him unable to understand the specific roles of each person in the courtroom—prosecutor, judge, defense attorney. Or when a person who has been accused of committing a crime suffers from dementia and cannot remember his charges, or even the event for which he's been charged. More often, however, competency evaluations are ordered by the court when the defense attorney or the judge has a concern that a defendant's mental illness may be interfering with his ability to understand or engage with his case.

As a psychiatric examiner, I am asked by the courts to give my opinion as to whether I believe a defendant meets the legal standards for competency. The "legal standards" part is important because competency is a legal, not a clinical, term. This distinction is a significant one. As a physician, I am capable of diagnosing patients. A judge is not. *Schizophrenia*, I may write in my hospitalized patient's chart after carefully determining that he meets the specific diagnostic criteria for the disease. Or *Major Depressive Disorder with Psychotic Features*. Or *Antisocial Personality Disorder*. These are medical diagnoses, made by trained clinicians. A judge cannot deem a person to have bipolar disorder or schizophrenia.

Similarly, as a physician, I cannot declare a defendant to be competent or incompetent to stand trial, nor may I render him legally sane or insane in the eyes of the law. The judge will take my expert opinion into account in rendering her decision. In most cases she will align her decision with my opinion, but she is not in any way mandated to do so. In the end a defendant's legal competence is the judge's—and the judge's alone—to designate. Indeed, the language utilized by the courts—the *legal* language of mental illness—is an entirely different language from the *clinical* language of psychiatry. And though to this day defendants can be found by the courts not guilty by reason of insanity, the term "insanity" in medicine is a linguistic relic. A nonspecific, pejorative, historical term that was used (and misused) in psychiatry in sweeping ways to classify not only illness but also deviance, disobedience, and even disability. However, the courts deal in standards and precedents rather than diagnoses and treatment. The discrepancy is noteworthy because it demonstrates how the system, from the outset, misapprehends what we know about mental health.

In addition to demonstrating a *factual* understanding of his case and of court proceedings, a defendant must also show that he is capable of a *rational* understanding. My work, then, is to methodically assess a defendant's capacity for trust and understanding. To do so I must create a lucid joining of the territory of medicine and the territory of the law. With a clinician's eye, I describe the symptoms I see and I determine the relevant diagnoses. Yet instead of formulating my medical conclusions with the intention to guide treatment, I must use my findings to answer the court's specific questions and meet its legal standards. I undertake this bridging of worlds with an awareness of the ways that mentally unwell people challenge our overloaded legal system. If unnoticed, their illnesses can easily cause them to get lost in the momentum of the court and the machinery of the legal process, resulting in unjust outcomes. My hope is that in lending my clinical expertise to the process I can ensure that the courts must pause to consider whether a defendant's mental illness might unfairly handicap him as the legal proceedings unfold.

On the morning I evaluated Frank, he had been removed from the general population of the jail and housed in the facility's mental-health unit for nearly a week. The materials I reviewed before the interview showed that on the jail's one-to-five mental-health classification scale, Frank had been deemed a five—the ranking that indicated the most serious active symptoms of psychiatric illness. The Connecticut Department of Corrections (DOC) definition of that highest designation reads as follows: *These individuals are severely impaired with an acute psychiatric condition such as major psychosis, affective disorder or major depression, or acute anxiety. These offenders represent a potential danger to self and/or others and are gravely disabled.*

Typically, competency evaluations—like legal meetings—are held in private rooms within jails' visiting areas. However, inmates who are housed in the mental-health unit are not considered psychiatrically stable enough to come to the visiting area, and so instead I wind through the locked concrete hallways, escorted by a correctional officer, to reach the jail's mental-health housing unit.

I am led into a small room where Frank is sitting in a wheelchair. During the interview I ask him why he's in the wheelchair, and he says, "I'm a mess. I'm in a fog," and then begins speaking nonsensically about how Satan interferes with his desire to obtain justice. There is no medical explanation for the wheelchair provided, no history known to me about his having used a wheelchair prior to his incarceration. Indeed, the police report that describes him yelling while entering and exiting the house also includes a section about his calling down to his father from upstairs.

Frank is wearing a prison garment called a "Ferguson gown": a thickly padded, army-green, sleeveless variety of hospital gown fastened with Velcro at the shoulders. I know this means he has nothing on underneath. This attire is one form of risk reduction. It is thick enough so it cannot be tied in a tight knot; it is fashioned with enough Velcro closures so that it can stay on but would come apart with any kind of weight or pressure. The design has minimized any way in which the cloth could be manipulated to be used as a noose or a weapon.

I have seen other male detainees wearing a garment that resembles a shower wrap—a padded rectangle of fabric that wraps around the waist like a sarong and has Velcro closures. I once saw a frail elderly woman with schizophrenia who was being held in the mental-health unit of the women's prison after voicing suicidal thoughts to an officer. The information I had gotten prior to the evaluation was that she was so disorganized that she was constantly walking around naked in her cell. When I evaluated her, however, she was relatively lucid and remained so throughout the interview. I asked her about the reports of her walking around naked, and she blushed with embarrassment.

"The gown is too heavy," she said. "I'm not strong enough to stand up with it on. So when I want to walk over to the toilet or to the door to get my meal tray, I have to take it off."

Frank sits wearing his Ferguson gown in his wheelchair behind a table. I sit down across the table from him. But his wheelchair is positioned so that he faces the side wall of the room rather than facing me. I don't know why he has turned that way, but I assume he's done so to avoid my gaze.

"Is it okay if we have the officers turn you so that we're looking at each other, Frank?" I ask. Frank does not respond, but the CO shakes his head no.

"Can't reach," says the CO, gesturing toward Frank's lap. I look to see what he means. When I do, I see that Frank's hands are cuffed at the wrists and that the cuffs are shackled to a metal loop on the wall by a chain strung between cuffs and wall. I look back at the CO.

"Is this the best we can do?" I ask, somewhat incredulous about the degree to which this wheelchair-bound man is restrained.

The CO tries to maneuver the chair, and after several jostling attempts we end up with Frank no longer facing the side wall but facing the corner of the room over my right shoulder. It is all I'm going to get.

Frank is distractible and irritable. He struggles to respond to even the most straightforward questions. After a few failed efforts to get him to discuss his charges, I move on to basic questions about his birthplace, his family, his upbringing. Sometimes when defendants become annoyed or angry when discussing their legal cases, they fare better on the psychosocial-history portion of the exam. Frank does not. When asked how many siblings he has, he responds, "Quite a few, that's all I can tell you." When asked how his mood is this morning, he says, "I plead the Fifth." He refuses to answer most of the questions I ask him. When he does respond to questions, he rambles on unintelligibly about God, about how mental illness is "a lie to pacify Satan," and how his attorney is a "turncoat" and a "traitor." At times in the middle of a sentence, he trails off, closes his eyes, and tugs at his unclean beard or greasy, disheveled hair.

I ask Frank whether he has been prescribed psychiatric medications, and he responds that he has been but that he stopped taking them some time ago. "My father thinks I should stay on them," he tells me, acknowledging that this very subject had been one of the recurrent arguments with his father. "Father doesn't always know best."

I determine quickly that Frank does not meet the legal standard for competency to stand trial. Though I attempt to guide him through the entire interview, his paranoia supersedes me. Before long he begins politely declining to answer my "nosy" questions. Eventually he refuses to continue the evaluation at all and asks to leave the room, a request that is completely within his rights.

Frequently the evaluees I see are more capable than Frank of tolerating the entire interview. Sometimes they are even less so.

When I see Shaniece Andrews, she is curled in a fetal position, lying on a thin white blanket on the concrete floor of her cell in the mental-health ward of a women's prison. She clutches the edge of the blanket beneath her in her fists and pulls it up beneath her chin. I peer through the window into the cell but cannot see her face. I see only her curled body atop the blanket. The crown of her head is closest to the door, closest to me, and through the window I see that her hair—matted in disorganized, three- to four-inch-long dreadlocks—is flecked with white specks. Lint, maybe. Or dandruff. Or something else I am not close enough to see.

The CO had tried to get Shaniece to leave her cell to come talk to me but had been unable to coax her to do so. I decided to see whether Shaniece would speak to me if I went to her cell.

"You want me to open the trap?" the CO asks, referring to the locked, rectangular opening in the cell's formidable metal door. The CO is a friendly young blond woman. She has a strong build, and her cheeks are pink, as if she's been out in the cold. She looks as if she cannot be more than twenty-three or twenty-four years old. Had I seen her on the street, out of uniform, I would have guessed she was a soccer coach, or an EMT, or a golf pro. I wonder how she ended up with this job.

"Thanks," I say. She leans down and pulls a key from a jangling set toward a lock on the door. She turns the key, slides a thick metal bar to the side with a loud clank, and tugs on the rectangular door of the trap, which opens out toward us like a breadbox, a mailbox, a garbage chute. The trap is at the level of my thighs. I squat down in front of it and call through it to the woman on the floor.

"Good morning, Ms. Andrews," I say. "I'm Dr. Montross, a psychiatrist."

There is no response.

I continue. "The judge has asked me to come and talk to you to make sure you understand some things about your charges and about what will happen in court. It's called a 'competency-to-stand-trial exam,'" I explain, "and I need to ask you some questions to get some information for the court. Do you understand what I just said?"

After a long pause, the woman props herself up from the floor on one elbow and turns her head slowly to look at me. She is young—twenty-two according to the papers delineating her charges and her attorney's concerns about her mental health. Maybe the exact age of the pink-cheeked correctional officer who has opened the trap for me. Shaniece is thin and wide-eyed. She is also trembling. She meets my gaze briefly, then fixes her own gaze on the corner of her cell.

"Ms. Andrews?" I ask again, peering through the trap. "Can you look at me?"

"Yes," she says, turning to me for a moment, then turning away again, still propped on her elbow, still focused on the place where the cell walls meet, up near the ceiling. A place where I see nothing but concrete and space.

"Do you understand why I'm here, Ms. Andrews?"

"Yes," she says, after a long pause.

"Why am I here?" I ask. "Can you explain it to me so that I know you understand?"

"Yes," she says. She pauses again. Then, "No."

We go on like this for a few minutes. I ask her basic questions through the trap. After long periods of silence, she answers in single syllables that don't reveal anything about whether she is following what I'm asking of her, whether she comprehends what I'm saying. As she quivers on the floor and squints her eyes at the corner of the cell, she seems terrified.

In the interspaces between her answers, I jot down notes, gleaning whatever information I can from my observations. *Internally preoccupied*, I write. *Prominent speech latency. Thought blocking. Responding to internal stimuli. Minimal eye contact. One answer contradicts the next. Paucity of speech.* I look around her small cell. There is a bare plastic mattress on a molded plastic bed. At the foot of the bed is a standard jail toilet, modular and stainless steel, without a seat. There is a drain in the center of the room. The walls are covered with scrawled names, drawings, numerals—an accumulation of imprints left by untold numbers of mentally ill women held in this room over the years. I think of each of them here in their isolation but somehow connected through time and space.

And now this woman, scared and huddled on the floor. I angle my face so that she can see me through the trap, see that I mean her no harm. The noise from the unit is so loud that after I ask a question, I turn my head to place my ear next to the opening of the trap and wait to see whether an audible answer will come.

Another woman yells from the cell beside us. Bangs loudly on her cell door. Yells some more. "Do you have a fucking identity card, you whore?" she is shouting at my back. "I see your badge, and I know who you think you are impersonating!"

Down the hallway there is a stretching group in progress for inmates who are well enough to come out of their cells. A Justin Bieber song plays from a portable speaker while a group of women do modified push-ups against the wall and sing along. COs shout down the hallways to one another, and voices buzz and break through the walkie-talkies they wear on their belts. With each loud noise, Shaniece flinches as if she is about to be hit.

She is incapable of answering the questions I pose. It is unimaginable that she could participate in her court case in any kind of a meaningful way.

Her charge is a minor one—assault in the third degree for getting into a fight with her adult sisters and throwing a tricycle at them. The maximum penalty associated with assault in the third degree is one year. Many people facing this charge would be sentenced to probation or to a program, without serving any prison time whatsoever. It's highly possible that for someone like Shaniece without a prior criminal record, such a charge would simply be dismissed.

But because her psychiatric illness has required sequestration on the mental-health unit and rendered her unable to participate meaningfully in any court proceedings, by the time I see Shaniece, she has already been in jail for four months. She is incarcerated when she should be hospitalized.

IT IS NOW WELL UNDERSTOOD that the closing of state psychiatric hospitals in the 1960s, '70s, and '80s led directly to the influx of mentally ill people into correctional facilities. In 1955 state psychiatric hospitals held more than 500,000 patients with severe mental illness. Today our jails and state prisons contain an estimated 356,000 inmates with serious mental illness, while only about 35,000 people with serious mental illness are being treated in state hospitals—stark evidence of the decimation of the public mental-health system. This reality is worth reiterating: ten times more people with serious mental illness are in our nation's correctional facilities than in our state psychiatric hospitals.

Deinstitutionalization—the term used to describe releasing large numbers of people from residential state hospitals—was born of the coalescence of social, economic, and pharmacologic forces. In the 1950s the landscape of psychiatry was changing. The first antipsychotic medications became widely available, with neuroleptic medicines like Thorazine showing remarkable promise in treating the hallucinations and delusional symptoms characteristic of psychotic illnesses. Chronic mentally ill patients who had been relegated to spend their lives in institutions began to improve; some could even go home.

The prospect of liberating tens of thousands of people from long-term psychiatric institutions was thrilling, especially given the egregious treatment and even abuse that many of the facilities' residents at the time endured in the name of psychiatric "care." Organizers and advocates saw life-changing possibility for mentally ill citizens to leave the isolation of their institutions and return to their communities, and federal law concurred. In 1963 the Community Mental Health Centers Act was passed, with the intention of shifting care for the mentally ill out of the asylums and into the communities. State mental hospitals across the country were closed, suddenly seen as relics of a bygone and backward era. But as is often the case with governmental progress, a critical component of the deinstitutionalization equation never came through. Funds for services that would provide essential care to patients in their communities were not adequately allocated, and the promises of resources that had been made—from psychiatric treatment to vocational training to social supports—never materialized.

In a further pendulum swing toward "patient rights," many states passed legislation making it more difficult to hospitalize and medicate patients against their will. A policy intended to honor individual autonomy and protect personal liberty in fact meant that people desperately in need of treatment—whose decision-making abilities were compromised by their illness and symptoms—languished, untreated, on the margins of our society. Civil libertarians fought not only for deinstitutionalization but also for psychiatric patients to retain an expansive autonomy in deciding whether or not to take medications. This fierce idealism lost sight of the fact that the affected organ in psychiatric illness *is* the decision-making organ. It also lost sight of the fact that severe mental illness can in itself be a form of imprisonment.

As Dr. Elinore McCance-Katz, the U.S. assistant secretary of health and human services for mental health and substance use, told me, "If mental-health advocates are still talking about civil rights" instead of fighting for access to treatment, food, and housing, "they have outlived

their time. I don't consider it advocacy to argue for the civil right to remain ill and to live under an overpass."

Without funds, without treatment, and suddenly also without housing, the population of mentally ill Americans that had filled the state
hospitals suddenly filled our urban streets. Begging for money, sleeping
in doorways, and causing disturbances due to their untreated symptoms,
our nation's most vulnerable citizens had fallen out of the auspices of
health care and into the realm of the legal system. The criminalization
of mental illness had begun.

SOON AFTER I begin performing competency evaluations, I arrange to
visit Rhode Island's Adult Correctional Institute (ACI) High Security
Center (HSC), described as a "super maximum security facility which
houses inmates who require close custody, control, and security." Held
in the HSC are detainees who have committed the most serious violent
crimes, who chronically violate prison rules, or who require a high level
of security and observation due to the fact that they themselves are being victimized within the general prison population, as well as mentally
ill inmates who become violent or self-injurious. The high level of security comes with a high cost. In comparison to the annual cost per detainee at, for example, the ACI's Medium Security facility, which was
$44,467 in 2017, holding a man in the HSC for that same year cost the
state $208,911, nearly five times as much.

John Adams worked twelve years as a CO, seven years as a lieutenant,
and five years as a captain at the ACI before being appointed the deputy
warden of the HSC, which the ACI staff and inmates call "the high side."
Like many Rhode Islanders, Deputy Warden Adams has spent his adult
life in the neighborhoods and community where he was raised. Over the
years he has seen firsthand the physical markers of what has come to be
called "transinstitutionalization"—the movement of mentally ill patients
from one institution to another: from hospitals to prisons.

When I meet with him in his office, Adams gestures out the window to the sprawling campus of brick buildings that surrounds us. "When I was a little boy, these buildings were almost all mental health," he says. "Now they're almost all corrections." The buildings are labeled differently; the people within them are the same.

Deputy Warden Adams introduces me to Lieutenant Macombe, a correctional officer who works on the high side. Macombe guides my visit through the facility, and as we walk, he describes how easily detainees with pathological symptoms can slip through the cracks. "The psychiatrists here are overextended," he tells me. "Of the ninety-three inmates who are in high security right now, sixty-five of them are seen by mental health. So I'd say the psychiatrist sees each inmate for maybe ten or fifteen minutes a week, if that. Sometimes that means it can take up to a year for the psychiatrist to understand what's actually going on.

"There was one guy not too long ago who was diabetic. He kept complaining about one of his toes and he didn't feel like his medical complaints were being taken seriously, even though the doctors were on it," Macombe continues, describing a particularly galling incident that had stayed with him. "The psychiatrist considered him to be just a management problem, just someone who was acting up. But the officers? We saw that he was drinking curdled milk, talking to himself in his cell, not bathing—I mean, there was not a lucid conversation to be had with him. But he denied all of this to the psychiatrist for eight, nine months, maybe. Then out of the blue said, 'I have to cut my toes off because they won't give me medical treatment.' And he did it. He actually cut one off." Macombe shakes his head.

"We're really good at gangs," Lieutenant Macombe says to me then. "We're good at assaults. But you throw mental illness in there . . ." He pauses. "These are sick men. We are designed to use force. This system is not designed to help them." He pauses again, then says, "Everyone tries."

Later that day I head to the administrative building on the ACI's campus to meet with A. T. Wall, the longtime director of the Rhode

Island Department of Corrections who has since retired. He emphatically says that the numbers of psychiatrically ill inmates are significant and that their presence in the state's correctional facilities has raised a chicken-or-egg question as to the moral responsibilities of prisons in the era of transinstitutionalization.

"Are we going to accept the fact that larger numbers are coming into the correctional system and fund it to provide treatment?" he asks me rhetorically, "or are we going to rebuild the community mental-health-care system? Right now the answer has been: neither one."

Some argue that at least correctional facilities provide an opportunity for ill people to receive care. But even when compared with locked units in psychiatric hospitals, correctional facilities have obvious fundamental differences. When the treating facility is a prison, safety, security, and punishment necessarily take precedence over recovery and care. This distinction—between a correctional facility and a therapeutic one—has moral implications. It also has practical ones.

The correctional system is designed around a logical framework. "We have rules," Wall says. "If you break those rules, then there are consequences. The consequences are meant to dissuade you from breaking those rules again in the future. When we get severely mentally ill people in our facility, they are not able to follow that logic. So there is a misalignment between our model and their processing."

As a psychiatrist, I recognize this concept of misalignment as a critical one. The patients I treat in my hospital have often been admitted to my care precisely because they are unable to conform to the expectations of their families and communities. A manic patient blows through his family's entire savings on a rapid binge of unwise purchases and investments, and his wife brings him into the hospital seeking help. His behavior is not only irrational and irresponsible but is out of line with what his family expects and needs. A psychotic patient repeatedly calls 911 insisting that she is being stalked by a construction company that is rearranging her furniture and sending poisonous gases through her heating vents. The police bring her to the hospital because her behavior is monopolizing the time and resources of the town's emergency services, which could potentially interfere with their ability to respond to citizens in true crises. A depressed patient cannot get out of bed and thus misses work for days on end, angering his employer and jeopardizing his job. A teenager begins cutting herself at her group home, violating the organization's rules about safety, and risks eviction. The very nature of mental illness is often defined in part by deviations from expected norms of behavior. Psychiatric hospitals perform a critical service, providing a safe, specialized environment for impaired patients to be treated and cared for as their psychological equilibrium is restored.

Within a correctional setting, the misalignment between the symptoms of mental illness and the expectations of the jail or prison has grave consequences. It renders the already difficult jobs of correctional officers more challenging still. Most receive minimal mental-health training, if any at all.

A Rhode Island correctional officer who has held his position for more than twenty-five years tells me, "We're not trained for that. We are trained in suicide prevention, yes. Otherwise, the mental-health stuff? Like when people break down or have psychotic breaks? I guess I'd say it's on-the-job training."

So in addition to their charges of maintaining order and safety, COs must now also handle the erratic—and potentially dangerous—behaviors of psychiatrically ill inmates. This contributes to burnout, frustration, and even fear among officers.

The misalignment also leads to unintended consequences for the incarcerated mentally ill. "Over and over again, I just watch them bury themselves for years in seg time," Deputy Warden Adams says with a tone of regret, referring to administrative segregation. If inmates break rules often enough—or if they break a serious rule like assault even once—they can be sent to seg. This form of punishment is assigned by neither judge nor jury but is rather adjudicated and administered entirely within the correctional facility. Detainees earn their way out of seg through enduring the mere passage of time and by adhering to specific behavioral rules and regulations as they do so. Conversely, violations of those rules can lead to additional infractions, thereby extending the duration of seg time.

This was the deputy warden's point. That if a mentally ill person is sent to seg in the first place because of his inability to conform to the rules and behavioral expectations in prison, he is no more likely to be able to follow the rules in seg, an environment that has been definitively demonstrated to exacerbate symptoms of mental illness. Failure to follow the rules leads to further discipline in the form of additional seg time—days, weeks, months, even years.

I once saw a man who'd been jailed for a minor charge but who, once incarcerated, began to intentionally ingest objects as an act of self-harm and strike out with aggression toward prison officers and staff. Despite the minor nature of his original offense, he quickly accrued additional charges for rule violations and assaults. The man posed a conundrum for the jail administration. Keeping him locked up only perpetuated his behavior and caused additional problems. But letting him go made the prison staff feel unsupported and unprotected and sent the message to the inmate that he could act in a threatening way without consequences.

As rules are broken and the period of incarceration is extended, this maladaptive cycle continues, racking up additional costs for taxpayers. The detainee is harmed by continued incarceration. The correctional staff is harmed by having to deal with a problematic, mentally ill inmate for a prolonged period of time. And society is harmed by paying ever-increasing sums of money to continue to incarcerate someone who never posed a significant danger to the community in the first place.

DURING MY VISIT to Rhode Island's High Security Center, Lieutenant Macombe takes me to a pod of cells within the prison called the Observation Status Unit (OSU). The OSU is a psychiatric observation area designed to house inmates with serious mental-health issues—"our most challenging mentally ill inmates," as A. T. Wall had described them to me. The detainees who are held here may be sent from any of the state's DOC facilities when serious psychiatric concerns arise. Floridly psychotic men shout at their voices and visions; paranoid men lash out against their cellmates; disorganized men climb into the wrong bed, or continuously disrobe, or defecate in the cell's sink. Some of the men here are so suicidal that they must be watched to be prevented from hanging themselves, or they are chronically self-injurious and so must be continuously monitored to be sure they do not bang their heads against cell walls or bite their own limbs or tear into their own skin.

The OSU is arranged in a line: a small number of cells facing an observation pod so that the COs can look into each cell at any moment, twenty-four hours a day. The men held here are single-celled—solitary confinement for psychiatric rather than punitive reasons, though of course the effects of isolation are indistinguishable, even when the motives differ. The officers stationed there point out different men to me who are behind the thick, clear windows of their metal cell doors.

"That's a guy whose water we have to limit," an officer tells me, gesturing to one cell. "He was trying to drink himself to death. Then that guy there ran over his wife with a car," he says, gesturing to another. I look through the window, and a man stands in the doorway rocking back and forth and laughing to himself. "He doesn't speak any English at all," the officer says. "Not a word."

"Then there's this guy," a lieutenant on the unit says, pointing to a young, heavyset man with what we in medicine would call "dysmorphic features"—an asymmetrical, atypical facial structure that can indicate some kind of underlying genetic anomaly. "He's mental health, but he's also mentally retarded," the officer says, using the archaic term for intellectual disability with sympathy and without any trace of malice. "He's basically here for his own protection. Other inmates would tell him how terrible he was, and they'd convince him the only thing to do was to hang himself. That ending his life would be the only way to solve his problems and that his family would be better off without him. Then he'd try to do it, and they'd rush in and rescue him. You know, be the Good Samaritan.

Because of that they'd get a reduction in their time." He curls his lip in disgust. "They used him as a toy."

The fact that the men in the OSU are under constant observation, or on "psych obs" status, means that on each shift each detainee has his own page assigned to him, which must be filled out by the COs in charge of the psychiatric surveillance. In bold letters across the top of the sheet is printed RHODE ISLAND DEPARTMENT OF CORRECTIONS CRISIS MANAGE-MENT STATUS (CMS) CHECKLIST. It reads as follows:

Date: _____ Reason for Observation: _____

Inmate name: _____ On Medication(s)? [ ] yes   [ ] no

Housing Location: _____

Items allowed while on CMS:

Item	YES	NO
Undergarments		
Safety Blanket		
Safety Smock		
Mattress		
Pillow		
One Book		
Legal Material		
Utensils		
Showers		
Attorney Visits		
Visits		
Phone Calls		

Item	YES	NO
Prosthesis(es)		
Eye Glasses		
Dentures		

Checklist to be completed every ten (10) minutes *on* each shift *by correctional staff.*

Time Checked	Code	Officer's Initials

Code Explanations				
1	Banging/Kicking	13	Meals/Fluids—Served/Eaten
2	Yelling/Screaming	14	Meals/Fluids—Served/NOT Eaten
3	Crying	15	Shower
4	Laughing	16	Toilet
5	Singing	17	Med Line

Code Explanations			
6	Talking	18	Seeing Mental Health
7	Mumbling Incoherently	19	Court
8	Standing Still	20	Reading/Writing
9	Pacing	21	Cleaning Cell
10	Lying Down	22	Smearing Feces
11	Sitting	23	Visits
12	Quiet	24	Other

This assessing and charting is time-consuming and expensive. But it is all observation. None of it is care.

PSYCHIATRIC BEDS ARE not readily available for many people who present to hospital emergency rooms seeking inpatient treatment. Mentally ill people who are brought to emergency rooms by police often undergo a cursory evaluation and are discharged without medications and often without a viable follow-up plan, sometimes mere hours after having been picked up by police. Unsurprisingly, without treatment the behaviors that led to police involvement in the first place recur. Over time police see this cycle of law enforcement response, emergency-room evaluation, and poor follow-up care as ineffectual, and they begin to consider jail as a better alternative.

I heard Portland, Oregon, police commander Sara Westbrook speak to a roomful of doctors about a call her department received about a mentally ill man at her city's downtown Waterfront Park. The man was large and muscular and had a gallon jug filled with fluid attached to a long chain. He was grunting loudly, swinging the chain in a large circle above his head, and charging at people. Onlookers began calling 911.

The police arrived, and the man began charging at the officers. Over the course of the next two and a half or three hours, the police officers worked diligently to get the man into custody with what Commander Westbrook described as "very little force." When they succeeded, they took him to the hospital.

"What do you think happened?" she asked the physicians in the room. "They let him go. He was out [of the emergency room] before we were done with our paperwork." Police would soon be called again, and this time they would take the man to jail.

When mentally ill people in crisis are not admitted to hospitals, Westbrook said, she and her officers view taking them to jail as an act of compassion. Given the lack of community services available for the mentally ill, she said, jail is at least "three hots and a cot, and I know somebody will check to make sure they're still breathing."

There is a cruel illogic to the fact that, across the country, jail is now seen as a treatment option—and sometimes the lone treatment option—for disadvantaged citizens with mental illness. There is even a term for this response: compassionate arrest. Whereas one cannot fault Commander Westbrook or anyone else in her position for utilizing jail as an option for treatment when it is the only practical option, the fact that such a strategy exists throws our unequal and discriminatory treatment of the mentally ill into full relief. We use compassionate arrests only for people who suffer from lack of access to care for their psychiatric illnesses. We would never incarcerate people in order to obtain treatment for their cancer, or their asthma, or their diabetes.

On my psychiatric hospital unit, patients are seen and understood within a framework of their symptoms, diagnoses, and treatment plans. Even with a very ill population, the focus is on fostering health. Incarcerated people who are mentally ill are viewed not within a framework of disease and treatment but within a framework of their past criminal behavior and their potential future threat to safety and security.

In the hospital, clinicians are trained to intervene when we see signs of agitation and fear brewing. We don't always succeed in averting episodes of aggression, but frequently we do. In addition to staff trained in de-escalation, we have scheduled therapeutic groups and activities. We have specially designed sensory rooms in which patients can lie under the comfort of weighted blankets or listen to calming music. A psychiatrist is in-house at all times, and a full range of medications to target psychotic symptoms can be adjusted within minutes if necessary.

These resources do not exist for the incarcerated mentally ill. Detainees with psychiatric symptoms are also particularly vulnerable to other inmates' brutality and are disproportionately victimized by both fellow inmates and by correctional staff. Seen as easy targets, they are viewed as raving lunatics whose accusations will not be believed. Their symptoms may also aggravate and provoke others—prisoners and officers alike—to lash out against them.

And mentally ill inmates frequently land in solitary confinement. As punishment for getting into fights. As protection from manipulation or sexual predation. To facilitate psychiatric observation. Some mentally ill detainees report feeling safer once they are removed from the general population. But many describe their time in solitary confinement as a deepening form of torture.

Even if we are aware that large numbers of Americans with severe mental illness are held not in state hospitals or supportive community environments but are instead housed in correctional facilities, I doubt that most of us know what that looks like. I suspect that few of us picture Frank, with his addled conspiracy theories about ISIS, in a wheelchair and chained to a wall. Or Shaniece, terrified and curled in a corner on the floor, unable to enter into even a basic conversation. I imagine we would not expect people this ill to be treated in the same ways that other prisoners are treated, to be held to the same expectations to which other prisoners are held. And yet, of course, they are. We do wrong by not asking ourselves whether locking our most vulnerable citizens into our most punitive environments is right. Whether it is moral. Whether it is just.

2.

HOW ARE YOU
ON THE FOURTH OF JULY?

Welcome to the Pit," Elli Montgomery says as she opens the door of what looks like an industrial loading dock at Chicago's Cook County Jail. Montgomery is a clinical social worker and the jail's director of mental-health policy. On any given day, the Cook County Jail houses an average population of 9,000 inmates, more than 2,000 of whom are mentally ill. Because of this, the jail has earned the distinction of being the largest mental-health institution in the country.

I have been invited to visit the Cook County Jail by the county's progressive sheriff, Thomas Dart, who had read an opinion piece on transinstitutionalization that I penned for *The New York Times*. "Our jails and prisons," Dart wrote to me, "have evolved into the new asylums."

Dart is a maverick in the field of law enforcement, trying ferociously and unapologetically to generate change from within. From his perspective he has no choice but to respond to the influx of mentally ill men and women into the confines of his facility. As a result, the jail now has within it a dedicated Office of Mental Health Policy and Advocacy, with Elli Montgomery at its helm. And when it came time for Sheriff Dart to replace the executive director of the jail, he took the unprecedented step of choosing a clinical psychologist to fill the position.

Dart also founded a Mental Health Transition Center on the jail's campus to provide vocational training and education for the jail's more highly functioning mentally ill detainees. Participants in the center's programming are required to attend intensive psychotherapeutic groups that focus on social, cognitive, and problem-solving skills. Dart's goal for the participants in the Transition Center programming is a straightforward one: to keep them from coming back to jail once they leave.

Sheriff Dart has no obligation to do any of this. The Cook County Jail is not a hospital, nor is it a prison. Unlike prisons, in which people serve lengthy sentences, jails hold a combination of pretrial detainees and people who are serving sentences of less than a year. Ninety-five percent of the detainees in the Cook County Jail are pretrial, meaning they have been neither tried nor convicted. The Cook County Jail is not a mental-health facility by any definition. Except, of course, it is, and given that fact, Sheriff Dart has charged Elli Montgomery and her team to do every possible thing they can to help. Dart does not view his actions as optional, given the realities that transinstitutionalization has wrought. "A community setting for mental-health care would be beautiful," he says to me during one of our conversations. "I'd also like for it to be Christmas every morning. Don't get me wrong . . . it's good to have these debates. It's just that I have a real sense of urgency. While these debates are going on, people's lives are being spent behind bars."

He's aware, however, that the fact that he has worked to build services within the jail contributes to a larger, worrisome trend. Providing psychiatric services in jail can unwittingly reinforce police impulses toward compassionate arrests. Meeting the needs of mentally ill people in the jails can also send the false idea to legislators that the larger problem of access to adequate care doesn't exist. "It's a conundrum," Sheriff Dart says to me. "If these weren't human beings, then we should do nothing and let the whole thing collapse—force the politicians to build these services in the community. But the problem is that the cost would be actual people's lives."

I follow Elli Montgomery into the building, and we walk quickly through a series of locked doors and tunnel-like concrete hallways as she begins peppering me with facts about the jail and the men and women who are housed herein. Montgomery has an intense gaze and seems to move with purpose in any situation. The hallways feel interminable, winding around corners, passing through doors, and crossing non-descript institutional rooms that are empty but for plastic chairs and the occasional table. I am told later in the day that the disorienting similarity of the route is intentional: signs and directional markers have been left out of these passageways to make it harder for anyone who might try to escape.

"Everyone comes to the Pit when they're first booked," Montgomery explains to me as we wind through the jail's hallways. "The police call it 'bringing in bodies.'" Eventually we enter the Pit, a cavernous space that feels like a warehouse. But it is not merchandise that is arriving, being sorted, and distributed. It is people—specifically everyone who was arrested in the city of Chicago overnight.

This is the jail's receiving area, where people are held before they have a bond hearing. A group of men file past me in a line, all but one of them holding their hands together behind their backs as if they were cuffed. "Hands behind your back!" shouts out one of the many COs positioned nearby, and the outlier quickly complies. Some of the arrested men appear anxious, some are visibly disoriented, some are talking to themselves or staring into corners. Many of them just look weary.

Around the room's periphery are cinder-block holding areas separated from the main room by floor-to-ceiling expanses of chain-link with chain-link doors in the center. There is no word to describe them other than cages. Inside each one, men sit or lie on benches. Some pace. Many appear to be in their twenties or thirties, but some look younger. Several are at least sixty, two of whom are lying down on the holding areas' wooden benches. Two or three men grip rolls of toilet paper. ("Because they are dopesick and our COs are nice," Montgomery tells me, explaining that the men are withdrawing from opiates. They use the toilet paper to wipe their dripping sweat and catch the contents of their stomachs as they vomit and retch.) None of the men have shoelaces, lest these be used to try to strangle someone or to hang themselves.

There are forty-four new detainees here today, half of a typical day's census, I learn. Even with the unusually low numbers, the cages are teeming with men. Not one of them is white.

"We're headed over there," Montgomery says, pointing across the room to a series of counters where her team of mental-health workers call up the arrested men one by one to talk with them in an abbreviated screening process. "But first I want to see why this guy is single-celled."

On the wall alongside us are a few smaller versions of the holding areas—cells designed to contain men who for some reason are not deemed safe to be held with others. Frequently this segregation is a red flag for psychosis or mania. Disturbed or paranoid detainees are often separated out and held alone as a management strategy. The pace and chaos of the room provides enough of a challenge for the COs without psychiatrically agitated arrestees creating additional disruptions. Montgomery walks toward the young man behind the fenced wall. He has neat rows of braids and is wearing casual, stylish clothes. He looks like a high school kid. He also looks totally bewildered.

"My job's to help you," Montgomery calls through the chain-link. "Why are you in here by yourself?"

It turns out he hasn't been sequestered for psychiatric reasons. "My leg's broke, and I need crutches, but I can't have them in there," he says. There's no sign of a cast beneath his jeans, but there's also no question that he's favoring his right leg and wincing every time he moves.

"Are you depressed?" Montgomery asks him.

"'Bout bein' in here," he replies.

"Got it," says Montgomery, moving on. It's a reasonable response and not an answer that concerns her. We make our way across the room to join other members of her team who are already at work behind the counters. Montgomery and the other mental-health workers call for detainees to come up one by one and be evaluated.

"Give me one out of five!" she shouts toward one of the holding areas marked by a sign bearing a large black number five. A young man emerges from the cage and approaches the counter. "Let me see your number," Montgomery instructs, and he holds out his forearm, revealing a grid of red numbers that have been drawn onto his skin with a marker. "Those you don't need anymore. Those are Chicago PD," she says. "This one," she says, pointing to a black *42* inked on the back of his hand. "Okay. Forty-two. DeJuan?" she asks, cross-checking the number with a photo-copied list of names she is holding.

"Yes," DeJuan says, confirming his name and date of birth.

"What are your charges?" Montgomery asks.

"Possession, and I think resisting arrest, but I didn't resist—"

"Possession of cannabis?" Montgomery clarifies, having identified substance abuse as a potential mental-health issue and now zeroing in. DeJuan nods. "Are you using anything else? Cocaine, heroin, pills, anything? How much are you drinking?" The two go back and forth. It was just weed, nothing else. He's been using it daily for years. He can't remember what the longest stretch is that he's gone without it. "What about when you were locked up before? How long was that?" Montgomery asks.

"Four months, but I still got it while I was in here," DeJuan replies sheepishly.

"You got pot in jail?" Montgomery turns to me. "I love hearing that," she says, rolling her eyes in frustration. She asks questions related to the pot use—"Do you need it for sleep? How's your appetite without it?"—and then segues into whether it's a means of coping with anxiety or post-traumatic stress, symptoms that can plague detainees who come from violent homes or neighborhoods, or who've been involved in or affected by gang activity. "Do you get anxious?" Montgomery asks.

"Nah, not really," says DeJuan.

She leans forward onto the counter. "How are you on the Fourth of July?"

"Oh, man." He chuckles softly. "I get jumpy, I'm not gonna lie." I'm watching Montgomery carefully with her rapid-fire assessment, and this is a deft maneuver. She's seen enough consistency in this environment to know which specific questions are more apt to get accurate answers. "Getting jumpy" when hearing fireworks in an urban environment plagued by gun violence is suggestive of post-traumatic hypervigilance. The sounds of bangs and pops register reflexively as threats, not celebration.

Montgomery moves through the remaining questions that her office has developed, including some about past treatment and medications, to help identify detainees who've already been diagnosed with psychiatric illness. Then Montgomery asks about current suicidality and symptoms that could indicate psychosis.

"Do I hear voices?" DeJuan repeats incredulously. "Lady, I'm not crazy, if that's what you're thinking."

"Nobody's saying you're crazy," Montgomery reassures him. With her assessment complete, she moves quickly. "Do you want to get help with the pot?"

"Yeah," he says, though it's hard to gauge his sincerity.

Montgomery hands him a card with the name of a care organization on it that offers substance-abuse treatment. "I'm going to have these people call you once you're out," she says, jotting down a number where DeJuan tells her he can be reached.

"Thank you," he says.

"You're welcome." She smiles. "Can I get another one out of five?" she calls.

One by one the men come up, and Montgomery runs through her questions. A homeless twenty-year-old who acknowledges that he feels scared much of the time and sometimes hears voices says to her, "I would like a safe haven." He was in foster care when he was young and has aged out of the system. He does not have any family members he can turn to for support. He has now been arrested for attempted robbery.

"Did you ever get any help with trying to find housing? Or with the voices?" Montgomery asks him.

"What do you mean, help?" he asks.

Montgomery shoots me a look that says she finds that question as heartbreaking as I do. This moment stays with me, an example of how many possible points of intervention exist in people's lives prior to incarceration and how often we miss every single one of them.

As one man after another comes up to the counter, I'm aware that I feel a tug of discomfort. The screenings are incomplete. Symptoms that are raised do not always get a thorough investigation. Montgomery sometimes must take stabs based on hunches. Because she is charged with evaluating so many detainees in such a compressed period of time, she has no choice but to do so.

"The quiet ones worry me," she says, telling me a story of a detainee in the jail who would not speak for days. "So one day I just said, 'How are the voices?'" He had not ever acknowledged hearing voices, but Montgomery had a feeling that he was and did not have the luxury—as I would in my hospital setting—of observing him at length or waiting for him to be more forthcoming with his symptoms.

Montgomery is relentless in her attempts to connect and provide help within the constraints of this environment. Still, the psychiatric needs of the men we're seeing this morning stretch far beyond what a brief conversation can provide. It appears that this is the first time many of these men have had any mental-health interventions or support at all. What the jail's mental-health program is able to provide is not anywhere close to the wraparound services of housing, food, medication, substance-abuse treatment, and social support that so many of them need. But it is more help than they were getting from the community before they were arrested.

We head to an area adjacent to the Pit where there are smaller, contained rooms. Montgomery walks past one of these caged areas with ten or twelve men inside who have completed county jail sentences and so are leaving today to go home. As we walk, she calls, "You guys are going home today, you all have plans for where to go? Where to get your meds if you need them?" One man speaks up that he does not. Montgomery gives him a quick set of instructions as to the prescriptions that should have been written and where he should go to fill them. Then, with more cages to check, we're off without knowing the status of any of the other men.

We come up to the female holding area—a similar small, contained room that has six women within it. Montgomery asks a general question about whether they are all doing okay. Two women nod, three do not respond, and one sits crying in the center of the room. Montgomery calls the crying woman up to the chain-link wall and begins to ask her questions about her situation, her charges, and whether she is feeling suicidal. They are kind and empathetic questions designed to get this woman help. In a hospital setting, they would be asked in a private room to protect her privacy. Here they are being asked in an area where all the other detainees and any officer who walks past can hear the conversation in its entirety.

Through her tears the woman says her charges are "something about my babies." She looks over her shoulder at the other women in the cell. Montgomery asks whether she would like to come out and sit down. The woman nods. An officer unlocks the chain-link door, and Montgomery directs me to sit on one side of a table and the woman to sit on another. Montgomery sits beside me. To be seated with this distressed woman is a gesture of compassion, but we are still only three or four feet beyond the cell, so our conversation echoes off the cinder blocks and the other detainees can clearly hear every word. On the table is a bag of maxi pads. There is nothing else in the room.

The woman is at most thirty. She could be younger. Her curly black hair is pulled back into a short, gelled ponytail, and she is wearing a navy-blue uniform with the logo of a local chain restaurant stitched onto the pocket. Her accent suggests she is Latina. In between sobs the woman recounts that she is a single mother of three girls, ages two, three, and six. She works ten hours a day, six days a week, to try to make ends meet. She gestures at the uniform she is wearing to emphasize the point. When she raises her arm, I see that she, too, has the grid of numbers written on it. Also on her hand is a script tattoo that reads "*Trust No Man, Fear No*

Bitch," and I cannot help but wonder about the hurt in her life that led her to make that message indelible on her skin.

"I was at work. My niece was supposed to be watching my girls," she tells us as she cries, describing how she has ended up in jail, "but I don't know what happened. The police found my kids walking in the street by themselves. . . . They took them into DCFS [Department of Children and Family Services] custody, and now I don't even know where my daughters is at."

Montgomery asks her gently again whether she is suicidal.

"Right now I have nothing to live for," the woman says.

"We can put you on suicide watch if we need to," Montgomery says. I wonder whether the woman knows what this entails in most correctional facilities—a smock with no undergarments, a cell with no sheets, round-the-clock observation by correctional officers, all until she is seen by a psychiatrist to be cleared—but she demurs. She has no plan to kill herself; without her daughters she just sees no point in being alive. Montgomery reassures her that DCFS will try to place the girls with family members if possible. She takes down phone numbers of a sister, a grandmother. She offers to call around and see what she can learn. It is a generous gift to a mother in a profound moment of crisis.

Just as with the rapid-fire intake screenings or the hurried aftercare planning of men on their way out of jail, I don't feel at ease as the CO lets this woman back into the shared cell and we turn to go. I want to ask more questions about the degree of her desperation, about what she thinks we'll find when we call her family members, about whether DCFS has ever previously been involved with her children. I want to be sure that none of the other women in the holding cage have issues that urgently need to be addressed. I want to pause and more carefully assess the voices in the young homeless man, to prescribe him medicines that could alleviate his symptoms, to connect him with resources to help him find that safe haven he seeks. I want to go back to the teenager in the single cell and ask him how his leg got broken and determine whether it needs medical attention now. I am overcome by the feeling that, though well intentioned and driven by the right impulses, the services that Elli Montgomery and her team are able to provide are *not enough*.

Then I realize that the standards I'm imposing are clinical standards. I'm looking at these men and women in crisis the way I look at the men and women I encounter in crisis in my hospital work. But this is not a therapeutic environment, despite the fact that many of the underlying reasons that the people we meet are here—including astronomical rates of addiction and trauma—are fundamentally issues of mental health.

At the end of our morning in Receiving, one of Montgomery's team members, Maggie, reports that everyone has been seen except an older man who refused to talk to anyone. Maggie thinks he might be paranoid, but because he won't engage, she can't tell for sure. Hearing this, Montgomery becomes even more determined to check in with him. She calls him over. He waves her off. She persists. "Just come here for a minute. Our job is to help you," she cajoles.

"I don't want any help. I'm not talking to anyone but a lawyer," the man says, but he moves toward her to say this, and Montgomery takes her opportunity.

"Let me at least give you this card," she says, "in case you change your mind and you think we can help you out in any way." She pulls out a bright red notecard that reads COOK COUNTY SHERIFF'S OFFICE, OFFICE OF MENTAL HEALTH POLICY AND ADVOCACY. Before she hands it to him, she circles the phone number and scrawls *Director Montgomery* on the top. "This is me," she says. "I'm on call on this number tonight. If you get out and you need help, you call me. Can you read that?" she asks, pointing to her handwritten name.

"Director," says the man. "You the director? You in charge?" She nods. He turns, looks at me, and raises his eyebrows to show that he is impressed. "What kinds of things you think you can help me with?"

"That depends," Montgomery replies, and now she is off like a shot. "What are your charges? What medicines are you taking?" Before long the man has dropped his defensive stance and is answering all the questions in earnest, acknowledging symptoms of depression that have plagued him in the wake of an injury that will require surgery while simultaneously emphasizing that he is a strong and proud man, not the kind of man who needs help from others. "I'm worried about you," Montgomery says to the man as the interview draws to a close. "I want you to call this number when you get out so we can hook you up with some resources."

"I promise you I will call," the man says. "I can't promise you anything beyond that."

WITH THE MORNING'S assessments finished, I next travel to a remarkable therapy group called "Thinking for a Change." I walk with Montgomery across the jail's extensive campus to the Mental Health Transition Center, a series of low-slung classroom buildings that house the program that attempts to reduce reincarceration among mentally ill detainees. The men inside, she explains, have all been identified as having mental-health needs but are also categorized as high-functioning enough to participate in job training, education, and therapeutic groups.

We slip into a classroom to observe the structured, research-based cognitive behavioral therapy (CBT) program. As with all forms of CBT, the exercises intend to raise individual awareness about one's own patterns of thinking and then to practice methods of changing the thoughts and assumptions in one's life that lead to problematic behaviors. This particular group meets two hours a day, five days a week—a therapy schedule that would be considered intensive even in a dedicated mental-health setting.

In this session of Thinking for a Change, ten men wearing standard correctional attire—tan tops and bottoms, white socks, and black slip-on shoes—sit at tables arranged in a circle. Two of the men look as young as nineteen or twenty. Two look as though they might be sixty or older. The others fall somewhere in between. A female counselor in her late twenties or early thirties sits in jeans and a cardigan at the head of the classroom and speaks to them in a voice that exudes the quiet calm of guided-meditation recordings. She asks each man to make a timeline of his life. Major events, she says. The things that stand out in retrospect.

The men write in silence. After a period of time, the counselor tells them to finish the sentences they are writing. She asks for a volunteer to share his timeline with the group. Several hands are raised. The counselor gestures to a man who is roughly my age. He begins to read aloud:

> *I was born.*
> *My brother was born.*
> *My mother went to prison.*
> *My father told me I wasn't his son.*
> *I saw* Purple Rain.
> *I started getting into trouble.*
> *I ran away to Chicago.*
> *I moved back in with my mom.*
> *I started running the streets and listening to rap and gangbanging.*
> *I got kicked out of high school.*
> *My son was born.*
> *I was using drugs.*
> *I went to jail and earned a custodian's certificate.*
> *My son graduated 8th grade.*
> *My brother and I became closer.*
> *Now I am back in jail.*

The counselor asks him how it was for him to make this timeline. "Not easy," he says. "By doing this I had to look at what my life has been."

A second man volunteers.

> *I was born,* he begins.
> *Went to grade school.*
> *Graduated high school.*
> *Bible college, one semester, didn't finish it, though.*

Went to prison.
Came out.
Worked.
Had kids.
Back in jail now.

He pauses several times as he reads. Looks down. "You seem bothered," says the counselor.

"It's more embarrassed," he says. "I was thinking about the way I was raised. I wasn't raised like this. I went to Bible study. I was raised in a Christian home." The counselor nods without speaking. She lets his words hang in the room.

"I feel you," says an older man, nodding. He begins to read from his own timeline.

I was born.
I graduated high school.
Went into the air force 1984.
Became a drug addict 1985.
My addiction kept me going back and forth to penitentiaries.
It destroyed my marriage.
It destroyed my life.

Another stands and reads:

Born sixty years ago now.
Graduated high school—a guy who graduated with me played with the
*   49ers and won two Super Bowls!*
Met my girlfriend. Her brother was a millionaire.
I became a mailman.
I started freebasing crack.
I was fired from the post office.
Then I just found out I have prostate cancer.

He starts to sit down. Then stays standing. Says to the room, "Them is a whole lot of years to not get back with nothing to show." His voice cracks, and his eyes well with tears. "My mother was sick and dying with cancer," he says with effort. "She wanted to see me drug-free, and I wasn't able to give that to her."

Another:

> *I was born.*
> *Four years later was abandoned by my mom.*
> *My grandma took me in.*
> *I started school.*

And here he looks up, wants to say more. He says more. The timeline has become the root of a larger narrative, and the room of men is giving him this space to elaborate, to give context to his life. "I was terrible— developmental and behavior problems. Maybe it was my mother. She was young. She was sixteen."

He looks to his timeline again and reads from it.

> *I remember being in the streets with my mother begging for money,*
>   *telling people it was my birthday to try to get them to give us money.*
> *In 1980 I ran away.*
> *I had bruises from playing football. The hospital thought it was abuse.*
> *I peed the bed until I was fourteen.*
> *My aunt used to whoop me.*
> *Home was unfit to live in—holes in the walls.*
> *DCFS took me away from my grandmother.*
> *I moved into a group home.*
> *I got suspended from school.*

He looks up again, adds, "I didn't want to accept what was happening. I wanted to be with my grandma. Not with these white people bringing me to school."

I discovered basketball—that was good. Basketball was such an
    important thing in my life that I started wanting to do good in
    school.
I made the honor roll.
But I could only stay in the group home until age fourteen.
I went back to live with my auntie.
I made the varsity team as a freshman.
But I started getting hooked up with the wrong people in the
    neighborhood—drinking, cigarettes, marijuana.
My grades dropped, so I couldn't play.
I quit basketball.
I quit school.
At age fourteen I started gangbanging, selling drugs.
I got hooked on drugs.
Ended up in the penitentiary for fifteen years.

He pauses. Points back to an earlier spot on his timeline. "Once I started hanging out with the wrong people and making the wrong decisions, it was a downhill spiral. And now I have trouble getting back to where I was before that time. I was too young—I was fourteen. Adults got me hooked on drugs, see. I was selling for them to make money after I dropped out of school, and it was easier for them to pay me with drugs rather than to pay me with money." He stops, sits. Looks up and apologizes to the counselor for taking up so much time.

"What I hear in your timeline," she says to him, "is how much you were alone."

What I hear, too, is how every single one of the men's timelines is riddled by addiction, a disease that our country treats as a crime.

The only two white men in the room sit apart from the rest of the men. From this fact and their appearance—heavily tattooed, thick goatees, shaved heads—I make an assumption that they are white supremacists, a faction with a large presence in many correctional environments. For much of the session, they do not participate; they are silent. I make the assumption that they are highly defended, that they are judging these other men, that they are ruthless, even cruel. At the very end of the class, one of them speaks. My presuppositions shatter. All I hear is vulnerability.

I was born, he says.
Biological father took off to California because I was crying so much that he thought I was a monster. He told my mother that he wanted to kill me.
My mother met my stepfather.
My two brothers were born.
Mom worked for AT&T.
We didn't grow up in a nice neighborhood, but my mother tried.
Eleven years old I joined a gang.
That same summer I smoked PCP.
I've been in love with it ever since.
In high school I got half of a credit for showing up for gym.
I went to school only because there were other gang members there who I wanted to fight.
I got expelled from school, and that same year I was shot in the head.
My brother and I were both in the pen together. He still has nine years. The night before I got out, we cried like babies. Then he said to me, "Don't worry, I'll leave the light on for you."

This gathering of ten men feels like a powerful place. As if the possibility of change dwells herein.

After the men each tell their stories, the counselor leads them through a mindfulness exercise to calm and center them before they return to the general population of the jail. They close their eyes. They regulate their breathing. Their stories suffuse the air of the room. I keep my eyes open and look intently at each of them, these men struggling to make meaning in this place and in the context of the mental illnesses that they've either alluded to or named—depression, anxiety, bipolar disorder, substance abuse, post-traumatic stress disorder. Somewhere down the hallway, a door slams. The oldest man in the room jumps. *How are you on the Fourth of July?* As I look at one man and then the next, the overwhelming sentiment I feel is compassion.

The paths charted in these timelines originate in trauma. The directions of the paths are locked fast by drugs. Once locked, the paths lead here to jail. They come here many times. They veer away and circle back. The pull is insistent. The drug pulls and the jail pulls. The destination is the same.

What does it take to resist the pull? Force in an equal and opposite direction? An opposing force that must pull against addiction, must pull against isolation, must pull against racism, must pull against poverty. It must pull against *mother left when I was four* and *no money to eat* and *stepfather beat the shit out of my brothers and me.* It must pull against *no good lowdown motherfucker* and *hands behind your back!* and gunshots and gangbanging. It must pull against nightmares and flashbacks, against your best friend lying in a pool of blood, against hopelessness and despair.

Once he's within the prison's orbit, what power does one man have to resist the pull of the dehumanizing fortresses of containment? What amount of force is required to tear away from these industrial complexes of trauma and punishment and exile?

We cried like babies. Then he said to me, "Don't worry, I'll leave the light on for you."

THE THINKING FOR A CHANGE therapeutic group is one end of the spectrum of experience at Cook County Jail. Before I leave for the day, Montgomery takes me to another: Division 10 in maximum security. Division 10, she tells me, is the "behavioral-management unit." The men held here have all been diagnosed with a mental illness. But they've also required separation from the general population because they have caused behavioral problems, they have been assaultive or self-injurious, or they have repeatedly broken jail rules.

When Montgomery and I enter Division 10, the COs are furious that we're there. An inmate has just thrown his urine onto one of the jail psychiatrists, and the officers have boatloads of paperwork to do as a result. It's almost the change of shift, and if we go in and something similar happens to us, then it will mean yet another incident report and the COs will be there later than they already have to be. Montgomery informs them that we are going in anyway. They shake their heads, look back down at their paperwork, and fume.

The room is the size of a basketball court. Men are locked in individual cells all around the unit's perimeter. The room initially resembles a small school lunchroom in disarray—concrete walls, modular stainless-steel tables in the center, trash and crumpled milk cartons strewn across the floor. This unit has clearly been designed for maximum containment and control, and the men held within it are pushing against those constraints. I feel the volatility of the environment. From the cells come the clang of objects smacking against the metal doors, and shouts: angry curses directed at the COs; frustrated pleas directed at Montgomery; and profane, lewd comments directed toward me—a new female stranger in this otherwise unchanging landscape. The noise is deafening, made worse by the fact that some of the COs shout threats and insults back at the men in the cells.

The inmates and the COs taunt each other through the cell doors, and the COs are eager to demonstrate to the caged men that they have the upper hand. It is an atmosphere of palpable antagonism.

In my own hospital work, I have had specific training for these sorts of moments that I lean on to keep from lashing out in a reflexive anger. I have physical and pharmacologic power over all my patients that I could abusively employ in the service of my own ego or my own fear or rage, at whatever instance I so choose. Years of training and years of practice prevent me from doing so, but I can understand how the volatility of these moments drives those with less training to assert control through whatever means they can.

It is not only a matter of skill set, however. The COs in Division 10 are in a fundamentally different position from the one I'm in. The role of the correctional officers is not treatment but control—a dynamic that is by nature an adversarial one.

It is also important to recognize that COs who work in units like Division 10 spend every day in an antagonistic atmosphere that many of us cannot imagine and could not tolerate. Thirty-four percent of U.S. correctional officers have post-traumatic stress disorder, more than double the rate than that among members of the U.S. military. Correctional officers are more than four times more likely to kill themselves than are members of the general population. Their suicide rate is double that of police officers. Researchers have looked closely to determine what renders officers so vulnerable to suicidality. Among the risk factors identified with working in corrections is the fact that officers constantly encounter aggression and injury; they constantly feel as though they are in danger. Yet they are reticent to share the trauma of their work lives with therapists or loved ones and thus shoulder the enormous stressors of their work environments on their own, sometimes for decades.

In 2011, thirty-six-year-old California correctional officer Scott Jones killed himself, leaving behind his wife and a young son. The note he left said simply, in capital letters, *THE JOB MADE ME DO IT*.

As I stand in the middle of Division 10, the officers and detainees alike seethe with hostility. The tension is palpable, and I'm aware of what a horrible environment this would be in which to work day in and day out: not only caging people, controlling them, and being hated by them but also tolerating incessant attempts at provocation and enduring perpetual threats of danger.

I look into the cells that surround me. I cannot see the men's faces. The cell doors are thick metal, the walls between them concrete. There is a slim piece of metal in each door, a kind of rigid mesh punctured by holes the size of pencil erasers to see out, to see in, for light to filter through, and this mesh screen passes for a window. When the men press their faces to the metal, press their eyes close to the holes, their brains adjust and they can see us fully. No matter what angle I strike, I can only see them if they are standing back from the grate. If they stand up against it, I see only shadows.

We have come here because one of the men in the pod has requested a psychiatric evaluation, and Montgomery walks over to his cell door to see how he is doing and let him know when the formal evaluation will occur. As in the receiving area, the questions about his symptoms—suicidality, hallucinations—are being asked through the cell door with no privacy whatsoever. Both the questions and the answers have to be shouted in order to be heard through the doors, broadcasting every word of the exchange to the other imprisoned men and COs who stand nearby.

Of all of the prison environments I've been in, this room is the single most hostile. Verbal threats and displays of strength and aggression fly in all directions from prisoners and officers alike. I'm aware of how exposed the men who share their psychiatric symptoms with us become and of how both officers and other detainees might make cruel use of those overtly expressed vulnerabilities.

And then, in an instant, I am the target. I am the one who feels suddenly exposed. "Get your hands up," Montgomery says to the man in the cell we have come to see. "Get them up where I can see them if you want me to keep talking to you."

The man smirks, looks at me, licks his lips, bites his bottom lip, and slowly raises his hands, palms facing out in a "don't shoot" gesture. With his expression, and with the laughter I hear behind me, my momentary confusion gives way to a sickening understanding. I look around, and several other men stand in their cell-door windows, one elbow and shoulder beating rhythmically in each rectangular frame, their mouths in open grins as they jerk off, staring straight at me. Several of them make jeering sounds alongside the foul sounds of their friction.

It's a problem in the jail, Sheriff Dart later explains to me. "We don't know what to do about it—we've tried everything. Even calling their mothers, their girlfriends. We tell them, 'He's doing this disgusting thing.' It does nothing."

Within an instant, a shift. An abrupt change. And though I did not just seconds before, I now feel afraid of the men in their cells. I see their faces watching me through the dark, windowed slits of their doors. *Leering* is the word that rises to my consciousness. They are caged. As they shout, some pace the short distance from one side of the cell to the other or from the wall to the door and then back. *Prowling,* the word comes unbidden. I try to stand in such a way that they cannot stare at me through the slits of window no matter how close they press their faces against the unbreakable transparency. I find their blind spots. I choose my angles. Despite my relative position of power and safety, I feel disarmed, which of course is the exact response the act is intended to evoke.

Working on the Intensive Treatment Unit of a psychiatric hospital means that I am not a rookie when it comes to startling behavior. Many of my patients are kind and appreciative of their care. Many are ambivalent or so sick that it is hard for them to engage. But some have been horribly traumatized and trust no one. And some harbor paranoid beliefs that I'm trying to hurt them. It is mostly my paranoid patients who lash out, who call me every kind of name you can imagine. They are my patients who are too ill to acknowledge that they need care, who have been hospitalized against their will because they are gravely impaired but who become furious when I refuse to discharge them from the hospital.

"Let me get this straight," I have sometimes joked with friends. "You don't get called a cunt at work every day?" I once told my colleagues that I should get my name tag reprinted, replacing my name with the name that one of my patients called me every time she spoke to me for nearly the entire course of her hospitalization: *Bitchus Maximus.*

Though some of my patients can be unpredictable, I have only twice felt physically threatened. Once, as I was bending over a patient who was having a seizure, a psychotic man came up behind me and groped my backside. Once a demented patient threw a full carton of milk at me so hard that an indigo bruise bloomed wide on my hip like an iris.

I take precautions, and in my hospital work I have highly trained colleagues who work to ensure my safety. But I also take pride in my ability to establish a rapport with patients, even those who are paranoid or fiercely defended. I trust my ability to soothe an agitated patient or de-escalate a situation that is heating up. I stay calm when patients try to provoke me. I am not easily unmoored.

Despite all this—my years of experience, my confidence in handling situations that might fluster or terrify people with less training—the masturbation had its desired effect. It threw me. It shifted the power dynamic. Although these men were in cages, I was the one who felt as though I could not escape.

BOTH OF THESE THINGS are true.

The classroom with ten deeply human men. Their fraught trajectories. Their palpable regret. Their vulnerability with one another.

And the fact that some of these men—perhaps many—have done evil things.

As I sit in the classroom with the men and their timelines, none of them feel evil to me. As I stand in the center of Division 10 amid jeers and shouts and men with jerking arms, none of them feel vulnerable to me.

What differentiates the men who write their timelines, who regulate their breathing, from those who throw urine and expose themselves and try to unnerve me?

The answer lies in part in the fact that existing within Division 10—or any of the countless places like it in our correctional facilities across the country—would destabilize any sane person. The environment itself is enough to breed a tenuous, self-protective hostility in the people who must work there. And Division 10 is *in* a place that is working hard to address the injustices in our criminal justice system, to acknowledge the presence and the needs of the severely mentally ill in jail. And even still there is this ward, the existence of which is evidence that despite all the hard work happening at the Cook County Jail to address the needs of mentally ill inmates, the volume and magnitude of the problem is too big for the jail to withstand.

Certainly there are people within our nation's correctional facilities who have committed truly evil acts, but the majority of those behind bars do not fall into this category. Instead most detainees fall within a Venn diagram of overlapping disadvantaged groups that include racial minorities, the poor, the addicted, and the mentally ill.

Not all of them are even guilty of the crimes with which they've been charged. But once they're behind bars, nuance is lost. The process prioritizes vengeance over social good, and in doing so it unequivocally renders vulnerable populations more vulnerable.

I think of the words of Bryan Stevenson, founder of the Equal Justice Initiative and one of the great civil-rights leaders of our time. "The opposite of poverty isn't wealth," says Stevenson. The opposite of poverty "is justice."

3.

SINCE ELEVEN

Savannah was a nineteen-year-old girl jailed in a women's prison. In the request for a competency evaluation, her attorney had written that "the defendant doesn't seem to care what happens to her or her case." The attorney had said that Savannah was "too depressed" to collaborate and thus appeared to be unable—or unwilling—to engage with her attorney in her own defense.

She had a slew of charges, some of which were minor (misdemeanor charges of drugs and disorderly conduct) and some more serious (felony charges for burglary and the violation of a restraining order). She incurred all the charges in the context of a long-standing addiction to crack cocaine and heroin.

The attorney had expressed no concern for the young woman's ability to understand court proceedings, and indeed Savannah sailed through that portion of the competency evaluation. She correctly answered questions about the roles of the prosecutor and the defense attorney, about what evidence is, and what a witness is, and what it means to take a plea bargain, and what happens if you violate probation. She knew the date and could list the current president and the two presidents who came before him. She could recite long sequences of numbers forward and backward and could correctly interpret lesser-known, abstract proverbs, like "Tell me who you walk with and I'll tell you who you are."

She could also answer questions about her personal and psychiatric history with clarity and logic—and when she did, a road map of trauma began to assemble itself piece by piece before my eyes. I asked her about where she was born and raised, who had lived with her during her childhood, how far she'd gone in school, where she'd been living prior to coming into jail. And just as matter-of-factly as she'd answered my routine competency questions, she explained that her own mother had been incarcerated when Savannah was very little and then Savannah had gone to live with an aunt but that the aunt had sexually abused her. When authorities discovered the abuse, Savannah was placed in the foster-care system, where she bounced from home to home without continuity or permanence. Often without oversight or basic safety.

I asked about what drugs she'd used. Her response was reminiscent of the men's substance-riddled timelines in the Thinking for a Change group at the Cook County Jail. "I pretty much used every drug you can think of at one point or another," she told me. "Crack was the thing that got me into the most trouble, though," she said, "and on and off some heroin." She'd tried to get clean a handful of times but without any sustained success. "I've really been using all along."

"All along since when?" I asked her. "How old were you when you started using?"

"There was this girl who was my neighbor at one of the foster homes," Savannah began. "She was seventeen or eighteen, I think. She's the one who gave me crack for the first time. I was eleven."

Eleven. A flood of images from my everyday life: my daughter and her friends buckled into the backseat of our car and keeling over with laughter while singing a goofy song they've made up for the last day of school; woven ankle bracelets and a host of colorful key chains hanging off backpacks; the way my girl is incapable of eating an ice-cream cone without leaving a telltale smear of chocolate on her chin; how she looks up from whatever Harry Potter book she's rereading for the umpteenth time and shouts a cheer of encouragement to her brother when he's up to bat in his baseball game; how just the day before she'd accidentally whacked her hip on the corner of the kitchen counter and crumpled in tears. How I'd knelt beside her, rubbing her back, and how she threw her arms around my neck.

Savannah continued talking as I was trying to square the giddy emotion of eleven and a neighbor who gives you crack. I heard her say, "Same girl taught me to shoot heroin, but that wasn't until I was thirteen. Pretty much have been using both ever since."

Savannah's substance dependency had then altered the course of her life in irrefutable and irrevocable ways. I asked her about her schooling, and she told me she'd gotten good grades for many years but that she'd dropped out of high school in the tenth grade. I asked her what had happened that she left school. "I couldn't stay off the drugs," she said quietly, suddenly shifting in her seat and dropping her gaze to the floor.

As a psychiatrist, I try always to remember that we cannot know with certainty what is going on in the minds of others. But we listen closely to what our patients tell us. We study what we see when we look at them, what we hear in their voices and in their stories. We look for patterns in their language. We gauge their expressions. We assess their lucidity, their degree of understanding. Often a constellation of these observations begins to cohere in a way that leads thinking toward a diagnosis— or lack thereof.

Patients in the throes of mania, for instance, may wear outlandish combinations of clothing and copious amounts of makeup and jewelry. They may exhibit "pressured" speech, which means that they speak so quickly and incessantly that it's nearly impossible to interrupt them. They may be disinhibited enough to make sexually inappropriate comments or racist ones. They may dance around the unit or rally the other patients into activities or shenanigans with an infectious exuberance.

In contrast, patients with intractable depression may lie in bed, unable to bear the idea of rising. They may go days or weeks without showering—*malodorous*, we write in our notes when the descriptor applies.

Their clothes may be unclean, their faces unshaven. Their speech may be slow, monotonous, as if uttering even a single syllable takes an extraordinary amount of effort. When they reveal the content of their thoughts, every moment of the future seems to them to be devoid of hope; every possible action to be taken is deemed impossible, with insurmountable obstacles looming on all sides.

So we are taught to pay attention, to interpret what we see and hear.

I read Savannah's abruptly downcast gaze and quiet voice as shame. She had described her drug use and trauma with candor and without self-consciousness, had spoken matter-of-factly about the vagrancy that defined her childhood and about her mother's incarceration. But now, when discussing the fact that she had dropped out of school, her steadiness faltered. These moments, too, are moments that psychiatrists are trained to examine for meaning. What was the content that brought about the shift in emotion? What happened in the conversation to change the relational dynamic? What question took the air out of the room?

Savannah had been a strong student, one with intellectual promise, even. Her grades had always been good, yet here she sat in jail. Maybe, had she been dealt a different hand, she could have been in college now, heading toward her own degree in social work, or psychology, or medicine. That was my sense of the origins of her ashamed reaction; that the line of questioning about school resonated, consciously or not, with her knowledge that had her life turned out differently, she might have been on my side of the table.

No part of me intended to make Savannah feel belittled, to feel less than. But it would be absurd to lose sight of the fact that I have power and privilege in these interactions. My recommendations sway judges to send the people I evaluate to the hospital for treatment or back to court for their cases to progress. I'm the one who calls the CO to the door when I've decided that the interview has ended. The officers come with cuffs, or they come with keys. The people I see are led back to their bunks, and I walk through the doors to the vast world outside. I gas up my car. Decide where to stop for lunch, and when. Pick up my children.

Have dinner with my family. Shame on one side, power on the other. Both Savannah and I understood which one of us was on which side.

I asked Savannah where she'd been living just before her arrest. Her mother was out of prison now, and Savannah had lived with her for a while, she said. But she'd stolen things from the home so many times to pay for drugs that her mother had kicked her out. They'd had a fight a few months ago that had gotten physical, hence the restraining order. Since that time she'd been staying in a motel, selling her body to pay for the room and to pay for drugs. "What else am I gonna do?" she asked me, resigned. "Can't get clean. Can't get a job if I'm not clean. This is just my life."

Savannah's attorney had sought a competency evaluation, concerned that her client was too depressed to engage in her own defense. It was, in the end, more complicated than that. It was true that Savannah's discussion of her case, the charges, and the possible outcomes that might result from them was characterized by a profound degree of apathy. Though she did have symptoms of depression, I thought her lack of engagement reflected the options for her life—or lack thereof—that she saw ahead of her. Which was worse? Serving several years in prison? Or returning to prostitution in exchange for drugs in a cheap motel?

Was she suicidal? I asked her.

"I'm always suicidal," she said, quietly. "There's not much to live for." Prison was hell. The motel room was hell. If those were the two paths her life could take, what did it matter?

What if she were offered intensive substance-abuse and mental-health treatment? I asked. Would she be willing to engage in such a plan?

"That's what I really need," she said to me with a look of earnest certainty. "That's the only way to change any of this."

I knew she was right. And I also did not know whether such a thing would be possible. The competency evaluation could indicate—as it eventually did—that Savannah would benefit from an intensive mental-health and substance-abuse treatment program, which she had not had in the past, and preferably one that focused on the treatment of trauma. But these decisions were in the hands of the courts. I could not direct

Savannah's care, as I would do for a patient I was treating in the hospital. And I knew that resources for intensive treatment, where they did exist, were scarce. Would the judge and the prosecutor lean toward treatment or punishment? I did not know. And if they opted for treatment, would there be a program available to truly help Savannah? With all the money available to fight the war on drugs, would there be money available to try to heal this young woman who became addicted to drugs as a child?

Meeting men and women in prison, I often found myself wondering where exactly the tipping point lies, where we go from feeling empathy for a person to feeling anger toward her, or fear. When do we stop seeing someone as a person deserving of our sympathy and care and start seeing her as a criminal in need of punishment who deserves to suffer?

Who do we think of as criminals, and when did Savannah become one? When she first tried drugs at age eleven? When she shot heroin at thirteen? Or do her physical altercations with her mother mark the moment we should stop feeling empathy for her; when we should start to feel angry or afraid? Do we fear the young man who is also given drugs as a child but who steals from a stranger rather than from his mother? Who uses a gun rather than his fists?

Where is the line at which our empathy turns to fury and fear? When the addict forces her daughter into prostitution? When the man kills for sport rather than defense? What if a childhood can be so horrible that it breaks a person irreparably? What then? What if someone gives an eleven-year-old girl cocaine and you can never, ever get her back?

The fact that Savannah is being punished rather than helped shines a light on the futility of incarcerating people over and over again without addressing the factors in their lives that lead them to break the law.

The philosopher Martha Nussbaum has written at length about this, classifying strategies of crime management as either *ex ante* or *ex post*. *Ex ante* methods are those that aim to prevent criminal acts; *ex post* methods are those employed in response to acts that have already been committed. Incarceration is definitively an *ex post* strategy, one that Nussbaum views as utterly ineffective at reducing crime.

If the goal is fewer offenses, Nussbaum asserts, then the focus of our efforts and our investments must be on deterrence—on preventing criminal acts before they occur. And deterrence requires that we look rigorously and honestly at how constructive policies that target nutrition, education, employment, and social welfare work to prevent crime.

Ex post tactics do not deter. They are what Nussbaum deems "fallback mechanisms" that automatically acknowledge and underscore that our *ex ante* strategies have failed. To illustrate the illogic of relying on an *ex post* response like incarceration, Nussbaum asks, "Let us consider elevators."

"A traveler to a distant country finds that elevators are very unreliable," she writes. "They are often badly constructed and maintained, and they break down often. There are no laws about elevators, no mandatory inspections, no licensing or certification. Never mind, her hosts inform her: we don't spend money on such things, but we do spend a great deal of money tracking down the offenders, and we give them long prison sentences at state expense, to show them what we think their bad behavior deserves. Our traveler would be justified in thinking that this is a very odd and irrational society, and one that, at some level, did not take the whole issue of human safety seriously. . . . But that . . . is how most societies treat most crimes. This neglect is even stranger in that criminals, unlike elevators, are equal citizens, among those whose welfare society is committed to protect and advance."

We need not rely on analogy to point out the folly in depending upon our *ex post* strategy of incarceration to eradicate criminal behavior. We can look straight at hard numbers: the current U.S. recidivism rate after nine years is 83 percent. *More than three-quarters* of people released from American state prisons go on to be re-arrested for committing another crime.

Once people are incarcerated, we can no longer employ interventions that are purely *ex ante*, but we still can and ought to aim for strategies that lie somewhere between *ex ante* and *ex post*. The goal of incarceration must be to have an opportunity to identify the deficits preventing the people from thriving—in Savannah's case addiction and unemployment and psychiatric illness and a history of trauma—and to use the time they are incarcerated to attempt to shore up those areas of weakness. Otherwise we fail to acknowledge a system that has failed Savannah since she was a child and we send her back to the motel, to a cycle of addiction and trauma and violence out of which she has been unable to break.

4.

YOU GOT KIDS?

In Connecticut I evaluated Kevin, a man in his late thirties who had already served several years in prison earlier in his life for a minor drug offense. When I met with him, he'd been arrested and jailed again on a similar charge. Until 2015 the state of Connecticut had some of the most draconian drug laws in the nation. A person's first conviction for mere possession—not sale—of small amounts of heroin or crack cocaine carried a sentence of up to seven years in prison.

As the interview progressed, Kevin easily met all the standards of competency we covered except that he seemed unable to engage in a meaningful discussion about a strategy for his defense. "It don't matter," Kevin said over and over, shaking his head. I continued to push at this question, trying to determine whether his nihilism about the sentence he was facing was rooted in a deep depression that would prevent him from working with his attorney to obtain the most favorable outcome. Or perhaps it was based in some kind of paranoia about a court conspiracy; perhaps he felt that his public defender was in cahoots with the prosecutor or with the police.

"Do you think that if you took your case to trial, that the trial would be fair?" I asked him, probing for paranoia.

He looked at me, eyes blazing. "Lady, what do you think?" he asked. I cocked my head and waited for him to say more. "You think a Black man with a prior conviction gets a fair trial in America? I been through this charade before. I know how it ends. Don't matter what I do or say. It's *irrelevant.*"

In my report to the court, I stated that I believed he was competent.

Whether defendants are mentally ill or mentally well, iniquitous and illogical punishments undermine our stated societal goals of justice, fairness, accountability, reconciliation, and safety.

Neuroscience and human development teach us a great deal on the subject of punishment. Children's behavior—and misbehavior—is shaped best when they face the natural consequences of their actions. A child refuses to eat her dinner because vegetables are "gross." If she is allowed to experience the natural consequence of her actions—that she feels hungry when getting ready for bed—then she can make the logical connection that her choice not to eat led to an undesirable outcome. Similar examples abound. A child refuses to put on his mittens on a winter day. The natural consequence he will experience is that his hands will be cold. A girl repeatedly takes toys away from her classmate when they play together. As a result the classmate soon chooses to play with another child and the girl realizes that if she does not play fair, she will play alone.

In contrast, when unduly harsh punishments are meted out for these infractions—when we spank a child for rudely refusing her dinner, for example—we bring about an effect that is the exact opposite of what we desire. A study that looked at fifty years of research on more than 160,000 children revealed that spanking did not increase a child's behavioral compliance one bit in either the short or the long term. Quite the opposite, in fact. Spanking children was "associated with unintended detrimental outcomes." Kids who were spanked were no more likely to behave well, but they *were* more likely to exhibit antisocial behaviors and manifest mental-health problems.

Overly harsh, illogical punishment is just as counterproductive in adulthood as it is in childhood. Evidence abounds that incarceration reinforces rather than reduces criminal knowledge and tendencies. In-equitable punishments convey the message to defendants that the justice system is anything but just. This understanding of the system does not promote adherence to its rules or compliance with its demands.

It's important to underscore that though the vast majority of the com-petency evaluations take place in correctional facilities with people who are locked therein, every single one of the people evaluated for compe-tency is a pretrial detainee. This means that although they are jailed, the men and women whose competency is in question have only been charged with crimes, not convicted of them. Pretrial detention, in fact, is a system that disproportionately holds people who are constitutionally defined as "presumed innocent" behind bars based not on dangerousness but on poverty. I routinely evaluate people who have already been incar-cerated for months by the time I see them, despite the fact that they haven't been convicted of a single crime. Often they remain jailed in-stead of out on bail because they cannot come up with a bond sum of a few hundred dollars.

In all but the most violent or high-profile cases, people who aren't perceived to be a flight risk are assigned bail at a hearing that takes place shortly after they are arrested. Bail is meant to serve as a guarantee that the defendant will return to court for his proceedings. The defendant gives the court the bail money, and once the court proceedings have finished, the money is to be returned to the defendant. In most states, regardless of the actual amount set at the bail hearing, defendants who are considered low risks for running away or skipping out on court must come up with only 10 percent of that amount in order to be released from jail during the pretrial period. The remaining 90 percent is covered by commercial bail bondsmen who put up the rest of the bond and charge interest.

Of note, the practice of bail bondsmen itself is rife with murky ethics. The United States and the Philippines are the only countries in the world that allow a commercial bail-bond market. Our continued en-dorsement of bail-for-profit is denounced as a human rights violation by many of our strongest allies. Some states—including Kentucky, New Jersey, and New Mexico—have taken measures to significantly reduce the cash-bail practices of their states. Washington, D.C., and California have become the first places in the United States to formally end their use of money bail altogether, relying instead on risk-assessment algorithms to help determine the likelihood that people will return to court.

But most states have not undertaken this kind of reform, and the numbers of people held in pretrial detention astound. On an average day, 451,000 people in America are being held in jail pretrial, at an annual cost to local governments of $13.6 billion.

The systemic, imbalanced incarceration of people based on poverty—people who have been convicted of no crime—is on its own an egregiously unjust punishment to suffer. But the personal costs of pretrial detention reach far beyond the endurance of incarceration itself. Jobs are lost as people languish in jail. As a result, rent goes unpaid, eviction notices are issued, and personal belongings are seized. People who cannot make bail have already proved themselves to be living without any kind of financial safety net. The cumulative implications of these additional losses, then, can be insurmountable.

And there are consequences of pretrial detention that are more wrenching still. The repercussions of imprisonment that plague those who've been sentenced to serve time ricochet in the same way through the families of pretrial detainees who are held behind bars without any determination of guilt. Nowhere is this grievous injustice more apparent to me than when I perform evaluations in the women's jail.

Nearly half the mothers who are incarcerated in America are single parents. Roughly a quarter million children in our country live with their lone caregiver in jail. Imagine, then, the trauma and havoc cast upon a family when a single mother is incarcerated without a conviction. When single parents are locked up, minor children are abandoned. In some fortunate situations, family members may be able to assume responsibility for their care, though even this best-case scenario may mean that children are forced to move homes and change schools. Often the circumstances of the extended families into which these children are thrust are bleak. If the family members were not already able—for whatever reason—to help provide a nominal sum of money to bail out their incarcerated kin, the environments that must absorb the care of one or more of the jailed woman's children are at best strained and at worst tumultuous, even unsafe.

Still, women who are unable to post bail may understandably choose to send their children into those strained environments rather than the alternative, which is to have them taken into foster care. For many incarcerated single mothers, there *is* no alternative to this brutal separation. The mothers go into jail and stay there, unable to post bail. The children are placed in state custody, living with strangers.

Even as I write this, I anticipate the pushback. Those who say, *Well, the mother shouldn't have gotten into trouble in the first place.* Those who say, *Maybe the children would be better off in foster care than with a parent who commits crimes.*

The presumption of innocence is a foundational element of the system of justice in our country. Our constitution stipulates that no one is guilty of a crime until adjudged to be so. Not one of the pretrial mothers I see who has been separated from her children has yet been convicted of any charges. These women are guilty only of being poor. If they could afford to post bail, they would await further court proceedings in their homes with their children.

And their convictions are not inevitabilities. Even the most cynical among us cannot pretend that culpability is universal among people who are arrested. Among those who do plead guilty, or who are found to be guilty, many will not be sentenced to prison time. They will get probation or community service. They could be mandated to attend mental-health treatment or substance-abuse programs. They could be fined. In these instances—as when people who've been jailed are found to be not guilty—pretrial incarceration is a punishment that has been endured without any just reason or cause.

Every day single mothers are locked up for nonviolent crimes that have no bearing whatsoever on the safety of their children, on their ability to care for their children. In countless cases the crimes they commit—prostitution, selling drugs, shoplifting—are desperate attempts to provide for the needs of their sons and daughters.

The brokenness of the system reverberates further. Children whose parents are incarcerated are more apt to abuse alcohol and drugs, smoke cigarettes, and engage in risky sexual behaviors as young adults. They also face increased odds of developing an anxiety disorder, dropping out of school, becoming a parent before the age of eighteen, spending time in jail, and being charged with felony crimes. These are all downstream consequences that weaken our families and communities rather than protect them.

In the United States, men and women charged with violent offenses spend an average of seven months in jail before being tried. For non-violent offenders the average is three months. This is wasted time and wasted money given that the vast majority of pretrial detainees pose little or no risk to their communities.

The psychiatric effects of pretrial detention—a period characterized by the brutal combination of helplessness and uncertainty—can also be devastating. People who've been sentenced to prison are three times more likely than the free population to commit suicide. Pretrial detainees fare far worse, taking their own lives at *ten* times the rate of the general adult population.

In a country that guarantees due process before punishment, the mental-health toll enacted on people who are locked up merely because of their poverty is a violation of our sacred principles. It is a sentence without a conviction. It is a miscarriage of justice that is, for many, too harsh to bear.

A PLEA BARGAIN affords a reduced sentence in exchange for a guilty plea. Plea bargains are deals offered by the prosecutor to the defendant. This arrangement is advantageous to the prosecutor because the case registers as a guilty verdict—the prosecutorial goal—and quickly re-solves the case, thereby reducing the prosecutor's caseload. It is advanta-geous to the courts because the deal staves off the need for a trial, saving the courts both money and time. It is advantageous to the defendant because it reduces the maximum penalty for the charges the defendant is facing and removes the uncertainty associated with what the outcome might be at the trial's end.

However.

Many countries do not allow plea bargaining within their legal systems out of a concern that it unjustly persuades innocent people to plead guilty. Nonetheless, the practice is on the rise. More than sixty countries around the world allow plea bargaining. In 1990 only nineteen did so.

Many of the defendants I see will take a plea deal not out of account-ability or even guilt but rather out of desperation to return to work or family or pets, to meet financial obligations, or to retain housing. Others lack faith in the fairness of the American criminal legal system. This is especially true of defendants of color, who are all too aware of the his-toric and modern-day racial prejudices reflected within our nation's courts.

Defendants may also lack faith in their legal representation. Though I certainly see people whose mistrust of their lawyers is based in a delu-sional paranoia, the reasons for most detainees' lack of hope are far more mundane. Nearly all the men and women I evaluate are represented by public defenders—attorneys whose overwhelming caseloads often result in a minimal amount of time and attention available to be devoted to any one individual defendant. Turning down a plea bargain in order to plead not guilty and take a case to trial, then, may seem akin to gambling. The stakes are often years of one's life.

Once I sat across from Jaylen, who was facing a maximum sentence of ten years in prison for an alleged assault related to a marijuana sales sting. Jaylen was six feet four inches tall, muscular, and heavily tattooed.

The public defender who'd requested the competency evaluation had said that he'd met only briefly with Jaylen because he felt afraid of him. Moments into the evaluation, as I was reviewing Jaylen's charges and their respective maximum sentences with him, it became clear that Jaylen and his lawyer had met so briefly that they hadn't even discussed the specifics of the charges. Jaylen was unaware of the amount of time he could be facing.

When I added up the maximum sentences of his charges and said that he could face ten years in prison, tears streamed down Jaylen's face; his body was racked with sobs. He laid his head on the table. When he raised it back up, his shoulders were still shaking and mucus ran from his nose. With his wrists cuffed, he tried several times, awkwardly, to wipe his nose on his shoulder. I reached into my pocket and offered him a crumpled tissue that he reached both cuffed hands forward to take while shaking his head.

He wiped his nose, then looked straight at me. "You got kids?" he asked, in a half shout, half sob. "What are you talking about, ten years? I got kids!" He choked, gasping for air.

"Ain't nothing right about the way this is going down!" he cried, still looking at me with a desperate urgency. "You know how they came to get me? Cops kicked in my door without a warrant in the middle of the night. My baby girl was screaming. They pointed a gun at my grandmother," he said, with tears still running down his cheeks. "She was in her pajamas, and she pissed her pants.

"They made my grandma piss her pants," he repeated, shaking his head in rage.

His voice broke here, and he closed his eyes tightly, as if to wish the memory away.

When he opened his eyes a moment later, he looked straight at me.

"My baby girl just turned two," he said, quietly now. "You got kids?" he repeated. "Ain't no way I can do ten years."

Guilty or innocent, I knew that if Jaylen were offered a plea bargain, he would almost certainly take the deal.

———————

AND WHO AMONG US wouldn't do the same?

How much would you be willing to gamble in pursuit of justice? How much of your life would you be willing to lay on the line as a wager?

Say you're thirty-eight years old. The parent of two children, ages five and nine. They're in kindergarten and fourth grade now, but the next time you get to spend more than a brief prison visit with them, the next time you get to sit down together for a meal, hold them in your arms for more than a perfunctory hug, sleep in the home where they've been raised, the five-year-old will be in high school and the nine-year-old will be nineteen—grown and perhaps already gone. When you get out at age forty-eight, your spouse might have remained faithful and waited for your return. Or she might have done so dutifully for the first few years but then ached with loneliness, strained to raise your children alone, struggled to pay the household bills with only her salary. She might have fallen in love with someone else. Or she might have fallen out of love with you. Maybe she stayed true for the whole decade, but maybe six years in she discovered a lump in her breast. You found out on the phone, listened to her crying, her voice trembling with fear, and you could do nothing. Couldn't hold her. Couldn't go to her. Couldn't sit with her in the hospital waiting room. Couldn't nurse her back from the surgery, tend her during the chemotherapy, shoulder the load of the parenting and the household chores when she was too weak to do so.

Does this feel too imaginary? Too hypothetical? It's easy to perform the exercise. Subtract ten from your current age and begin to list the major events that have happened in your life during the last decade. Here's mine, a partial list:

My daughter is born. My son.

All their preschool years go by. Kindergarten classrooms, each with a cage full of chrysalises that turn into butterflies for the children to watch in wonder and then set free. Elementary school—all of it. Every soccer game played. Every swim meet and music recital. Each of her school plays. All of his rapturous Christmases.

The stitches he got when the cousin he idolizes was tossing him onto a beanbag chair in glee and his head whacked the corner of a table. The nights of fever she had with pneumonia when I lay beside her, singing softly, a washcloth in my hand to wipe her fiery brow.

The weddings of two of my dearest friends.

My mother's mastectomy. The nights with her in the hospital. Helping her to untangle her surgical drain. Asking the nurse for pain medication, for a box fan to set in the window to move air through the sweltering room.

My father's hip replacement. Then his Thanksgiving Day stroke; my mad rush to fly across six states to get to his bedside. How I'd said to my mother, "He'll get better, these symptoms are temporary," with all the medical authority I could muster. How she—unflinching and always anchored in pragmatism—saw through my bravado, saw it for the desperate prayer it was, and, brushing away her tears of anguish, delivered a small rebuke. "You don't know that. We can't know that." How, in the weeks and months and years that followed, my brother and I would reach out to each other. *How do we help him? How do we help her? How are you doing with all this?*

A last visit with my son to my sweet grandfather before he died. A boat tour together on a wide Florida lake and dinner with my grandpa's chums in the dining room of his assisted-living facility and how my boy ate a huge ice-cream sundae and the octogenarians around him clapped and crooned in delight. How my grandfather zipped ahead of me in his motorized wheelchair so he could, chivalrous to the end, open every door for me to walk through.

The funerals of the parents of three of my closest friends. A toast of bourbon to one at a table overlooking Biscayne Bay. A Hindu priest kneeling before me and chanting as I tore white flower petals and placed them in the casket of another. My first-ever recitation of the mourner's kaddish for the third. At each of them, a chance to wrap my arms around my friends, to hold them as they leaned their weight against me.

The happy life that my wife, Deborah, and I built together. July evenings at the water's edge watching our children catch spider crabs and search for pipefish. Our anniversaries—ten of them. Hushed, sweet dinner dates over candlelight. And ten autumns of raucous football Saturdays—a period during which my beloved Michigan Wolverines cycle through three head coaches and hordes of forgettable quarterbacks, and a point in every season when I'm lying on the floor and moaning after yet another interception and my children giggle uncontrollably at my agony.

Here is what I say about all of it: Give me the forty lashes. Lock the pillory around my neck and wrists. The punishment will be cruel—of course it will be cruel—and I will suffer. But do not lock me away from my children for ten years. Do not block me from my marriage bed. Do not keep me from my parents as they are sick and as they age, from my dear ones as they grieve. Do not pretend that enacting violence upon my body is somehow less humane than wrenching me from all whom I love, than preventing me from living a life.

Wouldn't you, too, take forty lashes instead of ten years? Instead of five years? Instead of one? How is it, exactly, that we came to believe that ravaging one's life is less cruel than ravaging one's body?

OVER THE COURSE of a competency evaluation, I am asked to assess whether a defendant can rationally consider and weigh potential plea bargains. *What would you believe to be a really good deal in your case?* I ask them. *Or a really bad one? What do you think a realistic offer might be?* We are meant to be sure that they understand the risks and benefits associated with whichever course they choose, and to be sure that they are taking these risks and benefits into account in deciding to either plead guilty and accept a deal or plead not guilty and take the case to trial. It is relatively easy for me to assess whether a person is answering these questions with lucidity or whether his or her decision-making capacity is clouded by psychiatric illness. But the underlying legal question of what constitutes a rational response seems to me to be a thornier one when I consider the question outside the bounds of whether a person is mentally ill. How can we expect any of these men and women to think rationally in these most irrational of circumstances?

In these conversations a defendant's thinking is not about guilt or innocence. Instead the decision is often laced with fear of the maximum penalty, awareness of limitations of legal representation, and a lack of faith that the case will meet a factual, fair outcome. It is also invariably weighted by the time already spent in jail and away from one's family. Whether to accept or reject a plea bargain becomes almost entirely detached from the crime or from the person's responsibility for it. Instead the process is strategic, a game of chance. The question becomes, *How much of your own life are you willing to risk?* And, *What are you willing to endure?*

This is the calculus involved in plea bargaining. What injustice would you swallow, what punishment would you accept, in order to avoid the risk of being locked inside a cell for years?

Many times in the midst of my competency questions, men and women have asserted to me that the choice they're meant to have does not, in fact, feel like a choice at all. Even defendants I see whose claims of innocence are bolstered by a great deal of evidence that could lead to an acquittal are often so afraid of the prospect of losing at trial and receiving the maximum sentence that they express an anxious willingness to take a deal.

The short-term gain of such a decision, however, can pale in comparison to the long-term consequences. Pleading guilty to a felony charge— even a minor charge, even if it was done only to accept a deal—has far-reaching societal implications, the longitudinal repercussions of which are not always clear to those who do so.

A plea bargain is a deal, not a confession. This arrangement short-circuits the procedure of justice. No trial takes place, no witnesses are called, no evidence is presented. This is no longer a due process in which a jury of one's own peers examines the case with the goal of determining both truth (*is this person guilty or not guilty?*) and accountability (*if guilty, what should the punishment be?*). All citizens accused of criminal acts are constitutionally guaranteed the right to a fair trial by the Sixth Amendment. In circumventing this process, plea bargains strip away the importance of truth and culpability and dangle reduced risk before defendants like a lure. There is no space for rational consideration. *You got kids?* Jaylen asked.

Many of the people I evaluate admit their guilt straightaway. The fact that they are responsible for the act is often, to them, not in question. They don't deny the charges. But almost universally they are desperate for me to understand the context. Why they did what they did. The circumstances that led up to the moment that has changed their lives. When I review the maximum penalties with them, there is almost always some kind of outcry—an assertion that the correlation between the number of years they might serve and the crime committed is absurd. In so many cases, that incredulity is warranted.

The game of the plea bargain and the excessive looming punishments act in concert to move people from their initial positions of responsibility. The threat of an unjust, disproportionate punishment makes people back away from acknowledging culpability. It's one thing to acknowledge that you spit on a police officer when he arrested you for shoplifting. It's quite another to admit responsibility when the act of spitting has translated into assault on a public-safety officer—a charge that carries with it a maximum sentence of ten years in prison. The admission shifts from acknowledging having committed an offense to acknowledging having done something that merits a severe punishment. The change in terms prompts a reflexive, defensive stance.

This process is counterproductive to the aim of accountability and justice. When people feel as if the sentence they face is unjust and that they are being mistreated, they will not engage honestly with whatever mistreatment they themselves might have inflicted upon others. If the punishment does not suit the crime, there is an innate disavowal of the whole system.

There is more lost here than just the defendant's sense of fairness.

When we forgo an honest engagement in which accountability is accepted and a just consequence results, we lose a central tenet of justice. Punishment is intended in part to right a wrong, to reconcile an injury. A core principle of justice is that accountability and responsibility ought to be accepted. Victims' families speak of the hurt they feel in the absence of any kind of apology. How much more so when the act itself, and responsibility for it and for its implications, is not even acknowledged? No reconciliation is possible without this fundamental first step.

I am not an abolitionist. In my work I have encountered enough of the cruel corners of the human psyche to know firsthand that prisons in some version are necessary for people who harbor deep-seated desires to harm others and who lack the moral checks and impulse control to prevent them from doing so. Once, in a competency interview, a man wanted to make certain that I understood that though he had stabbed his girlfriend, he should not have been charged with attempted murder. "I wasn't trying to kill her," he told me. "If I had been trying to kill her, I would have taken her into the soundproof room I have. The one with all the guns." Then he grinned as he told me how panicked she became when she realized he was coming at her with a kitchen knife.

I am neither naïve nor overly idealistic. I'm not trying to make this fearsome world simpler than it is.

But I've performed competency evaluations on jailed men and women for years now. And I've treated thousands of psychiatric inpatients, many of whom themselves have come into contact with the criminal legal system and all of whom I must assess on a daily basis for dangerousness. Out of all these people—the whole mass of them—there've been only a handful who I thought were so dangerous, so likely to seriously injure other human beings, that I believed they needed to be kept away from the rest of society for a long time.

I can therefore subscribe to the way in which the author and legal scholar James Forman Jr. urges us to think about abolition. "What I love about abolition . . . is the idea that you imagine a world without prisons, and then you work to try to build that world."

Even people imprisoned for having committed acts of violence need not be locked away forever. The nonprofit law firm UnCommon Law develops long-term rehabilitation programs for people serving sentences for violent crimes. UnCommon Law has worked with more than two hundred people who have been released from life sentences—and not one of those people has gone on to commit another violent crime.

A study out of Stanford looked at people originally sentenced to life for murder who were subsequently released on parole. It determined that of all offenders, lifers who had been in for murder were the *least* likely group to return to prison if they were released on parole, with a recidivism rate of less than 1 percent.

Prison is and should be about safety. That's the logical application. And as such, prisons should contain only those people from whom society needs to be protected. The men and women who match this description are, in fact, a very small fraction of the enormous numbers of people who are incarcerated. The rest of those we imprison? We do so unjustly, and at our own peril. We cultivate hardened criminals out of people who might have been contributing members of our society.

Taking away someone's liberty as punishment is not in and of itself an egregious idea. It can instead be a pragmatic one. Imprisonment—like involuntary hospitalization—can serve as a means of protecting society from someone who is acutely dangerous. And like sending a child to time-out, it can be a disciplinary tool, expressing quite simply to someone that behavior that transgresses our societal norms will result in a temporary removal from society. Imprisonment needn't be degrading. If it were humane instead of debasing, constructive instead of destructive, it could be used as a moral mechanism to enhance the safety of our societies.

This is not the case today.

5.

JAIL, NOT YALE

I attend a meeting at Manson Youth Institution where the prison's discharge planner expresses her concern about the difficulties boys face immediately upon leaving the facility. She has a thorough understanding of the way those formidable obstacles reduce the boys' chances of reintegrating into their communities in healthy, law-abiding ways. The discharge planner tells me that one-third of the adolescents who are discharged from MYI are homeless when they leave. She then recounts a story about a kid she'd recently been preparing for discharge.

"He'd been a real asshole the whole time," she says. He'd been dismissive of her, dismissive of the idea of planning for his discharge.

But when the time finally came for him to go, she says she was getting his things together for him and he asked her, "Where am I going to sleep?" She said she didn't know, that she didn't have a place for him to stay. It was winter, and the temperature outside that day was fourteen degrees.

"I don't even have a coat, miss," he pleaded.

She looks at me and says, "Even though he'd been an asshole . . ." She pauses. Shakes her head. "This is where the job is really hard." She begins to tear up, stands up from the table where we're sitting, and walks quickly out of the room. I finish her sentence in my head. Even though he'd been an asshole, he is still a person. He is still a child.

After the meeting I walk through the hallways of Manson with a CO and four other psychiatrists. As I do, I notice that the only white faces I see belong to adults. Me. Three of the four psychiatrists. Some of the staff. There's a yellow line painted on the concrete floor that divides the prison hallways in half. One side, the one that I walk on with my fellow psychiatrists, is unimpeded. The other is the boys' side, and it is interrupted every so often by a metal detector, which, in order to continue walking, they must pass through. They're not permitted to cross the line. Some boys walk alone or in pairs headed to their jobs within the facility or to medical or legal appointments. Some walk in a line from their cellblock to the prison schoolrooms. Visitors provide novelty, and as we pass, they turn their heads to watch us. They crane their necks. One cracks a quiet joke to the kid in line behind him, covers his mouth with his hand, smirks, punches his friend playfully on the shoulder. The friend laughs, watching the CO out of the corner of his eye, ready to become stone-faced should the CO turn to spot them.

The boys wear matching baggy tan tops and bottoms that in another context I would have assumed to be scrubs. As we walk through the hallways, I notice a boy in a brightly colored jumpsuit, different from all the others. "That's high bond," the guard who's guiding us says. In this facility that means the boy's bond is set at over a million dollars. The CO tells us there are a handful of boys in here for which that is true. "Courts do it so that we keep an eye on them. Put them in a different color so we can see if they're breaking from the group or something. It's the court's way of saying they're like an extra-high flight risk. But you know teenagers. What it actually means is that in here it gives them crazy status."

We go into one of the prison housing units, and a jocular guard greets us at the door. We are collectively introduced as psychiatrists from Yale, and he breaks into a wide smile. "This is jail, not Yale!" he wisecracks.

"I used to work at an adult facility—maximum," the guard says. "When the inmates would ask for special favors, like books, we would say, 'Where do you think you are, yo? This is jail, not Yale!'"

All around us are the brown faces of teenage boys, looking through their cell doors. Their expressions are solemn. They pay attention.

"Oh, man," the guard says with a chuckle. "I haven't thought about that for a long time. You all enjoy your visit."

We move on, past a series of cells with boys held in them. I think of the ages between fourteen and twenty—middle school, high school, the start of college for some—and how much foundational growth transpires during those years. Everything from learning civics and writing English essays to going on first dates and figuring out how to spend earned money. This is the territory of cramming for final exams and not making varsity and breaking curfew and learning how to talk to teachers one-on-one. It is the period that bridges childhood and adulthood, encompassing puberty and, eventually, individuation from one's caregivers. All the discomfort I've ever felt about seeing men and women locked in cells is multiplied exponentially as I look at the staid expressions of these incarcerated kids, knowing they'll spend months or even years of their teenage lives here, separated from their families and removed from their school communities.

The CO takes us to a cell that is empty so that we can look inside it. The cell is tiny. We have to take turns walking inside because it cannot hold more than two of us at once. In the cell is a set of bunk beds, each with a two-inch-thick mattress. There is a small metal toilet. A small window in the metal door. A small amount of room to walk on the side of the bunk beds to the door or the toilet. There is nothing else.

We are then brought to the library. A young man is in there, holding a book, getting ready to leave. The officer taking us around introduces us to him. The young man greets us politely, then volunteers that he's spent four years here. "It was my first offense," he says. "First and only. I'm not coming back." I wonder what first offense gets you four years. I look at him, subtract four years from his face as best I can, and think he can't have been much more than twelve when he began his time here, though I know that the prison's youngest inmates are fourteen, so he must have been at least that old. Fourteen when he came in perhaps and eighteen when he leaves. His high school years all spent in prison. Some would hear his comment—*I'm not coming back*—as proof that the system works. A shining example of the goal of deterrence having taken root in a once-wayward youth. Cynical others would say, *We'll see about that.* Others still, *Either way, at what cost?*

There is a school area, and in the hallway the students' work is taped up to the walls. There are pages describing what a stereotype is. There is a paper on Down syndrome. There is an art poster—a photograph of a wooden African mask. Because we are on a tour, we're being taken to see the kinds of programming that happens here.

It is not nothing. I do not mean to say that it is nothing. But mostly the visit has been about the good that the prison is doing. Library. School. Art poster. I am glad these things are here. I do not doubt their legitimacy. But it has felt disingenuous that we haven't really discussed the punishment that happens here. The punishment at the core of why this place exists.

We attend a meeting with psychologists, teachers, social workers, correctional officers. We're given a chance to ask questions.

"What's the most severe punishment that can be leveraged against a boy held in this facility?" I ask a psychologist.

"He can be sent to segregation," she says, noting that the practice of solitary confinement exists for incarcerated children just as it does for adults.

"For how long?" I ask.

"Up to a year," she says.

Take the developing brain of an adolescent. Fourteen, fifteen, sixteen years old. Put him in seclusion for a year. He touches no one. Is touched by no one. He yells out, perhaps, or he stays silent, but he interacts with no one. His meals are pushed at him through a slot. We know that isolation changes and damages the adult brain. What about the effects of segregation on the still-developing brain of a child? And a child who presumably has already lacked the foundation for good decision making, has acted with extraordinary impulsivity, has perhaps enacted terrible trauma and perhaps also endured terrible trauma? What then?

We know that the brain undergoes critical periods of growth in adolescence as it changes to form the permanent neurologic structures of adulthood. The experiences and stimuli of adolescence affect the brain's neural circuitry and have a profound influence on the brain's development. This means that the sensory deprivation and the paucity of experience in solitary confinement would have lasting effects on a child's brain, not just psychiatrically but neurologically as well. Psychosocial deprivation in childhood has been demonstrated to *physically alter the brain's structure* at cellular and molecular levels. The results of these fundamental, structural changes in the brain manifest themselves in functional, behavioral, and psychological impairments. In other words, experience builds brain circuitry, and the way these circuits are wired is reflected in the ways that children learn, develop, and behave.

Robust literature on the neurodevelopment of children who were raised in orphanages has shown that these children have brains that differ markedly from the brains of children who were not "institutionally reared." Children raised in institutions have lower IQs. Their brains show changes at the molecular level: their telomeres—the protective caps on chromosomal strands of DNA that typically shorten with aging and disease—are shorter than the telomeres of other children. And the basic brain structure of children raised in institutions is altered—their overall brain volume is reduced. In addition, these children's brains demonstrate a "precocious connectivity" between the amygdala—the impulsive, instinctive region—and the prefrontal cortex, which plays a key role in rational decision making. Researchers believe that this "mature pattern" of neural connection occurs earlier than it should as a result of the children's having endured adversity without the protective buffering of a caregiver early in their lives.

It has long been accepted that the exposure to abuse or trauma can adversely affect a child's developmental trajectory. But neuroscience has come to understand that neural circuitry can be just as adversely affected by the *absence* of experience or stimulation. As a review on psychosocial deprivation in the journal *Neural Plasticity* notes, a "*lack* of experience can be particularly insidious, as the brain awaits instructions to guide its assembly that it fails to receive."

"The programming we've seen here," I ask the MYI psychologist, "the school, the library, the vocational skills—do the kids in segregation get that?"

"In theory yes," she says, "but in practice it's very hard to arrange." She says they have an hour of recreational time each day, during which they're also isolated from other inmates.

One of the fellows in my group asks, Do they have television in their cells in segregation? Do they have radios? Do they have books?

She says there are no electronics. She says sometimes, sometimes the mental-health workers will give them books.

I hear in my mind *When the inmates would ask for special favors, like books...*

In the meeting we'd observed, there had just been a school report from some of the prison's teachers. They had run through the names of a number of boys who were struggling in school. Many of them were mentioned as having substantial difficulty reading. Some could not read in English. Some could not read at all.

"Then what do they do if they don't have electronics? Or books?" the fellow asks. His question hangs in the air. It is not answered. There is no answer.

The American Academy of Child and Adolescent Psychiatry has been concerned enough about the answers to those questions that they've issued a policy statement on the solitary confinement of juvenile offenders. "The potential psychiatric consequences of prolonged solitary confinement are well recognized and include depression, anxiety, and psychosis," they write. "Due to their developmental vulnerability, juvenile offenders are at particular risk of such adverse reactions. Furthermore," they continue, "the majority of suicides in juvenile correctional facilities occur when the individual is isolated or in solitary confinement."

THIS TIME OF developmental flux renders teens biologically programmed to make mistakes and behave in a risky fashion. The transient neurologic and behavioral changes that characterize adolescence make teenagers more likely to try drugs and alcohol than people at any other stage in life. Some adolescents will become dependent on the substances they try. Some will commit crimes in order to obtain them. The adolescent brain also differs from the adult brain in its susceptibility and response to *reward*—the neurologic term for positive, reinforcing responses in all our brains that are elicited by seductive forces, from love to drugs to gambling. Current research suggests that adolescents who try cocaine become addicted more quickly than adults do. Related evidence indicates that compared with adults, adolescents go through a shorter time period from their first exposure to alcohol and drugs to dependence upon them.

There is a neurologic rationale to adolescents' tendency to ignore the consequences of risk. Studies of brain development have shown that the sensation-seeking drive in humans peaks around the age of fifteen or sixteen. But the ability to control one's impulses does not reach maturity until some ten years later. In fact, the frontal lobes of the brain, which are largely responsible for controlling our impulses, contain some of the last areas of neural circuitry to mature, with their development continuing into our midtwenties.

There are biological and evolutionary reasons that risky behavior spikes in the interspace between childhood and adulthood. Adolescence is a time during which important skills must be obtained in preparation for adulthood. Teenagers begin to separate from their parents and to assert their own autonomy. And they do so in predictable ways across cultures—and even across species.

This is age-normative behavior. There is a purpose to this time, after all. Adolescents must acquire self-sufficiency so that they will eventually be able to survive on their own without parental care. Risk, it turns out, serves an essential evolutionary role.

And it occurs during a precise neurodevelopmental window when impulsivity is on the rise but adult judgment and restraint have not yet kicked in.

Increased affiliation with peers, novelty seeking, and risk taking help adolescents begin to develop a foundation of skills they'll need to be independent. The behavioral tendencies also serve a secondary, evolutionary purpose. Teenagers' desire to stray from the nest expands both their social circles and the geographic territory they cover, guarding against inbreeding within the gene pool.

Regardless of potential gains and evolutionary benefits, with the developmental benefits of risk comes . . . risk. Compared with humans at other stages of life, adolescents are disproportionately reckless. One study showed that 80 percent of eleven-and-a-half- to fifteen-year-olds had had at least one episode of problematic behavior in the previous month, including school misconduct, disobedience to parents, substance use, and antisocial behaviors like theft or fighting. At least half of adolescents drive drunk, have unprotected sex, use illegal drugs, or commit minor criminal offenses. In fact, a review of antisocial behavior in adolescence found that it is "statistically aberrant to refrain from such behavior," with "actual rates of illegal behavior soar[ing] so high during adolescence that participation in delinquency appears to be a normal part of teen life."

Dr. Peter Ash, a forensic psychiatrist at Emory who conducts research on juvenile delinquency and questions of adolescent culpability, describes the neurodevelopmental mismatch thus: "Adolescent brains have got a foot on the gas, weak brakes, and leaky brake lines." They are, he says, "in a developmental stage of weakened self-control."

Dr. Ash points out that among all boys there is a high incidence of aggression in adolescence. In fact, he cites that by the age of eighteen the percentage of boys who've committed a serious violent offense—defined as an action that could have severely hurt someone else—is estimated to be between 35 and 40 percent. Which is to say that more than a third of boys commit at least one act of serious violence before they reach adulthood.

Lasting negative consequences of risk-taking behavior can be eluded—or they can be dire. Teenagers drive too fast, and crash their cars, and get into violent fights over trivial conflicts, and stupidly dive headfirst into too-shallow bodies of water. Some get pregnant. Many contract STDs. Some become dependent on drugs and alcohol. Some get thrown into jail. Developmental psychopharmacologist Linda Patia Spear writes that for certain adolescents the risk taking of adolescence becomes a more permanent, adult lifestyle characterized by continued criminal behavior. "Fortunately," Spear writes, "experimentation in risk taking is transient for most individuals, with the vast majority of adolescents surviving the lottery" of negative consequences that they have entered.

What, then, of those kids who are not the "fortunate" ones in the "vast majority" who "survive the lottery" of negative consequences? The fact that the vast majority of teenagers emerge from neurological immaturity relatively unharmed does not absolve us of responsibility to care for—or about—those, like Savannah, like the boys in MYI, who do not. Indeed, the fact that most *do* survive—and that most of us have—tempts us into the self-congratulatory position of seeing survival not as the result of chance in a lottery but as something that we've done right. It enables us to see those who have *not* survived unscathed as having done something wrong or as having some innately flawed element of their character.

In truth, the odds of surviving the lottery are influenced in part by luck but primarily by other established factors as well. Race, for instance. Gender. Socioeconomic status.

The odds also differ depending on where you live. If you are between the ages of thirteen and seventeen in the state of Georgia, for example, and if you are facing one of seven specifically identified charges, the "Juvenile Justice Reform Act" (I put the name of the bill in quotes given that there's very little justice and even less reform contained within it) passed in 1994 stipulates that you are automatically transferred to adult court. These charges—voluntary manslaughter, aggravated child molestation, aggravated sexual battery, aggravated sodomy, murder, rape, and armed robbery with a firearm—are known collectively as the "Seven Deadly Sins." For more than fifteen years, children convicted of these charges were also subjected to mandatory sentences, leaving judges with no ability to reduce or mitigate the punishment to be incurred. The law dictated that a first conviction resulted in a minimum ten-year prison sentence. A second conviction for any of these offenses automatically resulted in a life sentence without parole. Mandatory two strikes and you're out, for children.

Worse still, juveniles in Georgia who were sentenced to life in prison without the possibility of parole were automatically sent to serve their sentences in adult prisons, an arrangement well known to lead to sexual and physical victimization of child detainees at the hands of adult prisoners.

These practices were the law in Georgia until two landmark decisions by the U.S. Supreme Court in 2010 and 2012. In the first, *Graham v. Florida*, the court ruled that it was unconstitutional to sentence juveniles to life in prison without parole for any crime other than murder. In the second, *Miller v. Alabama*, the court deemed that mandatory-minimum life sentences without the possibility of parole constituted cruel and unusual punishment of juveniles in all cases, murder included. In 2013 the Georgia legislature finally passed a bill of its own, introducing a "safety valve" through which juveniles charged with any of the Seven Deadly Sins could be offered plea bargains rather than automatically receiving the mandatory minimum of ten years for a first offense established by the Juvenile Justice Reform Act of 1994.

Georgia may seem uniquely unmerciful, but the severe sentencing of juveniles is not an aberration. Deputy Warden Adams of Rhode Island's ACI told me that he and his correctional officers were "noticing more and more juveniles catching big time." I asked him what kind of sentences they were seeing. "Like forty/forty/ten," he said, meaning that they were seeing juvenile defendants who had three charges sentenced to forty years for the first, forty years for the second, and ten for the third. Kids being sentenced to ninety years in prison for charges stemming from a single incident.

Until the 2005 Supreme Court decision of *Roper v. Simmons*, juvenile offenders in America could be sentenced to death. The Court ruled in that case that capital punishment of children is unconstitutional. It based its decision upon the rationale that juveniles should be considered less culpable than adults because of their age-related impulsivity, their vulnerability to their environment, and the fact that the character of a juvenile is still in flux. We can't yet know whether a child's criminal act will prove to be "a marked deviation from an otherwise law abiding life."

In other words, is the kid a bad seed, a lost cause, a danger to society? Or did he merely draw a bad number in the lottery?

And it should surprise no one that the children who end up in prison do so disproportionately based on their race. Statistics, science, and anecdotal evidence all deliver this message with a grave consistency: racial prejudice influences criminal justice involvement from the moment of arrest to conviction, sentencing, and facility placement. Black kids are 2.3 times more likely to be arrested than are their white peers, a discrepancy that is higher than it was even ten years ago. At each stage of the judicial process, racial disparities among children multiply. Black juveniles are less likely to have their cases diverted before hearings than are their white peers; they are less likely to receive probation as a sentence; they are more than four times as likely as white juveniles to be committed to a detention facility.

Over the last two decades, the Supreme Court has repeatedly grappled with the constitutionality of extreme juvenile sentencing—life without parole, for instance, or consecutive sentences that add up to hundreds of years, thus avoiding the legal restrictions placed on life sentences but easily reaching far beyond the span of a life. Prior to the 2010 decision of *Graham v. Florida*, the state of Florida had led the nation in sentencing children to life in prison. As of 2009, researchers Jennifer L.

Eberhardt and Aneeta Rattan found that 84 percent of the juvenile offenders who received a life sentence without parole in the state of Florida for non-homicide cases were African American, though the population of the state as a whole is less than 16 percent Black.

Rattan and Eberhardt, along with their Stanford colleagues Carol S. Dweck and Cynthia S. Levine, have conducted research that begins to examine the disturbing role of racial bias in the severe sentencing of juveniles. They noted that Black children who went to trial and were sentenced in adult courts received punishments significantly harsher than those handed down to their white juvenile peers. "And," they note, "this practice is on the rise."

The Stanford team designed an experiment with a subject group of white Americans, a group that, they noted, is "overrepresented in jury pools, the legal field and the judiciary." They sought to assess whether the race of the defendant altered the way in which the white Americans in the study viewed the juveniles' individual guilt and responsibility. "In other words," they write, "we asked whether race influences the extent to which juveniles are viewed as less culpable than adults and, as a result, [whether it influences] the support for a punitive policy directed at them."

The nearly seven hundred white subjects were divided into two groups. Both groups were asked to read materials explaining that, at the time of the experiment, "life without parole sentences for juveniles in non-homicide cases were currently under review by the Supreme Court." They were then given identical information about the Supreme Court case, including the fact that "there was both support for and opposition to this sentencing option" and "that approximately 100 people had received life without parole sentences as juveniles for non-homicide cases." Within the reading materials, the researchers embedded a specific example of a case the Court had chosen to review in assessing the general constitutionality of such sentences: a fourteen-year-old boy, with seventeen prior juvenile convictions, who'd been convicted of brutally raping an elderly woman.

For the study the researchers altered just one word. In the materials presented to one group of subjects, the fourteen-year-old was described as "a Black male with 17 prior juvenile convictions." The materials for the other group described "a White male with 17 prior juvenile convictions." No other changes were made.

The experiment yielded two profound results. First, the subjects reading about a Black juvenile expressed "significantly more support" for dead-end sentences of life without the possibility of parole for juveniles whose crimes fell short of murder than did those subjects who'd read that the juvenile in question was white. Second, associating the crime with a Black child also affected participants' overall perceptions of juvenile culpability. The white subjects who'd read that the offender was Black were more apt to state that they thought the responsibility and blameworthiness of people who commit crimes was similar, regardless of whether the defendant was a juvenile or an adult. In contrast, the subjects who'd read about a white offender responded that juveniles who commit crimes should, by virtue of their age, be viewed as less culpable than adults.

ALL TEENAGERS MANIFEST the tumult of the transitional period of adolescence. But teenagers condemned to correctional facilities must do so within dire contexts and with iniquitous consequences. Enceno Macy was fifteen when he took part in a robbery during which a person was killed. Someone else killed the victim, but as a participant in the robbery Macy was charged as an adult with felony murder. Because he was a minor, Macy was put in "involuntary protective custody"—solitary confinement—in the adult county jail for nearly eight months, all before he'd even been tried, let alone convicted.

Of his time in solitary, Macy writes, "I was put there solely because of my age and 'for my own protection,' but I was treated the same way as adults who were put in solitary for serious rule violations.

"We received two books a week, two sheets of paper, and a golf pencil," he continues. "There was no access to any form of education or counseling for youth (or anyone else). In the wire cages we sometimes went to for exercise, the space was not much bigger than the cell and there was no room to run. I spent seven and a half months in those conditions."

Macy was convicted and sentenced as an adult, to adult prison. While incarcerated he endured several additional stretches in "disciplinary segregation," the official term for punitive isolation. These periods in "seg," Macy writes, "usually last[ed] a few months each."

With prescience Macy describes how normative teenage behavior—behavior that is neurodevelopmentally essential for individuation and establishing independence and which Dr. Ash would ascribe to weak brakes and leaky brake lines—is fundamentally misaligned with the prison environment. The disciplinary infractions that led to his time in segregation were "for fighting, leaving my job early, arriving back late from a meal, and copying out the lyrics to a song that they deemed 'gang related,' probably just because it was rap.

"Because of laws that gave mandatory minimums to teens charged as adults," Macy writes, "there were many of us in our late teens going through this mental gauntlet. It was as easy as using profanity when speaking with a state employee to get a couple of weeks in 'seg.' In other words," he continues, "actions that would qualify as everyday misbehavior for most American teenagers would get us placed in conditions that have been widely denounced as torture, especially when used on young people."

Child and adolescent psychiatrist Dr. Louis Kraus served for fourteen years as the chairman of the committee on juvenile justice reform for the American Academy of Child and Adolescent Psychiatry. Lest we lose sight of what we are doing when we put adolescents in solitary confinement, he asks us to look at it square in the face.

"Some solitary rooms don't even have a toilet," Dr. Kraus explains, underscoring that the conditions in many juvenile facilities are far, far worse than those I observed at Manson. "In those rooms there are just holes in the ground where the kids need to squat over a grille in the floor." Like Macy, Dr. Kraus asks us to consider the kinds of offenses that lead kids to be confined in these sorts of rooms for days, or weeks, or months, or a year.

"Picture your kid swearing," Dr. Kraus says. "You decide that as punishment you're going to lock him in his bedroom for the next week. You'll take away all electronics. Give him a pot to pee in. How long do you think would it take for child protective services to come in and take your kid away?" Dr. Kraus pauses to let the truth of his statement sink in. "We don't allow parents to treat their children that way. So why is it that for a group of kids who are especially vulnerable, we've decided that this kind of treatment is acceptable?"

In an era when the mothers and fathers of privileged children are cast as helicopter parents, chastised for protecting their offspring from even the most mundane slights and injuries, children who end up in the juvenile detention system are essentially handed over to the wolves. Adolescent risk taking is both normative and developmentally vital. But in these children we punish it, and we do so with particular ruthlessness in children of color.

Which kids in prison are the irrevocable criminals and which are those who just drew a bad number in the lottery? The question is not a viable one because the lottery is stacked. And kids who are placed in the rigid and intentionally punitive confines of juvenile detention facilities— or worse, in adult prisons—undergo a grievous disruption in the essential social and neurological development of childhood. This breach cannot help but render them different than they otherwise would have been.

Psychiatrists have long understood that children's development influences the trajectory of their adult lives—that attachment to parents or to reliable parental figures is an essential and irreplaceable need for a developing child. And it was well established decades ago that amid neglect, abandonment, even horrific abuse, the presence of a single reliable and loving adult in a child's life can not only mitigate lasting psychological damage but can also confer a kind of developmental protection.

Herein are the stories of children raised in poverty and violence by a single, drug-addled parent who emerge intact, apparently against all odds. In nearly every instance, a close look at the story shows the critical, consistent presence of a solid adult in their lives who helped rather than harmed the child. A grandmother who stepped in to provide periods of care and respite from chaos. A teacher or a coach who offered encouragement, stability, and purpose. An older sibling who supplied safety and nurturing where a parent had not.

"I was ruled by sorrow, fear, and anger," Enceno Macy writes of his time in solitary confinement, plagued by a "deep depression about missing people I used to know and," he adds poignantly, "my mom."

Adolescence is by definition a liminal time. Within it, yes, is burgeoning individuation and independence. But within it, too, is the residual child, still in need of love, still in need of constancy, still in need of protection and care. Our nation's justice system assigns punishment to children unevenly and unjustly. And our prisons too-harshly punish the individuating aspects of the adolescent identity, while offering no solace or succor for the unmoored child within.

6.

BORN ON THIRD BASE

Professional football player Malcolm Jenkins posted a tweet at the beginning of the 2018 NFL season. "Before we enjoy this game," Jenkins wrote, "let's take some time to ponder that more than 60% of the prison population are people of color." The comments he received in response to his tweet are identical in message and tone to the remarks I've heard in response to arguments for prison reform.

"Don't commit crimes . . . don't go to prison. And that goes for people of all colors," read one response.

"People go to prison for committing a crime not for being black," read another.

"And??? Don't commit the crimes," read a third.

This refrain—of any degree of punishment and maltreatment being justified by one's guilt—is perhaps the most common one I encounter in defense of our broken prison system. Sometimes people ask about my work and then tell me how it's hard to have sympathy for people who do things that land them in jail. They will say things like, "If you can't stand the time, don't do the crime."

"So you've never broken the law?" I ask in return.

"Nothing like *that*," is the inevitable response. "Nothing that would land me in *jail*."

This is of course patently false. I've seen a man jailed for shoplifting $11.88 worth of merchandise from Walgreens. I've seen a woman jailed for jaywalking and running away from cops after she'd had too much to drink. If people are incarcerated for offenses like these, then nearly all of us have broken the law in ways that would land us in jail. The difference is not our capacity to commit crimes. The difference is our ability to extricate ourselves from their consequences.

Cara Smith, an attorney and Cook County Jail's chief policy officer, powerfully illustrates this difference. "When my son was young, he was having trouble reading," Smith told me. "I took him to a neuro-ophthalmologist for an evaluation. She was a tiny woman, maybe four foot eleven. He went back with her in her office to be tested, and after the testing she came out and said there was nothing wrong with him. My first response was disappointment," Smith confessed. "I mean, if there was nothing that could be identified as the problem, then there was nothing we could fix. It meant that my son was going to have a struggle. He was going to need a lot of support, and it was going to be hard for him. My disappointment must have shown," she continued, "because the neuro-ophthalmologist said to me, 'Look, you don't *want* me to find something wrong with your son. Trust me.' I knew what she was saying— that she sees these devastating conditions, these chronic issues that children and families have to contend with, but I still worried about what this meant for my son. 'All people are born into one line or another,' the doctor said to me. 'I was born in the line without height. Your son was born in this line where reading is a struggle for him.'" Smith paused.

"Ever since then I've tried to use that example when people ask me what it's like to work in the jail. I tell them we were all born in these lines. I was born into a line with a loving family and resources. Most of the people in the jail were born in a different line—a line without family, or resources, or money. I tell them we all could have been born into different lines than we were."

If I were arrested, I would be able to read and comprehend the papers stating my charges. I would have a basic understanding of the nuanced mechanics of the system into which I was thrown. As an employed physician, I could most likely pay my bail immediately and without incurring significant personal hardship. In earlier, leaner times of my life—as a medical student on a very tight budget or as a graduate student waiting tables to make ends meet, for example—I had multiple friends and family members to whom I could have turned who would without question have stepped forth to loan me money to keep me from having to spend days, weeks, months in jail. If I were arrested, the concerns would be about my charges—of what was I accused? had I done it? what would the implications be? how was I holding up?—and not about whether I could make bail.

That is a luxury the vast majority of pretrial detainees do not have. I know this to be true when my patients are arrested. For many of them, prescriptions that cost four dollars per month are prohibitively expensive. If bail is set at three hundred dollars, it might as well be set at three million dollars. The two sums are equally unattainable.

It's easier to believe that everyone in prison belongs there. Easier to think that those of us who sleep at home and decide what we'll have for breakfast and decide when we want to shower and choose our clothes each day and get into cars and drive to Florida or Maine or Albuquerque and switch doctors if we want and decide between jobs and go to family weddings and bake pies for the holidays and order takeout and kiss our children every morning, belong where we are. And it's easier to believe that we are where we are because we are morally superior to the people who are not free to do these things. But the truth more often lies in the privilege of circumstance—or in sheer luck—than in any difference of moral character.

When I was growing up in Indiana, there was a phrase the adults in my life would have used for people who think that they are where they are because of their superiority and virtue. *He was born on third base*, they would say, *and thinks he hit a triple.*

"It's easy to do this job if you presume everyone's guilty," Cara Smith said. The unsaid part of her sentence: *yet of course everyone is not.*

The job—which is also to say the way we view our country's prisons and our prisoners—becomes more difficult when you allow yourself to consider uncertainty. Surely some of the people in jail are innocent, serving time for crimes they did not commit. And some are serving time for transgressions that others—including myself—have committed without consequence.

I was in the midst of mulling over these questions when Deborah and I joined some of our dearest friends for an autumn dinner party. There were eight of us around the table. Four married couples—five women and three men, all parents of young children. It is a group that gathers regularly enough that our evenings are light on small talk and heavy on contentment. This night we drank wine and talked about the books we were reading. We commiserated about the poor performances of our favorite college football teams. We brought up the struggles we were having raising our children, seeking advice, perspective, and humor from one another. There were flowers floating in a bowl of water at the center of the table as we ate. Short, stout candles burned themselves into pools of wax as they threw golden light onto our faces: the faces of beloved friends.

As the evening wore on, one of the hosts asked me how the writing of this book was going. A central challenge, I told him, was how to make people who are not incarcerated *care* about people who are. How to break down the false but persistent idea that the kinds of people who are imprisoned are fundamentally—morally and ethically—different from those of us who are free. People want to believe that you go to jail because you break the law and that if you don't want to go to jail, you shouldn't break the law, I told him. If you break the law and go to jail, then many, many people believe that you pretty much deserve whatever you get once you're there.

As I recounted the conundrum to my host, I decided that this group of friends provided the perfect test case for my hypothesis that all of us have committed crimes but only some of us go to jail. We opened another bottle of wine, and I suggested that we confess all the ways in which we'd ever broken the law.

These friends are among the closest friends I have. They are good people. Moral people. They coach youth soccer and manage car pools and responsibly prescribe medications and care devotedly for their aging parents and play on the church softball team. They are people I would entrust without reservation to stay in my home, manage my finances. People with whom I would—and do—entrust my children.

I led off by telling the story of how I'd once lost track of renewing my car registration. I drove with an expired registration for weeks. Eventually I was pulled over. The officer told me I had to get out of the car and come with him, that I could not continue driving the car. My son, three years old at the time, was in his car seat in the back of the car. The officer told me to take my son and the car seat, to leave my car on the side of the road where he would have a tow truck come and impound it, and to get into the rear of the police car. After three or four minutes of polite conversation, I convinced the officer to let me drive home and park in my driveway until I'd gotten the registration renewed. He agreed, drove behind me to my house, gave me a ticket, and said that to reinstate my registration I would need to go to traffic court. Then, just before driving off, he looked at the darkening sky and asked me if I'd heard whether it was supposed to rain.

On the court date, dressed in work clothes, I arrived in the designated courtroom, which was teeming with people waiting their turn. As more and more people filed in, an officer repeatedly called out that it was a busy court day and that we should all make arrangements preparing ourselves to be there for hours. I stopped and asked the officer where I should go once inside the room, having never been to traffic court before.

"Are you a lawyer?" he asked, presumably because I was dressed for work and thus looked as if I might be.

"No," I said, "a doctor."

"Come with me," he said. He took me to the front of the courtroom past rows and rows of people who had arrived before me. He handed my slip to another court official. "Have a nice day, Doc," he said to me.

I was the third person whose case was called. I explained myself to the judge, paid my nominal court fees, and with that the whole thing was done.

I disclosed some other offenses to my friends at the dinner party. Everyone else did, too. In less than an hour, here are the crimes we could collectively remember having committed without suffering any legal repercussions whatsoever.

Every day I text and e-mail while driving. Every day I speed. I've driven double the speed limit. I used to steal plates of cake out of the revolving glass tower in a deli. I knew where my parents kept their cash, and I stole money from them all through my childhood. I used to steal bulk candy every time I went into the grocery store. I drank underage. I drove a car before I had a license. We had scavenger hunts in college where we had to steal everything to win. I used a fake ID. I smoked pot. I used shrooms. I did cocaine. I took Ecstasy. I used speed. I took LSD. I've driven drunk. I snuck an animal through customs. I backed into a car in a parking lot and drove away. I've cheated on my income taxes. I forged a signature on a car title. I evaded police when they tried to pull me over. I forged a college degree to get a trade license. I bribed a police officer after I was caught drunk driving. I broke my car out of an impound lot and used a friend's license plates to drive it home. I carried a revolver licensed to someone else in my backpack across my college campus. I took a credit card that had been left in the copy machine at Staples and charged two thousand dollars' worth of stuff on it before I threw it away.

Only one of us had ever been arrested—for disorderly conduct after a bar fight. "What happened?" I asked.

"I pleaded nolo contendere and had it expunged from my record a year later," my friend said.

These are not all minor crimes. There are felonies herein.

After the dinner party, I told another friend about the question I'd posed and some of the answers I'd received. She told me that a few days prior she'd mailed a package of marijuana edibles to a friend. Marijuana remains illegal in both the state where my friend lives and the state to which she mailed her package. Interstate drug trafficking is a federal crime, I told her. She looked at me wide-eyed and gulped. Then she started to laugh. "So I guess it wasn't very smart of me to use my credit card to pay for the postage?"

It will be easier if we don't pretend that we who live free lives are morally superior to the people who sit in the cells I describe. If we instead acknowledge that privilege and poverty and race are determining factors that suffuse and define our encounters with the criminal legal system. It will be easier if we admit that there are people who are serving time for the very crimes that we ourselves have committed but from which we have suffered no ramifications. That we've all been born into different lines and that for those in the lines that lead to prison, the consequences are grim.

PART II

Our Prisons

7.

THE ARCHITECTURE OF CONTROL

J ails were not originally intended to be forms of punishment. Dungeons and prisons existed in antiquity and through the Middle Ages, but imprisonment was not yet seen as a penance in and of itself. These were holding cells only, used to contain offenders until their trials took place or until their actual sentences could be carried out.

The punishments themselves were corporal—the wrath of the state inflicted on the body of the condemned person. Gallows are mentioned, and pillories. Heads severed from bodies in more ways than a person can imagine. Bodies are branded. They are drawn and quartered. They are doused in oil and set aflame. Wrongdoers are strapped to slowly revolving wheels where their limbs are beaten with a hammer until the bones in the gaps between the spokes give way.

Dead or dying bodies throughout history are crucified or hanged in gibbets. They dangle from chains. They are suspended above roadsides or in public squares. Or they hang in cages at the sea's lowest edge and are left there until the tides have risen and receded three times. Dead bodies were used to set examples—bodies of sailors hung in pre-Revolutionary Boston Harbor as a warning to pirates.

Punishments were often designed so as to multiply agony and draw out suffering as long as possible. Death might have been inevitable, but the administration of the punishment was meant to maximize pain and prolong the anguish of the convict.

These historical punishments are notable not just for their cruelty and torture but also for the critical role that public exhibition and shame played in their implementation. Pillories served as a measure of both discomfort and humiliation, as their positioning in the town square or near the courthouse steps encouraged passersby to notice—and ridicule—the restrained criminal. Indeed, the definition of the word "pillory"—dating back to the year 1325—contains within it the purpose of evoking shame. *A device for punishment, usually consisting of a wooden framework mounted on a post, with holes or rings for trapping the head and hands, in which an offender was confined so as to be subjected to public ridicule, abuse, assault, etc.*, reads the Oxford English Dictionary. Three and a half centuries later—by 1699—the word itself could also be used as a verb, meaning *to abuse, ridicule, or defame.*

Burnings at the stake and hangings took place before cheering crowds. And during the French Revolution, more than twelve hundred people were executed by guillotine in Paris's famed Place de la Concorde, where the killings became a form of cultural entertainment. People brought their children to watch, and fully functional guillotines were sold as toys for use on dolls or for adults to slice bread and vegetables at the dinner table.

America, too, conducted spectacles of torture and execution. The bodies of recaptured slaves who had attempted to escape dangled visibly in cities and towns across slaveholding America to serve as deterrents to others who might have ideas about running away. In Paul Revere's account of his midnight ride, he writes of passing "Charlestown Neck . . . nearly opposite where Mark was hung in chains." Mark Codman, a slave, had murdered his master. The crime had been committed twenty years prior to Revere's famed ride, but as Revere rode past, Codman's desiccated body still hung. Our country's most notorious examples, though, are more recent extrajudicial ones—the more than four thousand lynch-ings of African Americans that took place from the late nineteenth until the mid-twentieth century. These executions were meant to inspire ter-ror rather than carry out the law, but nonetheless lynchings were carnival-like spectacles where white people would gather in the thousands. The dates of the planned events were advertised in white newspapers in advance. Community dignitaries and elected officials attended, joining the audience that had gathered to jeer at the victim as a gruesome mur-der took place. People brought picnics. They brought their children. Vendors circulated through the crowd, hawking food items and postcards that commemorated the event. Some people went home with pieces of the victim's clothing—or even of the body itself—as souvenirs.

In the late eighteenth and early nineteenth centuries, voices in Eu-rope and the United States eventually began to call for a more humane alternative to beatings, maimings, and executions. And imprisonment was portrayed as a more evolved option. As such it became a form of punishment in and of itself, rather than a mere form of containment.

This turn to incarceration marks a transition away from visible, public, bodily punishments meant to maximize physical suffering and shame. In-stead, punishment becomes something meant to restrict and control of-fenders rather than destroy them. From this point forward, the execution of the sentence is intended to affect a person's life rather than his body.

Yet bodily punishment served a purpose. In his seminal work *Disci-pline and Punish*, Michel Foucault writes that enacting power on the body of the criminal had meant that order was restored and the balance of power was re-equilibrated. "If torture was so strongly embedded in legal practice, it was because it revealed truth and showed the operation of power," he writes. It "reproduce[d] the crime on the visible body of the criminal; in the same horror, the crime had to be manifested and an-nulled. It also made the body of the condemned man the place where ... vengeance ... was applied."

The crime made manifest on the criminal. Justice restored by applying the injury to the injurer. This ideal of a body-centric philosophy of punishment is a familiar one throughout history and across traditions. With its "eye for an eye" logic, corporal punishment has retribution and recompense at its core. How, then, to determine the proper scale of punishment when it is no longer doled out in equivalencies? Serving time may be more palatable than torture or execution and theoretically more humane, but there is no easy formula for its calculus. How to pay back a wound with time? How to repair loss with the deprivation of liberty? The math of it does not square. I think of the analogy my medical-school professor gave when explaining the baseless marketing promises of collagen-containing beauty creams that claimed to repair aging skin. That method, he said, was akin to trying to fix a rotting barn by throwing plywood at it.

Like imprisonment, the practice of solitary confinement—the most oppressive form of punishment within our correctional facilities—was not initially intended to be punitive. The origins of American solitary confinement lie in a failed nineteenth-century model, known at the time as the "Philadelphia System." The principle—named because it was first employed in Philadelphia's Eastern State Penitentiary—arose from the idea that time spent in solitude would encourage reflection, penitence (hence "penitentiary"), and eventually reformation. Detainees held in Eastern State were housed in monastic conditions in solitary cells. Each cell was illuminated by a single skylight, representing the "eye of God." The isolation was unremitting: anytime prisoners were taken from their cells to be moved to another location, guards placed hoods over the penitents' heads.

This novel philosophy of corrections grew out of a predominantly Quaker group whose title now resonates with irony: the Philadelphia Society for Alleviating the Miseries of Public Prisons.

At the time, the desperate need for reform was indisputable, and attempting to effect reform was a noble pursuit. Accounts from late-eighteenth-century houses of correction describe incarcerated men, women, and children living together in vermin-infested conditions of filth and squalor. Communicable diseases in these dungeonlike quarters were rampant, and many historical accounts from the facilities mention periodic epidemics of "gaol fever"—now presumed to have been typhus— which was often lethal. Overcrowding was the norm, and in jails without adequate space or security, inmates were brutally restrained, their bodies chained to the floors or to the walls.

The Philadelphia System sought to reform such conditions. The project inspired great enthusiasm and the promise of significant rehabilitation. Such aspirational assurances drew visiting leaders from other countries eager to witness and learn from this revolutionary program. However, the Philadelphia System was quickly viewed for what it was: another catastrophic chapter in the history of American corrections.

"The system here is rigid, strict, and hopeless solitary confinement," wrote Charles Dickens, who visited Eastern State Penitentiary during a United States tour in 1842 and who evocatively described the haunted circumstances he observed therein. "Over the head and face of every visitor who comes into the melancholy house, a black hood is drawn, and in this dark shroud . . . he is led to the cell from which he never again comes forth, until his whole term of imprisonment has expired. He is a man buried alive, . . . dead to everything but torturing anxieties and horrible despair."

An editorial position taken by the *Times* of London described the psychiatric effects of the Philadelphia system more succinctly as "maniac-making."

Indeed, prisoners detained in solitary confinement were noted to become so psychologically disturbed—with some even committing suicide— that the Philadelphia System was eventually recognized as inhumane and was gradually abandoned.

By 1890 the United States Supreme Court had issued an opinion, *In re Medley*, that was decisive in its condemnation of solitary confinement. Justice Samuel Miller wrote, "A considerable number of the prisoners" in the penitentiary system of solitary detention "fell, after even a short confinement, into a semi-fatuous condition, from which it was next to impossible to arouse them, and others became violently insane; others, still, committed suicide; while those who stood the ordeal better were not generally reformed, and in most cases did not recover sufficient mental activity to be of any subsequent service to the community." Despite the Supreme Court's denunciation of solitary confinement in the *In re Medley* opinion, the fundamental constitutionality of solitary confinement had not been the issue at hand. Therefore the Court's strong statements about the ruinous effects of the practice had no bearing on its legality. Their assertions on the damage that isolation wreaked were largely ignored, and the use of it in corrections in our country continued, in new and evolving forms.

When Alcatraz opened in 1934, it was unique in that it had within it a hallway designed and designated for solitary confinement. Then in 1983 the warden of an Illinois prison unilaterally put the facility on permanent lockdown in response to the murder of two correctional officers. From that point forward, all of that prison's inmates were held in twenty-three-hour-a-day isolation. Other state facilities followed suit, and in 1989 Pelican Bay State Prison was built in northern California, the first prison in the country constructed with the intention of holding every inmate in solitary confinement. With that, the era of supermax prisons—facilities explicitly designed for "long term segregated housing"—began. There are now freestanding supermax facilities in forty-four states as well as an additional supermax prison within the federal correctional system.

The locked-down structure of the supermax contains within it yet further mechanisms of control. Elaborate strategies are put in place in order to restrict the movements and behaviors of prisoners. Just as often as these tactics are implemented, they fail, requiring new strategies of control or a never-ending modification of existing ones. In an earlier era of solitary confinement, for example, cell doors would be opened for the distribution of meals. Some detainees would take advantage of that time to act out in aggression or to attempt to escape from the confines of their cells. To counteract these behaviors, traps were built into doors, diminishing the risks that existed if doors were unlocked and opened but also further diminishing human contact and interaction.

Men intent on aggression adapted to the new challenges posed by the trap as men have always done, as any animal intent on survival—which is to say, any of us—finds a way to fulfill its instincts. Some would grab COs' hands as they came through the trap. There are accounts of serious injuries. Broken fingers. Broken arms. Others would throw cups of urine through the trap at officers, or handfuls of feces, spit, semen, even blood. Once when I was visiting the punitive administrative-segregation unit of a maximum-security prison, I leaned against the cinder-block wall across from an empty cell.

"Uh, Doc, you don't want to be touching that wall," the CO who accompanied me interjected politely. "Every bodily substance you can imagine has been thrown against it."

Double-door traps were developed so that the contents being passed through could be reached by the detainee only once the CO's side was safely locked closed. I imagine a new form of protest will now emerge, and then a new technology will quash it. On and on.

These measures are justified by the argument that the men held in solitary confinement must be so contained because of the wild dangerousness that is in their very natures. Only these drastic measures can contain the risk that these men embody. That logic, of course, does not track. We have now known for more than a century that the human behavior cited as the rationale for solitary confinement is consequence, not cause.

Although solitary confinement was present throughout the twentieth century in American corrections, the use of the practice expanded exponentially in the 1970s amid a confluence of changes in the legal and philosophical landscape of the United States. Sentencing policies— including guidelines for probation and parole—grew even stricter, giving rise to a substantial increase in the country's incarceration rates that would continue to spike during the "War on Drugs." Between 1985 and 1995, the government cut back dramatically on prison education and treatment programs where they were not completely eliminated. The goals of incarceration shifted from rehabilitation to a correctional strategy intended purely to "incapacitate and punish." The consequences have been lasting. A 2007 assessment of rehabilitation in the state of California, for example, found that half of all prisoners released in the year prior had not participated in a single program while incarcerated.

This move to incapacitate and punish also coincided with the country's push toward deinstitutionalization. Jail and prison populations swelled from an influx of the undertreated mentally ill. The overcrowding of prisons had a predictable consequence: violence in correctional facilities escalated. Prison systems responded with an unprecedented increase in the number and use of supermax cells, justifying this shift by classifying modern-day criminals as "harder" and "unable to be rehabilitated." The long-held aim of reforming prisoners was now classified as a fool's errand and therefore a waste of resources. The grim new management strategy for these "hardened criminals" was to isolate them from one another, often for the duration of their sentences, sometimes for the duration of their lives.

This ethos of incapacitate and punish is now dominant in the American corrections system, and its toll is devastating.

ACCURATE STATISTICS ON the use of solitary confinement in America are notoriously opaque. Because the practice is administered entirely within correctional confines, there is no public or judicial oversight of its use. No records exist to show how often—or for what durations— solitary confinement is employed. We do know, however, that America's extensive use of isolation as correctional practice has drawn consistent criticism from the international human rights community. Juan E. Mendéz, the United Nations Special Rapporteur on Torture and Other Cruel, Inhuman or Degrading Treatment or Punishment, notes, "The United States uses solitary confinement more extensively than any other country, for longer periods, and with fewer guarantees."

Despite the opacity of administrative-segregation policies and use, a joint endeavor between Yale Law School and the Association of State Correctional Administrators was able to conclude that in 2014 between 80,000 and 100,000 people in America were held in isolation in a cell for twenty-two to twenty-three hours per day for thirty days or more. These staggering numbers did not include juveniles held in isolation, nor did they take into account people in jails—like the men in Cook County Jail's Division 10—or those in military or immigration detention.

According to the United States Bureau of Justice Statistics (BJS), nearly 20 percent of all people detained in our country's prisons and jails in 2011 spent time in segregation or solitary confinement. This percentage is even higher for detainees with psychiatric illnesses. "The use of restrictive housing was linked to inmate mental health problems," the BJS report reads, citing the fact that nearly a third of prison inmates and a quarter of jail inmates who demonstrated symptoms of "serious psychological distress" had spent time in restrictive housing in the prior year.

Solitary confinement is presented in our country as a means of dealing with violence, of attempting to protect correctional officers and the general prison population from dangerous inmates. But the stated purpose plainly differs from the reality.

While major infractions in jails and prisons routinely lead to administrative segregation, the accumulation of multiple minor violations can also result in solitary confinement, or an extension of a person's time therein. Of the 13,000 times that detainees are sent to disciplinary segregation in the state of New York each year, for example, roughly *85 percent* are punishments for nonviolent infractions.

The kinds of nonviolent behaviors that can lead to administrative segregation in facilities across the country include the possession of contraband, a term that encompasses a wide range of forbidden items in prison, including the possession of too many envelopes in your cell or having more than five dollars in cash without permission. Detainees can be isolated for engaging in self-injurious behavior or attempting suicide, if either is interpreted as an attempt at manipulation. And in most facilities, tickets—the prison shorthand term for disciplinary infractions—can be administered, with punishment eventually rising to the level of administrative segregation, for the nebulous "not following an officer's instructions."

Five Mualimm-Ak, the prison activist, writes, "Anyone lacking familiarity with our state prison system would probably guess I must have been a pretty scary, out-of-control prisoner. But I never committed one act of violence during my entire sentence. Instead, a series of 'tickets' . . . were punished with a total of more than five years in 'the box.' . . . During my years in prison, I received an endless stream of tickets, each one more absurd than the last. When I tried to use artwork to stay sane, I was ticketed for having too many pencils. Excess pencils are considered sharpened objects, or weapons. Another time, I had too many postage stamps, which in prison are used like currency and are contraband."

Mualimm-Ak explains how easy it is for inmates to be found in violation of policies, with dire consequences. Often, he points out, people imprisoned in segregation are damned if they do and damned if they don't. "One day I ate an entire apple—including the core—because I was starving for lack of nutrition," he writes. "I received a ticket for eating the core because apple seeds contain arsenic. The next time I received an apple, fearful of another ticket, I simply left it on the tray. I received a ticket for 'refusing to eat.'"

Medical care provides another opportunity to be found in violation of unit rules. "During the five years I spent in the box, I received insulin shots for my diabetes by extending my arm through the food slot in the cell's door," Mualimm-Ak explains. "One day, the person who gave me the shot yanked roughly on my arm through the small opening, and I instinctively pulled back. This earned me another ticket for 'refusing medical attention,' adding time to my solitary sentence."

Mualimm-Ak's accounts of the kinds of infractions that could lead to—or extend—time in administrative segregation are galling and show

how quickly nonviolent rule violations can accumulate and combine, yielding unimaginable periods of punishment for minor offenses.

CARRYING OUT SENTENCES in public created gruesome spectacles, but it also allowed members of the community to witness the full extent of the retribution. What you see is what you get. The observable nature of the punishment was intended to send messages of both deterrence and the power of the state. The public knew the crime of which the convict stood accused. The people were informed of the sentence the criminal would receive. And they watched as the punishment was enacted upon the condemned man.

Imprisonment has quietly drawn an opaque curtain over punishment. The state's assertion of power over the individual, once demonstrated in public, is now hidden. And not merely behind closed doors but, in the case of modern-day prisons, behind multiple impenetrable locked metal doors, armed guards, and razor-wire-topped walls.

Secrecy—or at least intensive, careful control of all information that leaves our nation's prisons—is now a defining aspect of American punishment. Phone calls are monitored. Letters are read and are routinely redacted. The use of social media is forbidden, and illicit postings, if discovered, carry grave punishments.

A particularly shocking example of this sort of penalty was unearthed in South Carolina. The Department of Corrections in South Carolina, like those in many states, forbids inmates to post on social media sites while they are imprisoned. The rationale behind this policy arises from a concern that detainees could use such sites to coordinate criminal activity. That concern may be valid, but the responses to such violations are ludicrous.

Tyheem Henry, a man incarcerated in South Carolina, was caught having posted on Facebook on thirty-eight different days. As punishment, he received thirty-seven and a half *years* in solitary confinement.

He also lost the right to have telephone, visitation, or canteen privileges for the next seventy-four years and was forced to forfeit his sixty-nine days of "good time," earned days that are removed from the end of a person's sentence as a reward for good behavior.

A review of the heavy penalties imposed by the South Carolina Department of Corrections exposed that "Creating and/or Assisting with a Social Networking Site" was designated as a Level 1 offense: the category reserved for the most violent infractions of prison conduct. As a result, the *average* penalty administered for social networking was 512 days—nearly a year and a half—in disciplinary detention or punitive solitary confinement.

These consequences are imbalanced and inhumane. They are also ridiculous, as investigative journalist Dave Maass points out. "If a South Carolina inmate caused a riot, took three hostages, murdered them, stole their clothes, and then escaped," Maass writes, "he could still wind up with fewer Level 1 offenses than an inmate who updated Facebook every day for two weeks."

As a result of the stringent control of information within jails and prisons, families struggle even to find out basic facts about their incarcerated loved ones. Information on individual inmates is controlled. The ability of incarcerated people to send information out into the world is controlled. And information about these facilities and what happens within them is also carefully controlled.

Just south of the tiny town of Florence, Colorado (population 3,881), lies the only federal supermax prison in the country: Administrative Maximum Penitentiary, known as ADX. The cryptic moniker itself almost totally obscures the facility's true purpose. In fact, ADX is the highest-security prison in the nation and holds men whom the federal government has designated as the country's most dangerous prisoners. It also serves as a striking example of the institutional secrecy that can exist within American prisons.

ADX opened in 1994. It was built for $60 million and holds up to five hundred men in near-total isolation. A 2015 article in *The New York Times* describes the facility as "not just the only federal supermax but also the apogee of a particular strain of the American penal system, wherein abstract dreams of rehabilitation have been entirely superseded by the architecture of control."

ADX was "not designed for humanity," explained Robert Wood, a former warden of the prison. "Let's be candid here. It's not designed for rehabilitation. Period. End of story." In contrast to the chaos and mayhem described in many jails and prisons, Wood described the "very stark environment" of ADX, with "no noise, no mess, no prisoners walking the hallways," as "a clean version of hell."

Wood and the few prisoners who have written about their time in ADX describe it in similarly bleak terms, and their voices are vital because access to the prison and what goes on within it is systematically restricted. Jean Casella, the co-director of Solitary Watch, an advocacy group dedicated to ending the practice, edited an anthology of essays written by people in solitary confinement, including some from ADX. Casella says most prisoners at ADX are permitted to send and receive letters. However, all correspondence in both directions is opened and read. In addition, all incoming mail is scanned and then destroyed. The men receive only the scans of the letters that have been sent to them, not the letters themselves.

It is not only the media who are unwelcome at ADX. Those who would provide oversight are similarly rebuffed. "Since opening two decades ago," Jeanne Theoharis, Distinguished Professor of Political Science at Brooklyn College, writes, ADX "has allowed only a single visit by human rights groups." She continues, "Two UN special rapporteurs on torture have requested to visit and [have] been denied."

One of the voices that has managed to emerge from the impenetrable shroud of ADX is that of Jesse Wilson. At the age of seventeen, Wilson was convicted of larceny and sentenced to five years in a Mississippi prison. While he was incarcerated there, he describes himself as being "at war with the guards," resulting in an eventual transfer to Unit 32 at Mississippi's notorious Parchman State Penitentiary.

Margaret Winter, the associate director of the ACLU's National Prison Project, deemed Unit 32 one of the worst prison environments in the nation, citing its inhumane conditions, including a lack of mental and medical health care for prisoners held therein. The ACLU filed suit in 2002 against the Mississippi Department of Corrections on behalf of Unit 32's death-row prisoners. They charged that prisoners were "held 24-hours-a-day, seven-days-a-week, in cells where summer heat indexes reached 120 degrees, the toilets were non-functional, the housing areas were routinely awash in sewage from broken plumbing and they were subjected day and night to the ravings of severely psychotic prisoners whose mental illnesses were left untreated."

Through the legal actions of the ACLU and eventual court intervention, the population of Unit 32 was dramatically reduced, and in 2010 the ACLU and Mississippi DOC came to an agreement to close the facility for good, an outcome that Margaret Winter deemed "nothing short of a huge success story" for human rights.

But three years before that decision was made, Jesse Wilson fatally stabbed a death-row inmate who was also being held in Unit 32. The killing was the third murder in as many months within the unit's violent confines. Wilson received a life sentence for the murder and was sent from Unit 32 to ADX, or, as he called it, "the end of the line."

Wilson, who entered prison at seventeen with a five-year sentence for theft, is now serving life in isolation at ADX. "We the inmates are voiceless," he wrote in an essay about his experience at ADX. "Our voices are not heard. If they are heard," he continued, "the things we say are thought of as lies."

One such lie that Wilson cites is the government's claim that mentally ill inmates are not housed at ADX. "I heard the head of the Bureau of Prisons testifying in Congress (on [the] radio), saying they do not have insane inmates housed here," Wilson writes. "This is what should be thought of as a lie. I have not slept in weeks because of these nonexistent inmates beating on the walls and hollering all night. And the most non-insane smearing feces in their cells."

Jesse Wilson wrote his essay, called "Loneliness Is a Destroyer of Humanity," at age thirty-three. At thirty-three he has lived nearly as much of his life in prison as he did a free man. Once he reaches thirty-four, the columns will be equal. At thirty-five, and every year thereafter, the balance will tip further and further, irreversibly. The life becomes a life predominantly confined.

Wilson is a rare voice chronicling the harsh circumstances of his imprisonment and of his life in isolation, but his prose also reveals the human capacity to find beauty in the most stark and hellish of circumstances.

"Out my window I see into a concrete yard surrounded by red brick walls," he writes. "There is a drain in the middle of it and out of it weeds are growing. I thought they were weeds," Wilson continues, "until a few blossomed into these beautiful yellow and brown flowers."

8.

THE LOST PEOPLE

There is no direct way to get to Northern, the supermax prison Connecticut built in the 1990s during the national boom in supermax construction. Any route requires miles on state roads that wind through small towns, the kinds of places whose streets are festooned with red, white, and blue ribbons all through July and whose businesses line their awnings with strands of blinking lights come December. Before long the towns give way to neighborhoods, modest subdivisions with well-kept lawns, and then the subdivisions fade and the roads are flanked by rolling fields, some with crops, some with horses. Eventually the road curves, and one by one three prison complexes emerge on the horizon. A tall white water tower looms on a hill. Multiple rows of fences surround low, wide buildings. Curls of razor wire top the fences, reflecting the sun in sparkling shards.

One of these three prison complexes is Northern, where most of the detainees spend twenty-three hours per day isolated in their maximum-security cells. They are given one daily hour of "outdoor recreation" in individual cages within a walled concrete square, the open air above them traced through with loops of the same razor wire.

The stated goal of the Connecticut Department of Corrections' administrative-segregation program is the prevention of violence, achieved ostensibly through "behavior modification" but also through layered measures of control. The men eat in their cells, with food passed through metal traps in their doors. When they are walked to the recreation yard or to the shower, they are handcuffed, their legs are shackled, and a tether chain runs between their cuffs and their shackles. When they have competency evaluations, and sometimes even during legal visits, their tether chains are locked to metal rings sunk into the concrete floor.

Yet even this extreme control does not quell all violence within the walls of Northern. In fact, aggression and self-injury here are often far more severe—and more gruesome—than the prison violence that occurs in lower-security facilities. The explanation given for this truth is that the men held in Northern are, as the state commissioner of the Department of Corrections once called them, "the worst of the worst."

From the moment I enter, Northern feels palpably different from any other correctional facility I've been inside. It is intentionally stark and ominous. In a filmed interview for Yale University's Visual Law Project, James Kessler, the architect of Northern, says, "When we were designing it, there was a desire that [the detainees'] first experience [of the prison] would make an impression." Kessler, a Yale School of Art and Architecture graduate, is a specialist in a field I hadn't even known existed: criminal justice architecture. Of the DOC's goals for the overall prison structure, Kessler adds, "There's nothing soft. It's hard, and they wanted that."

Immediately inside the entrance at Northern is a metal detector, and for the first time in my prison work the detector is so sensitive that I must take off my wedding rings in order to pass through it without sounding the alarm. (A colleague of mine had cautioned me to take care in choosing my undergarments whenever I was headed to Northern— she had once driven two hours to the prison to do a competency evaluation only to have the metal detector go off from the underwire in her bra. Rather than begin the two-hour drive back home, she removed the bra, put it in a locker, and went without.)

The guard manning the entrance flips through my notebook and sends it through an X-ray scanner. Then a heavy metal door slides open courtesy of someone I cannot see to allow me to walk into the waiting room. Everything in the waiting area is concrete. Concrete floors. Cinder-block walls. Smooth concrete benches cemented to the floor. I'm the only one in the room. I clear my throat, and the sound echoes all around me.

After a few moments, a CO leads me to another thick metal door that slides open slowly to allow us to step into a concrete corridor. The passageway is so long that I cannot see the end. The door slides closed behind us, and though I know I've entered and remained on ground level, I have the unmistakable sensation of suddenly being underground.

"And what is that corridor like?" asks Kessler, the architect, rhetorically in his interview. "It's an interesting part of the design. . . . [The inmates] see visually it's a long road. . . . This is what [we] intend it to be—is to have a lasting impression."

There's no question that entering into the corridor carries with it a sense of foreboding, and this unease is calculated. The architect, the Department of Corrections, we as a society—we want these men to feel dread, and fear, and hopelessness upon entering. We say we want them to feel repentant for their actions, to feel regret. But we cannot mean this because the gaze down the corridor is not a gaze back in reflection but rather forward, into a future that is dark and fathomless.

In which case for whom, really, is this grave and ominous statement intended? Not for the correctional officers who must traverse this corridor each day, who must also exist in these stark, echoing, concrete tunnels. Kessler says it is intended for the prisoners, a purposeful intimidation to communicate to them that they are beginning a long, grim journey. But I know from my work in other prisons that Northern already has a reputation that looms large within the state's correctional system. The men imprisoned here surely knew of this bleakness that awaited them well before they stepped into this forbidding hallway.

The design must, then, have a societal purpose. It must be intended for those of us who will never walk down the corridors but who know that the men we've banished here will. The structure is designed to execute our desire that these men should feel daunted, should fear, should suffer. It is a message that transcends cultures and centuries. A message that communities through time have sent to their condemned, to their damned.

In his *Inferno* Dante envisioned a similar message inscribed upon the Gates of Hell: *Per me si va ne la città dolente, per me si va ne l'etterno dolore, per me si va tra la perduta gente. . . . Lasciate ogni speranza, voi ch'entrate.* "Through me pass into the painful city, through me pass into eternal grief, through me pass among the lost people. . . . Abandon all hope, ye who enter here."

I VISIT NORTHERN for the first time thanks to the invitation of Dr. Gerard Gagné, the prison's principal psychiatrist. At my request he has allowed me to spend some days observing his practice here.

Dr. Gagné meets me near the entrance to the subterranean-feeling hallway and greets me warmly. In our correspondence it has been clear that he is smart and affable. In person he's smiling broadly, crisply dressed, and wearing oxford shoes with bright orange soles. He makes a joke about the pace of the day to the officer who screened me and led me in, who guffaws. I like him instantly.

As we walk down the endless corridor, Dr. Gagné orients me to the facility. "The capacity here is two hundred and twenty men at a time," he explains. "There's a high-bond unit for inmates who have committed horrible crimes. There are eleven people on death row in Connecticut, and they're all here. Otherwise, men are sent here for problematic behavior within the system."

Men in the high-bond unit are pretrial detainees who have not yet been tried, convicted, or sentenced. But the crimes of which they've been accused are, as Dr. Gagné says, "horrible" enough that a judge has set their bail at a prohibitively high number to prevent any possibility that they might return to the community or flee while awaiting the progression of their legal cases. According to the prison's handbook, the bail number that could land you at Northern before trial is $850,000 or above.

The eleven men on Connecticut's death row are indeed housed at Northern. They are not, however, awaiting execution. Though they each were sentenced to death some years prior, the state of Connecticut then abolished the death penalty in 2009. For several years the men on death row were in a kind of legal limbo. Although no new death sentences would be handed down, it was not clear whether the ban on execution would be retroactively applied. Eventually, in 2015, the State Supreme Court ruled that the eleven men who'd been sentenced to death could not be executed without violating the state constitution. One by one these men are being resentenced to life imprisonment without the possibility of parole.

Some of the detainees who are referred to Dr. Gagné's mental-health service are not, in fact, psychiatrically ill but have constantly chafed against the authority of officers. These men refuse to submit or comply, despite the certain, unavoidable escalation of consequences. They pose chronic behavioral problems and up the ante as their infractions accumulate, accelerate, multiply. Others are psychiatrically ill and are too disorganized to adjust their behaviors to avoid punitive consequences, *fundamental misalignment* made manifest.

Quite often, Dr. Gagné tells me as we sit down together in his office, the people he sees embody some mixture of psychiatric symptomatology and oppositional defiance.

But whether it's been reached through the unwillingness to conform or the inability to do so, the end of the disciplinary line is Northern.

The first of the men that Dr. Gagné and I are going to see together falls into the latter of those two categories. His name is Mr. Ali. For someone who is imprisoned in a supermax facility built to hold dangerous criminals considered to be "the worst of the worst," Ali's charges do not seem to fit the bill. Other than his two charges of assaulting a public-safety officer while incarcerated in 2013—presumably both from the incident that landed him here at Northern that same year—he had only three convictions listed on the state's judicial website: one criminal trespass charge and two low-level felony charges related to an attempted robbery during which he was in possession of a firearm.

One of the prison's nurses joins us as we leave the mental-health office to begin rounds. We walk, escorted by a CO, through a series of indistinguishable concrete corridors, all of which share the buried feel of the hallway into which I first entered Northern. Eventually we come to a door that leads to the housing ward where Ali is held.

The heavy door slowly slides open for us to walk through, then closes behind us with a decisive slam. The ward spreads out in a two-story circle with cells on both levels. I hear shouting and look up to see a man in a bright yellow jumpsuit being walked along the upper tier's perimeter to his cell. His hands are cuffed behind his back, and his feet are shackled. A CO walks beside him, hand slid under the man's armpit, gripping his upper arm. The detainee talks loudly as he walks, seemingly calling out to the men whose cells he's passing. His voice echoes through the ward, obscuring my ability to make out any of the words.

I comment on the cacophony made by the slamming doors, the man's voice, and the yelling of other men in response. "I call this the monkey house," the nurse says. "It gets so loud, and the guys in here are the really bad guys." The comment hits me hard, both for the way it instantly classifies the men held herein as animals and also for the racist overtones a comment like this one has—intentionally or not—when spoken by a white woman about a unit full of men of color.

To my left is a large, open area encircled by the cells, a few modular metal tables within it. The tables are octagonal, bases sunk into the concrete floor. Four silver disks protrude on metal arms from the table base for men to sit on, but the room is empty. A black monitor is mounted high on the wall with the date and time illuminated in bright red digital numbers. Its addition was the result of a law, Dr. Gagné tells me, to help inmates in these extenuating circumstances keep track of what day it is and what time of day it is. A sign is taped to the floor-to-ceiling glass wall that encloses the empty dayroom. It reads: FOR PHONE CALLS AND HAIRCUTS ONLY. Here, protruding from the concrete floor beside the tables, are some of the thick metal rings, maybe three inches in diameter, to which the men's tether chains are locked when they're seated at those tables, shackling their bodies to the floor.

To the right is an examination room, into which Dr. Gagné leads me. The door is made of an indestructible-looking Plexiglas. This enables the CO to stand outside without hearing the content of the psychiatric session but near enough to come in in an instant if something dangerous were to occur. The two walls on either side of us are raw gray concrete, as are the floor and the ceiling. Behind me is a wall made entirely of stacked gray cinder blocks. Dr. Gagné and the CO pull molded plastic chairs into the room for us to sit on when we meet with Ali. I sit down, facing a bank of windows that look into the interior of the prison ward.

Before going to get Ali, the CO turns to Dr. Gagné and says, "Whatever meds you put him on, don't change them! Poor guy used to be talking all day to concrete in corners."

"It was tough to get him to accept medicine, even though he was really sick," Dr. Gagné says to me as we wait for Ali to arrive. "He would put an elaborate system of papers across his floor. He said he was making a map of the Middle East. He kept getting tickets for breaking rules, but it was for that kind of stuff—disorganized behavior. He wasn't assaultive, and he was eating fine, so I couldn't cite grave disability."

By this Dr. Gagné means that he could not forcibly medicate Ali. In order to administer psychiatric medication to someone against his will, a physician must demonstrate to a judge that the patient is either an imminent risk to himself or others or that he is "gravely disabled." This means that a person retains the right to refuse psychiatric treatment in almost all circumstances. However, if he is actively suicidal, with an intent or plan to harm himself, or homicidal, with a plan to harm others, a judge may determine that the ill person relinquishes this right. The third category of patient who can be forcibly medicated—those who are found to be gravely disabled—is the category I most frequently encounter in my own hospital practice. Herein is the patient who be-lieves her water supply is poisoned and so has stopped drinking, and the man who believes that CIA operatives implant devices into his brain as he sleeps and has thus nailed boards across his apartment door to protect himself. I seek to medicate these patients against their will when they are admitted to my care, though they sometimes rail against me when I do. In these instances I feel strongly that my patients' right to live a healthy life free of delusional fears and dangerous behaviors far out-weighs their right to refuse treatment.

The argument for patients to accept medications can be an even harder sell within the prison walls, as many detainees believe that psych meds make them sluggish, diminishing their ability to defend them-selves should they be attacked in a fight.

Since Ali was eating and drinking, he could not be deemed gravely disabled. Since he hadn't been assaultive, he couldn't be considered an imminent threat to others. And he wasn't suicidal. But he was—unquestionably—psychiatrically unwell enough that his untreated men-tal illness was affecting his life in a profound way. Prior to beginning the antipsychotic medication that Dr. Gagné had eventually coaxed him to take, Ali had accumulated 383 tickets, each one with the capacity to prolong his time at Northern. He was, in the words of Rhode Island's Deputy Warden Adams, burying himself in seg.

When Ali walks into the evaluation room—it is more accurate per-haps to say, "When Ali *is walked* into the room," because the CO grips his arm firmly and directs his gait as he shuffles, the shackles and tether chain jangling with each step—he is older than I'd have imagined. Older, in fact, than any of the men I would envision to be held in a supermax prison. This presumption of mine that supermax prisons hold primarily young men is one, over the course of my first few hours with Dr. Gagné, of which I'm quickly disabused.

Ali has very long fingernails. He is balding. He has a gray beard. He sits down, looks first at me and then at Dr. Gagné, and says bluntly, "That little pill gives me cottonmouth." It is one of only two intelligible things he says in the twenty minutes he's in the room with us. His speech is pressured, with one sentence tumbling out on top of the last, making it impossible to interrupt him. Despite the sheer quantity of his speech, the content is utterly incoherent. He rambles about constellations and conspiracies, about a man named Arthur, about a freeway. At one point, without any relevant context, he brings up Hootie & the Blowfish. If indeed this medicated version of Ali is the more psychiatrically well version, as the correctional officer attested, then it's clear to me how horribly ill he must have been before receiving treatment.

Eventually Dr. Gagné is able to speak enough to interject that it's good for Ali to keep taking the medicine, even though it makes his mouth dry. That it will help keep him out of trouble, and that will help him get out of Northern and back to the prison where he was before. Dr. Gagné motions through the windowed wall for the CO to come back in, indicating that we've finished. He writes down notes from the interview and—as promised—leaves Ali's current medication orders unchanged. The CO grips Ali's arm, and Ali stands. Just before he is escorted out, Ali utters the second lucid phrase of the session. He is looking neither at Dr. Gagné nor at me but rather at a space between us, so I can't tell to which of us the comment is directed.

"Get you a quiet cell in the middle of here," he says. "Get in there and see what happen to you if you just sit in one of those goddamn cells."

THE NEXT MAN on Dr. Gagné's list for us to see is Mr. Rivers, originally arrested for successfully carrying out a financial fraud scheme. Rivers was sent to Northern from another prison after assaulting a DOC employee during a period of delusional paranoia. Because Rivers was so high-functioning and had carried out a series of relatively complex crimes, Dr. Gagné tells me, it took some time for people to understand that he was also quite mentally ill.

"In fact, he has periods during which he's quite delusional. Sometimes it's about COs. Sometimes it's about other inmates. He feels very threatened," Dr. Gagné says. "And it's in those stretches when he feels very threatened that he's become dangerous."

Due to the fact that Rivers was assaultive, Dr. Gagné was able to obtain permission to involuntarily medicate him.

"Prior to being medicated, he received multiple, multiple tickets," Dr. Gagné tells me. "It was a hundred and thirty-one at last count. In retrospect the behavioral problems seem to have been almost entirely due to his mental illness. Once we could medicate him, the tickets stopped. Mr. Rivers doesn't think he's ill, but now he reluctantly agrees to be treated. You'll see what I mean."

Rivers is brought into the room. Like Ali, he, too, is bearded. He, too, is balding. He is thin and makes almost no eye contact. Even before he sits down, he walks over to the nurse who is drawing medication up into a syringe. He extends an upper arm toward her. The motion pulls his other arm across his body by virtue of the cuffs that bind his wrists. Some slack goes out of his tether chain. The nurse stands alongside him and rolls up the sleeve of his baggy, prison-issue jumpsuit. Rivers faces forward, does not look at the nurse, and does not flinch as she says, "One, two, three," and deftly plunges the needle into his deltoid.

Antipsychotic medications come in many forms. Most of my patients swallow pills once, twice, or even three times a day. Many of these same medications, often in identical potencies, can be given as injections at moments of crisis. I use injections in rare instances on my hospital unit when a patient becomes assaultive and must be quickly subdued or when a patient is so profoundly catatonic that she cannot swallow pills. There are liquid forms and pills that dissolve immediately upon contact with saliva, both of which I prescribe for patients who have a tendency to "cheek" their meds—pretending to swallow them but actually tucking the pill alongside their gums to remove later in order to throw it away or to give or sell it to another patient.

However, one of the most effective pharmacotherapeutic treatments for chronic psychotic illness is the administration of long-acting injectable (LAI) antipsychotics. These injections, typically given once a month, maintain therapeutic levels of medicine in a patient's bloodstream over the course of thirty days, and they eliminate the need for patients to remember to take their pills daily or multiple times per day. If a person is ambivalent about taking medication, it is easier and more therapeutically effective to engage in a struggle about the issue once a month rather than on a daily basis.

Once he has received his medication, Rivers sits down, and the CO leaves the room.

"How are you spending your days?" Dr. Gagné asks him. It's a fair question in a place with prolonged periods of time and few ways to occupy oneself. It is also, I note, a skillful question. Dr. Gagné has told me that Rivers does not agree that he is mentally ill, and the fact that his medications are court-ordered means that there's a high likelihood he also contests the fact that he's being subjected to them. In many instances a psychiatrist might open an interview by asking a patient about symptoms or inquiring as to how the medications are working. But in this case doing so would start the interview in a place of conflict, which Dr. Gagné wisely seeks to avoid. The question is also open-ended enough that it allows for a response that will yield information beyond the mere answer to the question. It will allow Dr. Gagné to assess the quality of Rivers's speech. Is it pressured, as Ali's was? Or soft, slow, and monosyllabic, which could indicate depression? In listening carefully to the answer, he can also begin to evaluate the process and content of Rivers's thoughts.

"I'm lackadaisical," Rivers responds to the question, and I'm immediately struck by the specificity of his vocabulary, an indication of intellect or education level or both. "I sleep all day every day." Then, despite Dr. Gagné's attempt to steer clear of contentious treatment issues, at least initially, Rivers says, "It's because of the medicine."

I can tell that Dr. Gagné is not convinced that the medicine is to blame, and for good reason. LAIs are less likely to sedate patients than are shorter-acting preparations of the same medications. But rather than challenge Rivers's assertion directly and risk setting up a familiar confrontation, he steers the conversation toward a truth he knows they can agree upon.

"Do you think you'd be out of bed if you were in a different facility where there was more going on?" he asks.

"Definitely," Rivers replies. The answer shifts the subject from an issue prone to evoke conflict, but it also gives Dr. Gagné more information— that whatever sedation Rivers may or may not be feeling from the medication, it's not so significant as to prevent him from engaging in activities if doing so were a possibility.

"My hope is for you to get out of here and back to a place where there's more to do," Dr. Gagné says, reiterating his alliance with his patient and doing so with sincerity. "And my sense is that things are going a little better for you recently in terms of moving toward that goal."

Here Rivers can only partially agree. "I haven't had any tickets. But, you know, the COs were harassing me. They were assaulting me. They were putting me in a metal cage to have me assaulted by inmates who were using cattle prods and shit."

"If I ever saw that," Dr. Gagné says calmly, "I'd report that to the warden. And I know the deputy warden would take action to prevent that from happening anymore. I also know that you seemed to feel like you needed to defend yourself more before you were taking the medicine, and since the medicine started, you don't feel that way as much. You haven't been getting tickets because you haven't felt like people are threatening you, so you haven't felt like you had to fight to protect yourself."

"Nah, man," Rivers says to Dr. Gagné. "I haven't gotten tickets because Officer Mendoza must be away. It's got nothing to do with the medicines." He pauses, as if momentarily considering that Dr. Gagné might be right. Then he shakes his head as if to shake off any emerging doubt in his own beliefs. "I don't feel I was misinterpreting nothing."

I'm aware of the difficulty here. This is a delusional man with paranoid beliefs and implausible-sounding accounts of assault. On the other hand, I know that assault of detainees by COs occurs and that mentally ill detainees are particularly vulnerable to victimization. When the session ends and Rivers is being taken back to his cell, I ask Dr. Gagné how certain he is that Rivers's assertions are delusional. He tells me that anytime reports of assault are made by inmates, he looks at the evidence on both sides to be sure he isn't making any erroneous assumptions. In Rivers's case, he says, security video was reviewed, which did not substantiate any of Rivers's claims. He tells me that there has never been any evidence to corroborate even one of Rivers's accusations.

"And the thing that makes me even more confident in this situation," he continues, "is that all of the accusations stopped—along with the aggressive behavior which accompanied them—once he started accepting the meds. He has had no tickets at all since he's been medicated."

Rivers, though, does not see it this way. He has a number of explanations as to why the abuse has stopped—a particular CO has been away, an inmate who was in cahoots with the CO was moved to another facility—none of which have anything to do with psychopharmacology.

When, during the session, Dr. Gagné had tried to draw the parallel between the LAI and the cessation of tickets, Rivers shook his head.

"If the order for you to take meds were to expire," Dr. Gagné asked him, "would you keep taking them?"

"No," was Rivers's reply. "For some reason all of this assaultiveness has ceased. But if it expires, I will not take it. No."

Rivers's complaint that he stays in bed all day is a common one. I hear it frequently from detainees when I perform competency evaluations. To screen for mood disorders, I routinely ask how much the person is sleeping. Both sleeping too little (insomnia) and sleeping too much (hypersomnia) can indicate psychiatric disturbance, and both are common in correctional facilities. Hypersomnia can merely be a coping strategy—a way to pass the time in a boring environment. But it can also be pathological, accompanied by depressive symptoms such as hopelessness and helplessness. Men like Rivers who are serving long terms in isolation are particularly prone to endorse this kind of apathetic or depressive hypersomnia.

As I listen to Rivers, I'm reminded of Harry Harlow's mid-twentieth-century research that demonstrated the shattering psychological and behavioral effects of isolation on primates. Harlow's experiments became famous, both for their groundbreaking and durable scientific findings but also for the cruelty of the circumstances to which the animals in the research were subjected.

Using monkeys as subjects, Harlow altered experimental variables to look at the consequences of different stressors, durations, and environments of isolation. Over and over again, he demonstrated the destructive and debilitating effects of isolation on the development and behavior of monkeys.

In one notorious experiment, monkeys were confined in an apparatus officially known as the "vertical-chamber." The vertical-chamber was an upside-down metal pyramid covered by a mesh-screen top. Unable to climb up the slippery sides of the contraption, the monkeys would slide to the bottom. They spent the first few days trying to climb without success. Eventually they gave up.

These studies "demonstrated the effectiveness" of the chamber "for rapid production of pronounced and prolonged psychopathological disturbance." Of note, Harlow specifically designed one of the vertical-chamber experiments to look at three-year-old monkeys who already had established maternal and social bonds. The experiment was designed to examine whether the isolation and hopelessness of the chamber was strong enough to evoke psychopathology even in primates who had an established foundation of wellness and connection. The answer was a resounding yes. As the Philadelphia System had demonstrated on human primates more than a century before, hopeless isolation damaged individuals indiscriminately.

Like many of Harlow's experiments, the design seems borne of cruelty, and reading about the methods and the findings is almost too much to stomach. But such an experiment should never have been necessary in the first place. Pulitzer Prize–winning journalist Deborah Blum describes the experiment as yielding "common sense results" that were already well understood: that primates are inherently social animals and that extreme isolation can damage them in devastating and potentially lasting ways.

Yet we have not applied this common sense to our carceral policy. Administrative-segregation programs are routinely described as constructive means of ensuring safety and shaping behavior. Harry Harlow designed his vertical-chamber with the specific hypothesis that such a design could induce hopelessness and despair. Decades after Harlow, and more than a century after the Philadelphia System, it is difficult to take seriously James Kessler, the architect of Northern, who asserts that "the limited environment, the lack of stimulus" in the prison's design is "all about essentially the hope, the belief, that these individuals can change."

DR. GAGNÉ'S NEXT PATIENT is not only held in solitary confinement at Northern but has been in solitary confinement at Northern for the last seven and a half years.

"I'll be interested to hear what thoughts you have on this next guy," Dr. Gagné says to me. "I've been seeing him for seven years, and I'm still not sure diagnostically what's going on with him. He wasn't supposed to be on my list this morning, but I added him on because I thought he'd be interesting for you to see. I also thought maybe you'd see something in him that I've been overlooking."

The man's name is Chen Yu, except it isn't. Dr. Gagné tells me that he is Chinese and that he speaks very little English. He doesn't think that this is actually his name, but it is the name under which he's listed in the DOC, and it's what everyone calls him.

Many years ago Chen Yu was incarcerated on a relatively small charge. Solicitation, Dr. Gagné thinks. Something like that. When he was first incarcerated, he would repeatedly spit on correctional officers. Spitting on correctional officers is considered assault. For that behavior he was sent to Northern.

"He's been a real diagnostic puzzle," Dr. Gagné reiterates to me as we wait for Chen Yu to be brought to us. "Right now I'm thinking about him within the context of somatoform disorder," he offers, raising the possibility that the man suffers from a condition in which people are preoccupied with bodily sensations or physical symptoms to such an extreme degree that it interferes with their functioning.

"You'll see when we talk to him. He has all of these physical complaints, none of which make any kind of sense from a medical standpoint. He spends hours every day on the toilet and is totally preoccupied with his bowels. He's had a bunch of medical workups—very thorough ones, in fact, because we've all been worried that we're missing some medical etiology—and none of them has revealed anything. Every test has been negative."

Chen Yu is so preoccupied with his bowels and his need to be near a toilet that he almost never leaves his cell, Dr. Gagné tells me. He doesn't go to rec time. And though all detainees at Northern are offered showers three days a week, for which they're walked across the tier to a single enclosed shower stall, Chen Yu never goes. Dr. Gagné says he can't remember ever hearing of him showering.

"I asked him once about this," Dr. Gagné says to me, "and he just said, 'I shower in my cell,' which obviously isn't possible. That was it. No further explanation."

The CO and Chen Yu arrive. When Chen sits down, he does so wearily and with impatience. He is preoccupied—annoyed, perhaps, at being called to see the psychiatrist when he prefers not to leave his cell. Dr. Gagné introduces me, then asks Chen to explain to me what he's been going through here, how his problems got started.

"CO use a medication on me, makes my elbow hurt," Chen begins abruptly. "In 2014 make my left elbow hurt. Then it stopped. November until now CO gives me medicine that makes my right elbow hurt."

I notice several things right away about these complaints. First and foremost, COs don't administer medications; prison nurses do. Chen's claim that COs are giving him medications that cause him pain immediately makes me wonder whether he, like Rivers, has paranoid beliefs. Second, of all the various complaints I've heard about medication side effects, shifting unilateral joint pain limited to one extremity has never been one. Certain antipsychotic medications can cause acute-onset muscle stiffness called *dystonia*, but this is easily observed and recognizable by clinicians. It is also temporary—and in most cases can be quickly reversed by the administration of a medication that counteracts this effect. Even if the description—"pain" as opposed to "stiffness"—could be viewed as a possible issue of vocabulary in someone who isn't a native English speaker, the shifting nature of the discomfort and the fact that no one could see what Chen was talking about made a dystonic reaction unlikely in my mind. Finally, untreated dystonic reactions tend to worsen and increase in frequency if the offending agent is continued. The symptoms would be unlikely to wax and wane.

Once Chen has begun discussing his physical complaints, he is unable to move on to other topics. Anytime Dr. Gagné tries to ask him other questions—about his sleep, or his mood, or his energy level, or his appetite—Chen responds by circling back to bizarre complaints about his joints and his bowels. Before long he starts telling us that he has "to shit." He repeats this several times, growing increasingly uncomfortable-appearing. I know this is his preoccupation and that he might not even be able to produce stool if he were sitting on a toilet right now. But still it strikes me as yet another moment of the surreal existence that is imprisonment. In order to go to the toilet, Chen must wait for Dr. Gagné to signal to the CO and for the CO to walk Chen back to his cell, undo his shackles and cuffs, and lock his cell door. Chen is not even in control of his most basic bodily functions, a truth that must certainly contribute to his preoccupation with them.

The one comment unrelated to his physical symptoms that Chen makes comes as the CO enters to take him back to his cell. "I want to go to population," he tells Dr. Gagné, referring to the general population of detainees as opposed to those who are segregated here at Northern. "Can you talk to the warden?" he asks. "I've been here too long, man."

Seven and a half years. An initial minor infraction compounded by poverty and mental illness and, in this case, language and cultural barriers balloons, taking on a life of its own.

After Chen leaves, Dr. Gagné tells me a story that is striking for its deep compassion and even more so because it happened within a supermax prison, a place that is punitive by its very design.

For years, Dr. Gagné tells me, Chen Yu was imprisoned at Northern and had no contact with anyone on the outside. He had no commissary money. No visitors. No phone calls. As Dr. Gagné struggled to understand what was going on in Chen's mind, he would ask him from time to time whether he had any family, whether there was anyone Dr. Gagné could call to learn more about who Chen Yu was and what his psychiatric history might be. This year, out of the blue, Chen Yu mentioned a sister. The name he gave as his sister's was a common one, and so Dr. Gagné and his team reached out to one woman after another until they found someone who recognized Chen Yu's description and date of birth.

The reaction was utter shock. "His family thought he had been dead for ten years," Dr. Gagné tells me. "It was really an emotional thing. They were stunned to hear that he was alive." Chen and his sister and mother have since been reunited as a result of Dr. Gagné's perseverance; they've since been to visit him at Northern. However, they've been unable to shed any light on the question of Chen's psychiatric diagnosis. According to Chen's sister, Dr. Gagné says, Chen had no mental-health issues that the family knew of when he was arrested and disappeared.

I ask Dr. Gagné why Chen is still at Northern, whether he's still assaultive. The answer is no, but it's complicated, he tells me. Chen has become an administrative issue. He's classified as an inmate with "special needs." This classification is for men who are perceived as unable to succeed in the general population but who are also not benefiting from repeated stretches of administrative segregation. Although they have some more privileges than other inmates at Northern—for example, they're not chained when they come out of their cells—they are difficult to place at other facilities.

Dr. Gagné tells me that in his opinion Chen should go to the prison from which Rivers has come that specializes in inmates with mental illness, but because Chen is classified as special needs, that prison was refusing to accept him.

A year later I write Dr. Gagné to schedule another visit to Northern. I ask him whether it would be possible to meet with Chen Yu again when I come, explaining that his story is one that has really stayed with me and that I'd appreciate the chance to see how he was doing and perhaps to ask him some follow-up questions.

"He was actually transferred to another facility," Dr. Gagné writes back, naming the specialty mental-health prison that had eventually accepted Chen. "I think it's a more appropriate placement. He's okay there." I am touched by the implication that Dr. Gagné has checked on Chen despite the fact that Chen is no longer his patient. "Of course," Dr. Gagné continues in his e-mail to me, "there are others we can meet when you join me."

MY SECOND VISIT with Dr. Gagné is in the wake of a brutal attack one inmate made against another.

Although the stated goal of Northern's construction was to quell violence, the prison's purposeful architecture did not immediately have the desired effect. In fact, in the first many years of its operation, the facility was plagued by regular attacks and acts of aggression. "It used to be a hell of a lot worse than it is now," one of the COs at Northern says, echoing the sentiment I hear from many of the staff members who describe the violence within the prison's walls for many years as "out of control."

"Every day it seemed like there'd be something," the CO tells me. "Inmates would start floods, set fires, attack the staff and each other. I'd just be waiting to see someone running through the halls—and then we'd know it was an emergency and we'd all take off running. It might not have happened every day. . . ." The officer pauses. "But it felt like it did."

Through a series of strategic steps, and in collaboration with Dr. Gagné and the mental-health service, the prison administration made reducing the violence at Northern a priority. The number of inmates held at Northern was cut. A unit designated for gang members was moved from Northern to another facility. And it worked. Over the course of the eight years that Dr. Gagné has been at Northern, he tells me, they've seen a decrease in restraints and many fewer instances of self-injurious behavior. The frequency of episodes of violence has also declined dramatically.

But violence was not eradicated entirely. The victim of the recent attack, a man named Alvarez, survived, and Dr. Gagné has been asked to see him to assess the psychiatric effects of the assault.

Anna, the nurse who is working with Dr. Gagné today, joins us. Accompanied by a CO, the three of us walk to the ward where Alvarez is being held.

When we arrive, Dr. Gagné tells one of the officers on the ward that we're here to see Alvarez. We learn that he is in the middle of his recreation time. "Let's see if he wants to stay in rec or wants to talk to you," the officer says, passing behind us and gesturing for us to turn and follow.

The CO leads us through a set of doors into the rec yard—a small outdoor concrete area enclosed by the tall prison walls and divided into three room-size cages. In each of them stands a man in a gray prison-issue sweat suit. The area looks like the fenced concrete run of a dog kennel. This is where the men come for their one allotted hour per day out of their cells. Unlike rec yards in other prisons I've seen, there is nothing here. No basketball hoop, no weights, not a single pull-up bar.

William Blake, a man in his twenty-ninth year of solitary confinement in the New York State Security Housing Unit (SHU), wrote of these spaces, "If you look up you'll find bars and a screen covering the yard, and if you're lucky maybe you can see a bit of blue sky through the mesh, otherwise it'll be hard to believe that you're even outside. If it's a good day you can walk around the SHU yard in small circles staring ahead with your mind on nothingness, like the nothing you've got in that little lacuna with you. If it's a bad day, though, maybe your mind will be filled with remembrances of all you used to have that you haven't seen now for many years; and you'll be missing it, feeling the loss, feeling it bad."

The three men in Northern's divided yard eye us as we walk along the concrete path in front of their gated cages. When we pass, I hear the first two men make comments to each other, but I can't tell what they're saying. One laughs. The other chuckles, and his sidelong gaze follows us.

We reach the third cage, and the man within it approaches the locked gate. He's short but muscular. He has tattoos on his forearms, on his neck, on his cheekbone, on his eyelids.

"Alvarez, you wanna talk to mental health or you wanna stay out?" the CO asks the man.

"I'll come talk," he says. And with that we turn back.

I follow Dr. Gagné and Anna out of the rec yard and into a stairwell that we climb until we reach the locked metal door at the top. Meanwhile, the CO recuffs and shackles Alvarez and leads him from the rec yard back into the prison ward. The door at the top of the stairs has not yet opened when the ground-level door we've come through slides open with a bang. Alvarez's leg chains clank along the floor and onto the metal stairs. He climbs the first few steps up toward us, and the CO walks behind him.

"I hate when they do this," says Anna, nodding at the CO. "He's supposed to be between us." I realize she means that we're at the top of the stairs with a locked door ahead of us and a prisoner who merits incarceration at a supermax facility is climbing ever nearer. Even in the psychiatric hospital, I make sure that when I'm meeting with patients, I always have a way out behind me. I understand Anna's concern. Later in the day, she'll tell me that since she started working at Northern, she has begun sitting with her back to the wall whenever she goes into restaurants. "I get nervous now if anyone's behind me," she says. "My girlfriends make fun of me, but I just say to them that if they want me to relax, this is how it's going to be."

"That happens to people when they work in here," Dr. Gagné concurs. "I've talked with COs who have retired from here, and they've told me that it takes two or three months after retirement for them to stop being edgy, to stop feeling like any sound or sudden movement could be a threat."

Anna looks down the stairwell at Alvarez as he climbs. "Ummm . . ." she says, looking pointedly at the officer.

"Alvarez, yeah, come down here until we get the door," the CO says. Alvarez turns around, steps back down the three stairs he's come up, and waits below us. After what feels like several minutes, the door in front of us opens. Dr. Gagné, Anna, and I head through, and Alvarez and the CO again begin to ascend.

We enter an evaluation room, empty but for a single table and five plastic chairs. Dr. Gagné arranges the chairs so that he and Anna and I sit in a semicircle behind the table, along with Dr. Mark Frayne, a psychologist who works on Dr. Gagné's team, who has met us in the room. Dr. Gagné situates the fifth chair, the one that Alvarez will sit in, so that it's positioned across from us but pulled four or five feet back from the table. Alvarez enters. The tether chain that runs between his handcuffs and leg irons dangles behind him like a looped metal tail. The CO asks him, "You want the cuffs in front?"

"Yeah," says Alvarez, and the CO unlocks the cuffs from behind the prisoner's back. Alvarez reflexively brings his wrists in front of his body and holds them so that they press against each other. He does not clasp his hands. The officer relocks the cuffs so that now Alvarez can sit without his arms pulled behind him. A chipped red padlock secures the cuffs to the tether chain. My eyes follow the metal links down to his shackled ankles. The image evokes gladiator battles, the slave trade, chain gangs. Chapters of history that feel barbaric and distant.

Alvarez sits down in the chair across from us, the wall of windows behind him. "You're Alvarez, 685773?" Dr. Gagné asks him.

Yes.

Dr. Gagné explains to Alvarez that he's going to ask him many questions, that they are questions he asks every inmate he sees, that Alvarez should not take offense or think that Dr. Gagné is suggesting that all of these questions apply to him. Does Alvarez understand?

Yes.

This preface to the interview is a familiar one to me. When meeting a patient for the first time, it's important to strike a balance between normalizing symptoms that may seem notable without implying something about a person that will alienate him and disrupt the rapport you're trying to establish as a clinician. If a person is experiencing hallucinations, for instance, you want to make room for him to disclose that. But if he isn't, you don't want him to feel judged or belittled by the question. I do a version of the same dance when I'm evaluating patients, and still I've had my share of outraged responses. "Do you ever hear things that other people do not hear? Or see things that other people do not see?" I ask. "Do you ever feel like the television or radio or stoplights are sending messages meant only for you? Do you feel paranoid or think people are out to get you?" *What? No! Why did you ask me that—do I look crazy to you?*

Dr. Louis Marino, a geriatric psychiatrist and a mentor of mine, taught me his kind way of assessing whether the demented patients he treats are oriented enough to know where they are. Instead of asking his hospitalized patients, "Where are we right now?" or "Do you know where you are?" he asks, "Did anyone tell you the name of this place?" If they say no to his question, it saves them the shame of admitting they have no idea where they are. It also avoids focusing their attention on the fact of their disorientation, which could evoke anxiety, fear, or agitation. In a prison atmosphere, inmates are defined by accusations. They must be guarded about their vulnerabilities in order to protect themselves. In addition, they may well be in prison because they are prone to impulsive anger and aggression. For all these reasons, initial reassurances that the questions the doctor is asking are not meant to demean or accuse take on even greater importance.

And so Dr. Gagné begins, asking questions about Alvarez's medical, psychiatric, and personal history. Alvarez tells us that he's been healthy. He saw a therapist of some kind for anxiety when he was a kid, he says. Then he served six and a half years in prison, from the ages of nineteen to twenty-five, for what he describes as "running guns." He had no mental-health treatment during that period of incarceration, he says, "Really nothing else until 2010, when I tried to hang myself."

"You tried to hang yourself?" Dr. Gagné asks. "What was going on then?"

"I was twenty-six," Alvarez explains. "I had just gotten out the year before, and I got locked up for this. I didn't think I could do the time."

I don't have any information about Alvarez in front of me, but Dr. Gagné does. He flips a page and checks Alvarez's sentence. I will learn later that Alvarez and his twenty-one-year-old roommate robbed a small store. In the course of the robbery, the roommate shot and killed the college student who was the cashier. Alvarez grabbed the cash register and ran out the door. For his role in the crime, he was found guilty of felony murder.

"You're serving thirty-eight years?" Gagné asks him matter-of-factly.

"Yeah," Alvarez says. "I've done seven. Thirty-one left. Twenty forty-eight."

I look up from my notes, not understanding the sequence of numbers. Then I realize that Alvarez has said the year he will be released, thirty-one years in the future. A year I've never yet even contemplated: 2048. I reflexively do the math in my head and realize that when Alvarez is released from prison, I will be seventy-four years old. The thirty-three-year-old young man I'm looking at now will be sixty-four. He will not have been outside a prison since the age of twenty-six. (I was once caught in a downpour on my way into a prison. As I waited to pass through a set of doors, I groused to an inmate on work duty who was mopping the hallway that even my socks were soaked. "They cancel outdoor rec in storms," the man said to me with a soft smile. "I haven't been in a rainstorm in eighteen years.")

Alvarez's account of attempting suicide at the start of his lengthy sentence correlates with the data we have on suicide in jails and prisons. The highest risk for suicide in jails occurs within the first twenty-four to forty-eight hours of confinement. In prisons the first thirty days are considered to be a particularly high-risk period. The length of a person's sentence is also an important factor, as long sentences induce hopelessness, a factor that has an even stronger correlation with suicide than depression does.

There are times in my work as a psychiatrist when I see patients who have made suicide attempts that come out of long struggles with depression, or psychotic illness, or substance use. Occasionally I will note that a patient's suicide attempt is a situational response to a moment of acute grief or substantial trauma. A mother whose child has been murdered and who cannot fathom continuing to live falls into this category. Or a middle-aged man who is diagnosed with an incurable, rapidly degenerative, and eventually fatal disease. Alvarez describes no history of depression, no psychotic symptoms, and only minor episodes of substance abuse. Trying to kill yourself when you've just spent the first six years of your twenties in prison and are newly facing the next three and a half decades of your life therein is a situational response.

"It was rough at first," Alvarez says of his sentence, "just wondering if I could do the time. But eventually I got used to the idea, and then I was okay, just doing my thing from day to day."

The psychiatrist in that prison had put him on pills for depression after the hanging attempt nonetheless. Alvarez took them for a year or two, then started refusing them. "They made me feel like a zombie," he says. "I didn't care about nothing. I only wanted to sleep. I stopped the medicine, and ever since then I feel great."

"It's different now," he says tentatively. His eyes up to this point have been downcast, but he raises them now to meet Dr. Gagné's gaze. "After what happened to me with this situation, I feel different."

"Let's talk about what happened," Dr. Gagné says gently.

"I live in 220," Alvarez begins. "But the door broke, so they wanna move me into 219. I feel more comfortable by myself. I say I don't want a cellie. But I don't wanna catch no tickets. I don't wanna get in trouble, so I say okay. They move me on a Saturday, and not enough people work on Saturdays."

How quickly we're in an alternate world. When where you live is a cell with a number. When you know the rhythms of a prison well enough to know that the weekday staffing is different from the weekend staffing and that there is risk associated with those rhythms.

Number 219 is the cell of another inmate: Soto. Alvarez says, "Once they move me in with him, I hear Soto say if he has to have a cellie, he'll jump to anyone. I tell him I don't want no trouble, I don't want no cellie either. He acting normal. We listening to music. We talking about the street. Then the captain passed. Inmate Soto started talking about his property to the captain, started getting mad. I could tell he was getting mad, so I jumped in my bunk to give him space. About three thirty they pass razors for shaving. He tell me I can go first. I go to the sink to shave my mustache. All the sudden I feel burning in my back. It happen too fast for me to even realize he's cutting me. I turn. He punch me in the head. He cut my throat. I think he is going to kill me. I see his face. His eyes. I never see anyone like that."

Alvarez pauses and looks back down at the floor, ashamed. His left knee bounces continuously in the baggy gray prison garb, making his leg irons jingle faintly. "I'm scared of everybody now. I feel like everybody wants to hurt me. Even the COs. I react like they're going to slap me or something. I'm not that kind of guy, never been afraid of anyone before." Dr. Gagné has not even had to ask a question. Has not had to say a word. It's as if Alvarez has been holding in this torment, waiting to have a chance to tell someone, waiting for this release.

"My hands is always shaking now," he says. "And I dream this every night. Every night I see his face, his eyes, and I think I'm gonna die. And ..." He takes a look at me and blushes, then pushes on. "And when I wake up, I've pissed myself. I don't talk to nobody about it. I get up and wash my clothes. Every morning is the same now. But that was never me before.

"It's messed up," he says. "But also now I worry I'll get in trouble. If I have another cellie, I might wake up from a nightmare thinking he might hurt me, and I might hurt him to defend myself even though he wasn't even thinking that."

I know that what Alvarez fears could actually come true. And I wonder what traumas lie in Soto's past that have rendered him able to enact his own horrible violence. Lines from an Auden poem come into my mind:

> *I and the public know*
> *What all schoolchildren learn,*
> *Those to whom evil is done*
> *Do evil in return.*

Alvarez has taken a breath, and Dr. Gagné waits to see whether he will keep talking, allowing this pent-up fear to continue to cascade forth. The pause lengthens, and Dr. Gagné begins to speak in a clear, even voice.

"The kinds of things you're experiencing are not uncommon reactions when someone has been through some kind of trauma," Dr. Gagné begins. "The nightmares, the flashes of seeing his face, the feeling that you're reliving the episode over and over." He pauses to be sure Alvarez is following, and he is, intently. "Sometimes people even associate a certain sound or smell with the attack, which can trigger feelings of panic," Dr. Gagné explains. "Like if a woman was raped by a man wearing a certain cologne, she may smell that cologne years later in a department store and feel like she is right back in the moment of the rape again."

Little by little I notice a shift in Alvarez's expression, from anguish to something different. If not full-fledged relief, then at least toward a version of it—a kind of lifting. An awareness that he is not going crazy. He's been holding on to these symptoms, and they've festered within him, foreign and terrifying. The fact that Dr. Gagné hears them calmly and without alarm provides the beginning of reassurance to Alvarez. The fact that Dr. Gagné is describing the response as something known and not atypical—maybe even something to be expected after an encounter as extreme as the Soto attack—imparts a measure of calm to Alvarez. And at the same time, I can tell that Dr. Gagné is not just trying to lend Alvarez some relief. He is also starting to educate him about anxiety and how it works.

"You might feel right now that these fears are never going to go away. That you're going to feel jumpy and afraid because of this for the rest of your life. But there are things we can do to help, and if you only remember one thing that we talk about today, I want you to remember that you will not feel like this forever." Alvarez nods a little. He looks as if he wants very much to believe what Dr. Gagné is telling him but finds it impossible yet to do so.

Whenever I'm in a prison environment, I'm struck by an odd duality within it. On the one hand, it's a human society, and because of that there are aspects to it that feel very familiar. I hear Dr. Gagné talking with Alvarez about trauma and how the body and mind respond in a series of predictable ways to a horrific event. And within this interaction I hear echoes of conversations I've had with innumerable patients—even with friends and family members—whom I have counseled in the wake of significant trauma. Trauma is a human experience. Anxiety is a typical human response when the body or spirit has been under assault.

On the other hand, there's a moment within every one of my prison visits during which I am slammed by the fact that this world is like no world I've ever known. That the rules and realities of correctional facilities have no equal in the world I live in.

Even as Dr. Gagné is providing education, counsel, and relief to Alvarez, I'm aware that the ways the two men view the context surrounding the attack differ dramatically. These men have different vantage points, and the views from the vantage points skew sharply, each in its own direction. This difference is compounded by the uniqueness of the prison environment and its essential unknowability. The evasiveness of *truth* within its walls.

Dr. Gagné's view is that Alvarez fell victim to a random act of prison violence. Soto, I learn, is serving a fifty-one-year sentence for murder.

When he attacked Alvarez, Soto had already lived the last fourteen years of his life in prison.

"After ten or fifteen years, the sun never sets nor rises in a prison," Jack Abbott wrote in his prison memoir, *In the Belly of the Beast*. "There are no seasons: no wind or rain or sunlight in your hair. There are no children to give you a vision of life, no women to comfort your soul. I have never walked beneath the sky at nighttime on prison grounds."

No seasons, no wind or rain, and most of all no hope. Prolonged sentences can throw the people who receive them into despair. With little or no prospect of ever regaining one's freedom, there is no incentive to behave in any way other than that which might yield the maximum personal gain.

Dr. Frayne says that the kind of sentence Soto is serving means that he and men like him have nothing to lose.

The threat of added time is meaningless when you're already effectively sentenced to die in jail. For the men who live their lives within it, the world of the prison becomes the only world. And the things that are their own, the things over which they have control, are so few that their importance is out of proportion to what we would perceive their value to be. Thus Soto, who does not want a cellie, is willing to define himself as an imminent threat to anyone housed with him—and is willing to perform the heinous actions necessary to render himself classified as such—just to keep his small space his own. And things that seem unimportant to those of us who live free lives—immediate access to specific belongings, for example—take on heightened meaning for men whose every move is controlled and constrained.

"Guys in for life get violent about their property," Frayne tells me, using the prison term for "possessions" that Alvarez had also used when describing Soto's escalation. "It's a phenomenon we observe. They get obsessive. They fixate on things. After a period of time, they lock in. Then it's very hard to redirect them."

These are rational explanations: Soto has a history of violence. He has attacked other inmates before. But he had not been violent for an extended length of time, and the correctional staff thought his behavior was in good enough control that he could temporarily tolerate a cellmate. Alvarez's door breaks, and as a result the officers have to move him into a different cell, and they move him in with Soto. It goes fine at first, but then Soto, who has demonstrated the capacity to be easily provoked, to become assaultive very quickly, has some altercation with an officer about his property and his tenuous control simply breaks.

These are rational explanations, and they're the explanations given and believed by the mental-health team. But they're not the only explanations. They're not Alvarez's explanations.

In the unknowable world of prison, these are also rational explanations. "I think the COs made the situation happen," Alvarez says when Dr. Gagné asserts that the attack was a random act and one that Alvarez must work toward trusting will not recur. "I'm thinking this shit was orchestrated," he begins. He looks at me. Blushes. Says, "Sorry, miss"— an apology for cursing in front of me. Then he continues. "Before this I got caught with cell phones. The COs were interrogating me: *Who's the CO bringing me this? Where am I getting this? Who's bringing it in?* But I don't rat on nobody. Then all the sudden they move me in with Soto, who they know will jump to anyone. I feel like they made this happen."

"I don't think the captain set you up—" Dr. Gagné begins, but before he can say more, Alvarez interrupts him.

"In 2009 Soto cut somebody," Alvarez says. "In 2012 he try to kill another inmate and told the judge he'd try to kill any cellie they give him. So why they put me in there if they *know* this?" Alvarez asks. "He straight-up *told* them he was going to do this. So they *knew*."

Alvarez was not psychotic. He was not paranoid. His fears—though they might not have been based in fact—were nonetheless conceivable, given the violence and opacity of the environment in which he exists.

In September 2017 *The New York Times* ran an article describing just these sorts of allegations at Rikers Island. The article revealed that prison guards allegedly gave a notorious inmate access to victims by unlocking their cells and even providing the aggressor with materials—like a rubber glove on entering the shower—with which to sexually assault other inmates. Aaron M. Rubin, the lawyer for one of the victims, says that guards purposely put the accused assailant in a segregated cell with his client and then "paid no heed to what was happening," according to surveillance video from inside the facility, which recorded, among other episodes, two days' worth of sexual assaults within one cell. The attacker, Mr. Rubin claims, was used by officers "as an enforcer to intimidate" other inmates. These kinds of abuses by officers have been documented in jails and prisons across the country. Which makes Alvarez's belief—that he was put in a cell with an inmate who was known to be assaultive because he had refused to confess about his cell phones—sound less far-fetched.

After the evaluation, when Alvarez has gone, I ask Dr. Gagné about Alvarez's fears for his safety, about his sense that the attack itself was one of retribution. Dr. Gagné says that he knows the captain well, that he is certain that moving Alvarez in with Soto was not a vengeful act meant to hurt or kill him. Dr. Frayne agrees.

Then the men politely shift gears away from my questions and begin to talk between themselves, questioning whether the attack on Alvarez could have been avoided. They wonder whether they could have foreseen the risk better, could have identified that risk and communicated it to the COs. They wonder whether they missed something that could have prevented this young man from being traumatized. It is a familiar moment to me. I've seen this kind of earnest reckoning among surgeons at the morbidity and mortality conferences I attended in medical school, poring over whether there'd been anything in a patient's history to have indicated she might be susceptible to the catastrophic hemorrhage she suffered on the operating table. I've seen it in the pediatric resident who had an ominous gut feeling in the room with an injured child but brushed it aside with no evidence to back it up and who learned years later that the child had been removed from her mother's custody due to documented abuse. I've seen it in my friend, still in training as a fledgling therapist, who calls to say she's bringing me coffee on a whim and then stands in my kitchen to say she didn't know that spring sunshine could exacerbate mania and that her patient had tried hard to kill himself and survived, but barely, and why on earth had she not recognized the risk that was emerging right in front of her?

In other words, Drs. Gagné and Frayne feel true regret and sadness that Alvarez was attacked. They do not believe at all—not for a moment—that the attack was planned as retribution. I suspect they're right. And yet I begin to see that the fact of who is "right" in this particular circumstance is immaterial. The "truth" of what happened is unimportant. In the clinicians' world, there is no way that the correctional staff intended for Alvarez to be brutally assaulted. In the prisoners' world, you can be talking with your cellie about the street one moment and have your throat slit by him the next.

"I can't sit still now," Alvarez said toward the end of the session. "I'm always walking. In the cell. In the rec yard . . . I jump at every sound." His voice was insistent, pleading. "I sleep with my light on and everything. What if the COs want this to happen to me again? What I'm supposed to do? I can't refuse to go where they tell me. I can't say no to them. What if they want to hurt me?"

"What if you never get an answer to that question?" Dr. Gagné asked. Alvarez shook his head slowly, looked at the floor, defeated. "I don't think the captain set you up," Dr. Gagné continued, "but I don't think me feeling that way makes any difference to you. I will tell you, though, that whether or not you ever get an answer to that question, you can be okay again. You can get a handle on this anxiety and start to get past this awful thing that has happened to you."

"The task of medicine," wrote sixteenth-century French surgeon Ambrose Paré, "is to cure sometimes, to relieve often, and to comfort always." Dr. Gagné was offering compassion in a place whose very intention—whose very design—is to be devoid of warmth and human connection. Alvarez looked up at him, reticently, and I saw that he was fighting back tears. "You can be okay." And in that moment all of us in the room—Gagné, Frayne, Anna, Alvarez, me—in that moment all of us wanted to believe it.

As the CO took Alvarez from the room at Northern, I knew that he and Dr. Gagné would continue their work together and that he would receive treatment from a good and devoted doctor. I also knew that he would spend the next thirty-one years of his life behind bars and that his fear of unwittingly hurting another—because he is now afraid of being hurt himself—is valid and could be realized. I watched Alvarez until I could no longer see him. He rounded a corner and was gone. Still, the sound of his chains echoed from wall to wall and back to my ears as he walked.

AS I LEAVE NORTHERN, my brain fires. My body senses the world: temperatures, colors, voices, shafts of light. As I drive, I pass a horse farm on a rural road with a beautiful old gray barn sagging on the hill's horizon. I spot a red-tailed hawk perched on the uppermost branch of a fir tree; the sky is a fierce, unwavering blue around the bird's feathered edges. I reach a town. At the lone traffic signal, a man in a steel blue pickup truck idles across from me in the oncoming lane. The light turns a sharp green, and as he passes, the man nods at me, raises his hand hello. I drive on, onto a highway that rises above a steeply pitched valley and winds between stone hills once blasted through with dynamite. Faster and faster the images of the world cascade around me. The places I pass churn by: *drive-in movie theater, gas station, tollbooth. Starbucks, strip mall, graveyard.*

A song on the radio from my adolescence pulls me into nostalgia. This constant stream of sensations provokes thoughts and emotions without any awareness on my part. This richness of each free moment of my life. The drive from Connecticut home to Rhode Island takes me across Massachusetts. I've been in three different states in one day, and Chen Yu has been in a six-by-nine-foot cell all day every day for the last seven and a half years.

9.

MINNOWS AND KILLER WHALES

There's no shortage of accounts of horrific brutality in prison, and many correctional facilities have far more assaults than Northern does. Beatings, rapes, and murders occur on a daily basis in penitentiaries around the country, and the violence flows in all directions. Inmates attack correctional officers. Officers attack inmates. Inmates attack one another. They attack their own bodies. Nineteen percent of men held in U.S. prisons report that they've been assaulted by fellow detainees. Twenty-one percent report having been assaulted by prison staff. In some states the problem has reached epidemic status, as in Alabama, where the U.S. Justice Department launched an investigation into all the state's male prisons, citing reports of "rampant violence and sexual abuse at the hands of both inmates and staff members." The inquiry began in the context of severe prison overcrowding in the state—with facilities operating at around 172 percent of capacity—and in the wake of a reduction in the number of correctional officers by 20 percent. Daily violence was routine. In February 2017 one Alabama county's correctional facilities reported three unrelated inmate murders within ten days.

Justice Anthony Kennedy rightly asserted that psychiatrists have a particular insight into corrections. We also have a deep understanding of human violence. Indeed, much of psychiatry is dedicated to deciphering, predicting, and preventing acts of aggression. And this research is conducted from a stance of objective analysis. In an attempt to rigorously investigate the foundations of violence, psychiatry's scientific inquiry pares away the moral and emotional contexts through which acts of aggression are typically—and retroactively—seen. Our goal is to preemptively identify methods of intervention; to identify the points at which we, as clinicians, might be able to intercede so that we can prevent injury or, worse, tragedy.

Looking at prisons through this lens—and contrasting the approach to aggression taken in prisons with the methods we use in the hospital to anticipate and combat episodes of violence—has convinced me that correctional environments exacerbate and foster aggression rather than diminish it.

Jungle. War zone. Hellhole. Devil's Island. Pit of despair. The perilous atmospheres that constitute our nation's prisons are described in like terms by those who live in them and those who work in them. These institutions, meant to prioritize and protect safety, are among the most dangerous environments in our country.

Derrick Hutchison, who is serving 120 years at Missouri Eastern Correctional Center for armed robberies, describes the prison hierarchy as a marine ecosystem. "You've got the minnows, and you've got the killer whale. Minnow being the lowest, killer whale the highest. I mean, that's how it is."

Consider Jehan Abdur-Raheem, originally imprisoned for twenty-five years to life for a murder he did not commit. After twenty-four years and eight months in prison, he was exonerated of the crime for which he'd been charged. However, his sentence was extended by nine years for a murder he *did* commit—the killing of another inmate in prison. "There are some rules in prison that are nonnegotiable," Abdur-Raheem, who is now a mentor working with Yale University psychologists to assist ex-offenders in their reentry into the community, explains. "You have to decide when you go in whether you're predator or prey. That's just the way it is." *I mean, that's how it is.* A man who had never before committed murder was not only transformed in prison into someone who felt he needed to kill another man in order to preserve himself, he was transformed into someone capable of doing so.

Reading or hearing about even a small handful of these incidents of violence in prison can be enough to tune out, turn away, put the pages down. There are bricks involved. And razor blades. There are shivs fashioned from broken silverware. And the jagged metal edges of soup-can tops. Some of the attacks involve prison gang members carving out territory or settling scores. Some are calculated and repeated assaults on the most vulnerable men in the facility: the psychotic or intellectually disabled inmate, the transgender inmate, the juvenile serving time in the adult prison. Some are random and vicious attacks on correctional officers, like one at Northern in which an inmate feigned a diabetic seizure and, when a CO entered his cell and leaned over him to help, the inmate stabbed the officer in the neck, nearly severing his jugular vein. Some, like Jehan Abdur-Raheem's, are desperate acts of self-defense. Some are petty squabbles—like Soto's—over property or privileges.

I once performed a competency evaluation on a man who sailed easily through the questions I posed, answering each one with clarity and logic. Just before the examination finished, I asked him about the fact that instead of the tan top and bottom the detainees in this facility routinely wore, he was dressed in a baggy red canvas jumpsuit that Velcroed down the front. His hands were cuffed in front of him at the wrists, and he was wearing leg chains. This evaluation was taking place at a high-security facility—not a supermax—so this degree of restraint stood out.

I knew that these things—the cuffs, the jumpsuit, the chains—were disciplinary markers. They meant that he was in segregation within the facility. Something he'd done had gotten him into trouble. I asked him about this, not to pry but because problematic behavior, too, can reveal psychiatric symptomatology.

"What happened that you got sent to seg?" I asked.

"Fighting," he said. "I went to seg for fighting."

"Over what?" I pressed him, intent on making sure that he had not lashed out at someone due to delusional beliefs.

"I started it," he explained. "It was lunch. I had cookies on my tray. We had made a deal. Two cookies for one soup. Then I ended up with an extra cookie, so I said to the guy, 'What about three cookies for two soups? Okay?' He said, 'Yeah.' Then he took the three cookies and only gave me one soup."

"Did you know you would get sent to seg for fighting?" I asked.

"Definitely, yeah," he responded.

"So why go to seg over soup?"

"Pride," he said quickly. "I had to make him understand. If you make a deal with me, you have to stand by it." He paused. "It sounds crazy, to go to seg over soup," he continued. "But it's jail. It's what happens."

By overcrowding and understaffing correctional facilities, we have created environments in which men must become predators, lest they become prey. We place these men in a facility whose primary stated aim is security, and we fail to keep them safe. And by restricting them as fully as we do, we limit the ways they can protect themselves. We create houses of law enforcement that are shot through with lawlessness and a kind of guerrilla warfare. It's all well and good to hypothesize that you and I would behave differently were we held within this world, but as Jehan Abdur-Raheem would tell us, from the outside it's impossible to ever truly know.

Dr. Stuart Grassian is perhaps the world's leading expert on the psychiatric effects of solitary confinement. In a fascinating breadth of research, Grassian has drawn from many sources to forge an understanding of how humans respond to circumstances of prolonged seclusion. In doing so he has determined that the human mind responds in predictable ways whenever its exposure to stimulation is markedly restricted.

By looking at a wide range of divergent circumstances, from shipwreck to polar exploration to imprisonment, Grassian discovered that similar psychological states have appeared in people isolated in each of these realms.

During the Korean War, for example, the United States government feared that Korean captors were using methods of profound sensory deprivation to brainwash American POWs. In response to this concern, the U.S. Department of Defense and the Central Intelligence Agency funded experiments aimed at learning what happened to human beings when sensory stimulation was reduced as much as possible. Subjects were placed in lightproof, soundproof rooms. Their limbs were fitted inside cardboard to reduce sensation and proprioception, the awareness they had of their body's position in space. The results were consistent—and striking.

The subjects in the experiments grew restless and anxious. They reported intense, terrifying hallucinations. Some described vivid, "primitive aggressive" fantasies. They struggled to know with certainty where the lines of reality lay. Others experienced paranoid, persecutory delusions. Still others became stuporous and mute.

The symptoms reported were not merely subjective. Measurable neurologic changes were noted in the participants. EEG studies conducted on the subjects' brains were abnormal. Without regular sensory stimulation, *their neurological activity had changed*. The studies of these previously normal brains now showed electrical impulses consistent with brains in the throes of stupor or delirium.

As Grassian looked across studies of isolation and sensory deprivation, a characteristic set of symptoms began to emerge. Sailors who had undertaken long solo sea voyages consistently reported experiencing dramatic hallucinations and fears. Pilots who flew long distances in darkness or above the clouds without sensory input for orientation recounted nearly identical experiences. Analogous findings surfaced in other, unrelated disciplines. When subjected to unrelenting sensory deprivation and social isolation, regardless of the circumstance, the human mind responded predictably: with aggression and fear.

Admiral Richard Byrd wrote of witnessing suspicion and paranoia in a fellow explorer on one of his famed Antarctic voyages. The man was taken to "the verge of murder or suicide over imaginary persecutions by another man who had been his devoted friend." A half century later, the United States Navy Medical Neuropsychiatric Research Unit issued a report on symptoms it had noted in its Antarctic researchers as the long winter progressed. Scientists were experiencing depression and anxiety. Their sleep was disturbed. As Chen Yu had, the researchers began to focus on physical sensations and bodily complaints. Their social relationships deteriorated. And the report noted that any psychiatric problems the researchers had beforehand worsened as the length of their confinement increased.

In reports from nineteenth-century penitentiaries, Grassian found descriptions of isolated prisoners in "an agitated confusional state" that resembled a delirium. The condition was characterized by paranoia, hallucinations, and panic attacks, as well as "random, impulsive, often self-directed violence."

These findings mirrored studies of modern-day detainees who quickly lose alertness and attentiveness once held in isolation. And like the subjects in the Korean POW experiments, today's isolated prisoners—even after only a few days of solitary confinement—show EEG patterns that have shifted to reveal markings consistent with a stuporous, delirious brain.

The consistency of these observations in a broad range of circumstances lent context and continuity to Dr. Grassian's research. He found that these common symptoms reliably emerged in prisoners held in solitary confinement, from the Philadelphia System to today's supermax facilities. By linking these disparate accounts, Grassian had discovered a specific psychiatric syndrome that develops in the isolated human mind, a syndrome indicative of grave psychiatric harm.

Grassian describes "The Specific Psychiatric Syndrome Associated with Solitary Confinement" as having the characteristics of "an acute organic brain syndrome—a delirium," marked by the following:

- hyperresponsivity to external stimuli
- perceptual distortions, illusions, and hallucinations

- panic attacks
- difficulties with thinking, concentration, and memory
- overt paranoia
- intrusive obsessional thoughts and the emergence of primitive aggressive ruminations
- problems with impulse control

Cesar Francisco Villa spent eleven years in solitary confinement in the SHU of Pelican Bay, part of a sentence of 348 years to life that he received after his third robbery conviction. His description of his own experience aligns with Grassian's syndrome. It also drives home how fragile the veneer of civilization is for us all.

"Waking is the most traumatic," Villa writes. "The slightest slip in a quiet dawn can set a SHU personality into a tailspin: If the sink water is not warm enough, the toilet flushes too loud, the drop of a soap dish, a cup . . . In an instant you bare teeth, shake with rage. Your heart hammers against ribs, lodges in your throat. You are capable of killing anything at this moment. This is the time it's best to hold rigid. This is not a portrait you wish anyone to see. Take a deep breath. Try to convince yourself there's an ounce of good left in you. And then a gull screeches—passing outside—another tailspin and you're checking your ears for blood."

The culmination of Grassian's research as an identifiable psychiatric syndrome with significant relevance for our current prison practices should not surprise us. It is merely the reinforcement of principles we have known since the failure of the Philadelphia System and the opinion of *In re Medley*. That we continue to use solitary confinement, then, means either that we do not care that it damages the people so contained or that we think the damage is worth it because the practice is effective or some combination of the two.

In the mid-twentieth century, the governments of Australia, France, and the United States sought to predict how individual scientists would adjust to isolated living conditions in remote research stations in Antarctica. The studies correlated Antarctic researchers' personality traits with their demonstrated ability—or inability—to tolerate the unrelenting conditions of isolation in the environment. The goal was to maximize efficiency and minimize conflict among the work groups sent to this most distant of lands.

"Lack of respect for authority and aggression," one of the studies found, "were important markers for poor isolation adjustment." Another concluded that "persons with antisocial and psychotic tendencies were poor risks for efficient functioning in conditions of isolation."

Grassian had also found that when held in isolation, people with preexisting personality disorders or impaired psychosocial functioning were particularly likely to develop the more volatile and dangerous symptoms of his syndrome, including paranoia, agitation, and "irrational aggression toward staff."

Lack of respect for authority. Aggression. Antisocial and psychotic tendencies. Impaired psychosocial functioning. Personality disorders. These are the hallmarks of many of the men in our prison system, and certainly of many of the men who behave so dangerously in prison that it lands them in administrative segregation. In other words, we are taking people who are *uniquely ill-suited to isolation* and we are placing them in solitary confinement, asserting that we're doing so to improve their functioning and behavior.

Antisocial personality disorder has been found to correlate with a higher-than-normal need for stimulation, and people diagnosed with the condition are described in the clinical literature as "pathologically 'stimulation seeking,' 'impulsive,' and 'unable to tolerate routine and boredom.'" This makes logical sense when we consider the high-stress, high-stimulation ways that sociopathy manifests itself in action: relentless rule breaking, thrill seeking, ditching out on the monotony of school or work, pushing at the boundaries of pain and pleasure. These are impulsive people who thrive on chaos. And the very traits that define people as antisocial also render them increasingly likely to react in violent and dangerous ways when placed in restrictive, low-stimulation environments.

People with antisocial personalities are also especially likely to challenge authority and break rules in prison, which means they're more apt than other detainees to wind up in solitary confinement. *Those who may most merit segregation and isolation by the standards of our current prison system are predisposed to fare the least well within it.* Here our desire for punishment and control may, in fact, cause more damage than good, fueling a vicious cycle of impulsivity and increasingly maladaptive behavior. Nonetheless, the use of isolation continues because departments of correction claim that the practice is necessary to reduce violence in correctional facilities. Such a claim is not merely misguided, it is false. Recent studies examining solitary confinement have shown that it does nothing to reduce levels of violence in prison and may, in fact, exacerbate them. The inverse is also true: prison violence diminishes substantially when solitary confinement is used less.

In the nineteenth century, we thought that isolation was cleansing and productive. We now know it to be psychiatrically devastating and rage-inducing. And yet our use of it as a tool meant to quell violence persists.

I KNOW HOW to diminish violence from my own work on the hospital units where my mentally ill patients frequently behave unpredictably and with aggression. If staff members or I have come to know a patient well, we have more tools at our disposal to use in order to help agitated patients calm themselves. Often a trusting personal relationship is the most powerful tool of all, and aligning with a person in a moment of opposition can de-escalate a crisis. There is a counterintuitive nature to this—it's in our human nature to adopt a defensive stance when we feel antagonized or threatened. But sidestepping conflict rather than bracing to meet it head-on can avoid a negative—or even a disastrous—outcome.

Perhaps the most familiar example of this kind of interaction is the response of an irritated parent to escalating insolence in a child. The more stubborn and rude a child becomes (think here of a toddler screaming her demands for candy in the checkout line of a grocery store), the more infuriating—and embarrassing, even—it is for the parent. As the parent grows louder and becomes more adamant in his insistence that the child behave herself, the child becomes more irate, dropping to the floor to writhe and wail. The two match each other's fury, and the conflict grows until parent and child are locked in a miserable conflict that ends in a foreseeable mess: the parent wrenching the child from the floor, abandoning his shopping cart, and storming to the car drenched in rage with the essential family shopping undone. It is here that I think of a phrase I once read in a parenting book advising caregivers in these moments to let the wind out of the sail. The metaphor was a useful one to me in my children's early years, and it remains relevant to me in my medical practice. Pulling the sail tight and fighting against the wind engages in battle with the misbehaving child. Loosening the sail— ignoring the child's screams and behavior in this particular example and deliberately forging ahead to the checkout—robs the wind of its power. Without anything to blow against, the force of the wind is gone.

I recently treated Heather, a patient with a severe personality disorder. Personality-disordered patients have developed ways of thinking and behaving in the world that are rigid and maladaptive. In Heather's case her disorder caused chaos in her personal relationships and was often characterized by verbal intimidation and self-injurious behavior. Heather would come into the hospital threatening to kill herself and, once admitted, would treat everyone around her—staff and patients alike—with derision. She did not participate in therapeutic groups, did not leave her room for unit activities. She stayed in her bed all day every day, getting up only to help herself to food from the meal cart and then returning to her room with her plate. On the second day of her hospitalization, Heather began taunting her roommate with a vulgar and relentless fervor. I spoke to her. My staff spoke to her. The provocation did not abate, and we began to worry that a physical altercation between the two women could ensue.

My clinical priorities at moments like these are twofold—I needed to treat Heather with appropriate care while also protecting her roommate, herself a patient who was psychiatrically ill enough to be hospitalized. Intervening to manage Heather's behavior was in part about setting healthy limits with her, but it was also about preserving the therapeutic environment for the other patients on the unit, all of whom were in their own moments of crisis and fragility.

Our unit was full, so moving either Heather or her roommate to another room wasn't a possibility. I made the decision that if Heather was unable to regulate her behavior, she would need to go into the Quiet Room, a space on the unit used for the seclusion and constant observation of aggressive or self-injurious patients. Though the room's euphemistic name conjures grim images of padded walls and historical maltreatment, or perhaps even some shared territory with solitary confinement, it is used on my units for a maximum of two hours at a time, with care, and as a last resort. A staff member remains outside the door at all times, and patients can come out as quickly as they can calm themselves and be safe—often after only fifteen or twenty minutes. It is exceedingly rare for someone to remain in the QR for the full two hours—so rare that I can't remember the last time in my work when it occurred.

In the majority of cases, people are asked by staff to go there to settle down, and they do so willingly. Often, in particular for patients who are hallucinating or paranoid, the QR can be a welcome reprieve from the high-stimulation environment of the unit. The room has a door that locks, but in all except the most dangerous situations it is left ajar. It was this scenario we offered to Heather, explaining that if she wasn't able to share space with her roommate in a safe and nonconfrontational way, the other option available to her was to have a space to herself in the Quiet Room. We would keep the door open, and she would be free to go out onto the unit just as she was in this room, but she couldn't continue to stay in this shared room, terrorizing her roommate. Heather made clear that she refused either option, and the situation started to escalate. She began to shout, accusing us of treating her unfairly and with cruelty. She doubled down on insulting her roommate, and she began threatening to hurt herself—something she'd done in the hospital many times before. Heather was backing us into a corner—we'd given her two options, both of which she refused. Our options now were to reverse our position and let her stay or to force her out of her room and into the QR. The first wasn't tenable—retreating from our limit setting and from the basic rules of the unit would embolden her to continue her behavior, perhaps even escalating it without consequence. But in light of her refusal to co-operate, the second option would require a staff escort to the QR, poten-tially even requiring staff to physically transport her there, which was a tactic we tried to use rarely and typically only in moments when patients posed an acute danger to themselves or others.

I stepped outside Heather's room to discuss our difficult position to-gether with the nursing staff so that we could reach a decision and come up with a plan. One of the staff on duty that day was Summer, an expe-rienced nurse who never ceased to surprise me with the matter-of-fact way she extended kindnesses to the ill patients with whom we worked.

Outside Heather's room Summer and I were weighing our options, frustrated that neither leaving her in the room nor physically transport-ing her to the QR seemed like the correct path.

"You know," Summer said, "I think Bre's working on another floor, and she knows Heather well. I could call her and see if she could come up?"

I had worked with Bre for years and knew her to be an unflappable nurse with a soft spot for our sickest patients. When a round of state budget cuts demolished programming and cut staffing at local group homes for adults, a string of patients with autism and developmental dis-abilities ended up on our units for prolonged stretches. Lower budgets meant that fewer people staffed the group homes at any given shift. Those workers that remained at the group homes were less experienced, since wages had dropped. Low wages and a high-stress work environ-ment translated into high turnover and lower-quality patient care. That reality, paired with fewer options for programming and therapeutic activities, predictably resulted in a rise in acts of agitation and aggression by patients whose conditions often rendered them particularly sensitive to routine and particularly intolerant of change. Once they became aggressive in the group-home setting, the patients were brought to our hospital and the group homes would not accept them back, even after the patients were stabilized, citing an unacceptable level of risk.

Bre was magic with these patients, for whom the hospital—with its flux of people in and out and its propensity for unpredictable noise and disruption in the milieu—was simply not an optimal environment. Her patience was unending, and she had an intuitive sense of what could calm a patient in a crisis.

"Hang on a sec," Bre said to us when she arrived. She disappeared into Heather's room for several minutes. When she reemerged, she was laughing and looking behind her at Heather, who was laughing, too, and following Bre to the QR. The two chatted as they walked. Bre asked a security guard to please put one of the unit's chairs in the QR so Heather would have a place to sit.

Moments later, with Heather calmly ensconced in the QR and her roommate safely in her room again, Bre swung through the nursing station on her way back to the unit where she was assigned.

"Hey, thanks, Bre," I said. "That could have gotten much uglier than it did. How did you get her to do that?"

"She loves to color," Bre responded. "She's actually really good at it. I told her I'd find her some of those intricate coloring sheets and some colored pencils. I'm going to grab them from the supply closet before I go."

Herein was de-escalation made manifest: knowing the volatile people in an environment personally, knowing their coping mechanisms, strengths, and weaknesses, allows for the capacity to calm potentially dangerous situations to the benefit of all involved. I've witnessed firsthand—and participated in—countless moments like these on my hospital units. Some, like Heather's, are moments that serve to defuse obstinacy. Other moments have been scary rather than merely frustrating. In both scenarios, however, careful engagement by experienced staff members introduces the possibility of a safe, calm outcome.

During one such example, I had just finished doing my rounds and had begun writing notes when I heard a screech followed by loud yelling on the unit. Seconds later a call for security presence to the unit came over the hospitalwide intercom, which meant that one of my staff members had hit the ward's emergency button to call for help: *Code Gray*, a mechanical voice repeated with urgency. *Code Gray.* I rose from the computer and stepped back out into the nurses' station on the unit, knowing that the intercom call would mean that security officers and mental-health workers from across the hospital would be running through the halls on their way to provide extra manpower and support to my staff for whatever crisis had prompted the alarm.

As the door closed behind me, I saw that Javier, a young intellectually disabled man with autism was screeching and hopping around one side of the unit in distress. A nurse and a mental-health worker both followed him, speaking firmly but quietly, attempting to calm him down. Twenty feet away from Javier, on the other side of the unit, stood Abraham, an intensely paranoid and muscular man. Abraham was thrusting a pointed finger at Javier, shouting, "I will kill him! If he comes near me again, I will kill him!" Several staff members stood in front of Abraham, keeping the two young men apart, but Abraham was pacing quickly back and forth and looked like he could easily break through the line of staff with no warning. The nurse in charge of the unit came over quickly to the nursing station when she saw me, knowing I'd want an assessment of what was going on. "Javier was fine all morning," she said. "He ate lunch and then sat down to watch a movie. Out of nowhere he stood up and ran over to Abraham and hit him on the head.

"It wasn't a hard hit, but it definitely was unprovoked," she continued. "And then Abraham just exploded. We can't get him to settle down." Acts of random aggression happen from time to time with our intellectually disabled patients and almost never arise out of malicious intent. In nearly all circumstances, the actions are manifestations of distress—perhaps an upsetting sound comes from the television or a parent fails to answer the phone when called—and as a result an arbitrary physical outburst is indiscriminately applied toward whoever or whatever is nearby. These are the kinds of behaviors that might have first led the families of these patients to seek residential care and then caused disruptions at the group homes. In this instance Abraham had been the unfortunate target.

But Javier was no longer the problem. Though he'd been screeching and hopping, a quick promise from staff of a Disney movie and a favorite snack in an out-of-the-way conference room quieted him and redirected him down the hall, out of Abraham's furious gaze. All of Abraham's ire now focused on the growing number of nurses and mental-health workers who'd arranged themselves in a loose arc in front of him, ready to intervene together if need be.

Eyes blazing with intensity, Abraham began bellowing threats toward the staff members standing in front of him. His body showed the unmistakable signs of the adrenaline coursing through it. He was breathing deeply and fast. I could see the strong, rapid flick of his pulse beating in the carotid artery of his neck. This was fight-or-flight, and Abraham had nowhere to run.

Abraham then began posturing, adopting stances I can describe only as warrior-like. Because of his strength and athleticism, the display was breathtaking. He leaped and spun, punching and kicking at the air. I'd never seen anything like it, and I knew, regardless of the fact that the staff far outnumbered him, that if we had to physically restrain him, injuries would occur. But I also knew that if a patient opened a door or crossed the hallway at the wrong time, that person, too, could become a target. We had to get Abraham to calm down, one way or another, or else someone was going to get hurt.

Watching his poses, I remembered that Abraham had immigrated to the United States several years before from Liberia, where he'd been conscripted into a militia to serve as a child soldier. The traumas that children in these military factions both endured and enacted are horrifying and well documented. As a result, their formative years—and the responses and reactions that take root during that time period—were shaped by trauma. I suddenly saw Abraham's actions in a different light. Already in the grip of paranoid delusions, Abraham was struck unexpectedly by Javier, which activated a primal neural pathway, galvanized in the trauma of his childhood. He had been thrown instantly into defending himself in battle. What we were seeing was not aggression for aggression's sake but rather an instinctive physical expression of terror. This was a human display no different from the puffer fish that inflates itself to scare off predators or the frilled lizard whose neck flaps splay to make it appear instantly menacing. If Abraham had wanted to harm someone, he could have done so by now. Instead his leaps and kicks were intended to ward off threats and protect himself from harm.

I knew not to be naïve—Abraham's show of aggression could turn into real danger at a moment's notice. But I also saw the scene differently in the context of his past. And because I was behind the nurses' station on the unit, there was a counter between Abraham and me that provided some degree of protection.

"Abraham," I said, firmly but just loud enough so he could hear me. "Abraham, it's Dr. Montross. I'm right over here, and I need you to look at me for a second."

"I will kill anyone who gets in my way!" he shouted.

"Abraham," I said again, "I need you to look at me. No one's going to touch you. I'm in charge here, and I will not let anyone touch you if you turn your head and look at me." He did. His flashing eyes met mine. His body still tensed and on alert. Fists raised.

"No one is going to hurt you," I said. "You're in a hospital, and our whole job is to help you. That's the only reason we're here."

"I will kill these men if they come at me!" he yelled, swinging his arm to gesture toward the staff members still standing in an arc in front of him.

"They're here because you were scaring us a little," I said quietly. "We were afraid you were going to try to hurt someone, and our whole job here is to keep people safe. If you can calm down, they will go," I promised.

Abraham glanced warily at the line of men. I nodded at John, a tall, soft-spoken mental-health worker in his late twenties, who was terrific in situations like these—so much so that he'd helped design de-escalation education and training for his colleagues. Despite his imposing physical presence, his demeanor was unwavering and calm. He knew that my nod to him was a kind of a signal that he should reinforce what I was saying.

"Listen to the doctor, man," John said, gently and with care. "No-body's gonna hurt you. We just need you to settle down, and then she's right. We'll all go back to what we were doing and give you some space."

I had learned over the years two key truths about patients on my units who became aggressive. One was that they were often acting out of their own fear. So despite their bluster and shows of strength, the most effective thing was often to speak directly to the fear beneath the volatile anger. *No one's going to hurt you. Our whole job here is to keep people safe.*

The other was that in most cases people do not want to be aggressors, even when acting as such. They escalate, often feeling the need to defend themselves, as Abraham believed he must, and they lose awareness that they're terrifying others. Frequently if a patient starts to become agitated and I feel myself becoming uneasy, I will name that feeling. I'll say, "You're scaring me," or I'll ask, "Do I need to be afraid right now?" Either way the patient's reaction provides good information. If the attitude persists and the patient says "Good!" when I tell her she's scaring me, or if he appears oblivious to the comment I've made, I know to keep my guard up and extricate myself from the interaction. But oftentimes when I name my own fear or unease, it serves to jar the patient into a kind of self-awareness. The intent isn't to threaten me, and the realization that the behavior *is* threatening can bring about a quick retreat.

Abraham looked back and forth between John and me, his breath slowing. I leaned toward him, resting my elbows on the counter. "If you head back to your room," I said, "we will leave you alone there. We will make sure no one bothers you, and you can just relax for a little while."

"Abraham," John said, "why don't I walk you there." It was a statement, not a question, but as he said it, John made a careful step out of the line of colleagues. A step closer to Abraham. He did this intuitively, a kind of reaching out, but it also served as a test. Abraham could perceive this as an intrusion. He could be too paranoid or fearful at the moment to tolerate anyone coming closer. If this were so, he would rev back up, in which case the other staff members would still be right there. But Abraham didn't move. He lowered his fists.

"Just you," he said to John. "I'll walk with you, but not all these other guys."

"I can't do that, man," John replied wisely, knowing the unpredictability of circumstances like these well enough to avoid putting himself in a potentially dangerous situation. "They have to keep everyone safe. But I'll have them stay a step behind us while we're walking, and if you're willing to hang out in your room and can get to where you're feeling more calm, then I think Dr. Montross will feel like you're good, and they can go." He nodded over his shoulder at me. It was as if he were passing back a ball. *Your turn.*

"Absolutely," I said. "John, why don't you and Abraham head to his room now. Guys?" I said—to the line of security guards and mental-health workers but, in fact, entirely for Abraham's benefit—"once Abraham's in his room, let's give him some space. He's doing exactly what we've asked him to, so once he's there, then we're all set. Thanks for your help."

John and Abraham walked down the hallway, Abraham went into his room and settled, and it was over. A situation that had the potential to be one of the most dangerous episodes I'd overseen was resolved without incident.

My hospital is not a prison, but as workers in both facilities will tell you, there's significant overlap in the people we see and the problems we face. A psychologist who works as a therapist both in the community and in a prison once expressed this to me plainly. "The work is the same inside the prison as outside," she said. "You meet the human being in either place. The people are very much the same. They're more traumatized in the prison, perhaps, but otherwise they are very much the same."

If in his activated state of psychosis Abraham had lashed out and attacked Javier, or a mental-health worker, or me, we would not have seen that action as a criminal one, as evidence of his "badness." But how that action—and thus how Abraham—is read depends significantly on where the action takes place. In a correctional atmosphere, an attack would have been seen only through the lens of security and aggression. Abraham could easily have been maced, restrained, even beaten. He would certainly have "buried himself in seg time."

De-escalation in the hospital doesn't always work. But the combination of a constructive environment and people who know the patients well enough to defuse violence before it happens makes so much sense when dealing with a volatile population. In contrast to the ever-amplifying exertion of control in prison, reaching out and aligning with the person exhibiting aggression is a preventive solution. It is an *ex ante* maneuver that anticipates violence and tries to defuse it rather than responding to and punishing it after the fact. It also allows the agitated person to retain some measure of power and thus some responsibility for his own behavior and his own self-control.

Knowing the patient allows staff members to know what will activate versus calm in a moment of crisis. Knowing that Abraham had been a child soldier allowed me to understand how a person with his history would respond predictably with adrenaline and escalation when facing a line of men, no matter how well intentioned the men might be. Speaking to his fear allowed us to shift the tone and shift his attention away from a perceived threat. In doing so we prevented altercation and injury. It also prevented us from adopting an adversarial stance, allowing us to remain on Abraham's side, working with him and trying to help, as opposed to having to subdue or restrain him.

In contrast, when conflict escalates and maximum control is the aim, a kind of malignant evolution—a *devolution*—of tactics and behavior can occur.

Thomas Bartlett Whitaker, on death row in Texas, won a prize in PEN America's Prison Writing Contest for his essay "A Nothing Would Do as Well." In the essay Whitaker describes a man he calls Mad Dog, who personified malicious aggression. Whitaker recounts relentless and galling acts of violence that Mad Dog routinely commits. The essay opens with Whitaker describing how Mad Dog, who has the bloodborne—and until recently incurable—liver disease hepatitis C, retaliates against officers who take away his radio. In vengeance, Mad Dog shoots correctional officers with darts from a homemade blowgun that he'd intentionally infected with his own blood.

It's hard to find sympathy for Mad Dog, let alone ascribe logic to his violence. But Whitaker attempts to do both. Whitaker explains that he has the reputation as a jailhouse lawyer and, as a result, that inmates will give him copies of grievances they've filed and of their disciplinary files in the hope that he can provide some legal assistance for them. In "A Nothing Would Do as Well," Whitaker reveals that Mad Dog's knees were both broken by police during his arrest and that he had subsequently slipped on water in jail, injuring his back. The medical braces he'd been given prior to his trial are confiscated upon his arrival on death row. When he asks for Tylenol or ibuprofen for pain, he's told that in order to obtain these medications he must purchase them from the commissary.

Whitaker writes of the detailed, even polite grievances that Mad Dog submits in attempts to receive medical care for his pain, noting that Mad Dog "had never received a single response from anyone."

Mad Dog writes a letter to the warden explaining the extent and severity of his pain and the fact that it is worsening. He writes that he does not feel that anyone is listening to him. Then Whitaker draws a conclusion he finds to be "particularly chilling." The end of Mad Dog's letter to the warden reads, "I have followed the rules you gave me when I got here. Yet you still will not respect that. What do I have to do to be heard around this camp? Do I need to share my pain with you?" Whitaker notes that fifteen days after Mad Dog submits this letter to the warden, he assaults an officer for the first time.

"Mad Dog had come to see pain as an antidote to death and impotence," writes Whitaker. "I am certain that the prosecutors and the wardens and the public will shout until they are blue in the face that Mad Dog was a dead thing long before he arrived on the Row, but I know better. He had been a man when he arrived—a broken one, perhaps, badly in need of growth and redemption, but a man nonetheless. . . . In his role as a monster he finally found an audience willing to notice him."

10.

IMAGINE YOUR BATHROOM

We have become a society that has developed rings we use to chain men to the floor. Trapdoors to keep feces from being thrown or arms from being grabbed. Tether chains. Handcuffs. Leg irons. We support a constant stream of innovations in control. And in the face of all these, the human spirit flexes and rebels. It chafes and maneuvers. It fakes left and goes right. It morphs in a relentless search for autonomy, connection, agency, and self-expression.

If we continue to ignore what neuroscience has to teach us about human needs and human behavior, we do so at our own peril. Yet all too often, fear undermines our ability to see situations clearly and address them rationally.

Once while I'm performing a competency evaluation with two other clinicians at Northern, the evaluee's nose begins to itch. Because his hands are cuffed behind him, he cannot scratch it. He tries to raise his knee to his nose. With the chains it does not reach. He leans down at the waist, raises his knee, leans over further, and at last rubs his nose on his knee.

When the evaluation ends, we're supposed to call the CO by opening a wall-mounted plastic box inside which there's a metal button and an intercom. I'm seated beside it, so when we finish, I reach over to initiate the call. I try to flip open the clasps on the plastic box, and they don't budge. I try harder to pry them open with my fingers. My colleagues and I all laugh nervously. The man we have interviewed watches with a dispassionate expression on his face. Eventually the psychologist who's with me comes over and, using both his hands, manages to pry the box open. I press the intercom button and say, "We're all set." We wait for the CO. There's an awkward silence. For what feels like several minutes, no one comes.

"Suppose I was gonna injure one of y'all," the man in chains slowly drawls, looking me straight in the eye. "They take this long?"

It is a comment meant to provoke. Its intention is to unnerve, to make me feel afraid. It works. In this fleeting moment, I understand the limitlessness of fear. I am across from a man so profoundly restrained that he cannot even scratch his nose, let alone attack me. And yet I watch the door apprehensively, waiting for the CO to arrive.

Herein is evidence of this cycle of endlessly escalating repression. In retrospect I understand the man's comment as a way of highlighting the ridiculousness of what he observed. Our nervous laughter. My fumbling fingers and skittish glances. All this despite the fact that his every limb was manacled. We might have been respectful of him during the interview, but our actions in these final moments conveyed an underlying truth—that we viewed him, consciously or not, as someone worthy of fear. His comment was a response to our hypocrisy. If we were going to judge him as a monster anyway, then he'd go ahead and fulfill the prophecy. And in return his comment made me fear him even more. Worse, it made me grateful and relieved that he was restrained. The environment galvanizes just this sort of damaging and misguided rationale. The unnerving dynamic of the supermax ensures its own existence. If we feel afraid even within this supremely high level of control, then we will continue to feel as though we need the supermax, and all the mechanisms of control within it, in order to keep us safe.

SEVERAL TIMES A YEAR, I'll have a patient on my hospital unit who has served ten years or more in prison. I do not ask him to tell me about the crimes, but the patient frequently tells me anyhow, and they are the offenses you would imagine to be commensurate with lengthy sentences: sexual assault, manslaughter, assault with a deadly weapon, murder. Most weeks there are also patients on my unit—like Javier or like Abraham—who are prone to aggression. Recently a young paranoid man was brought in after he punched a random man in line at Dunkin' Donuts. The next day he approached a patient on the unit and, without warning, did the same.

However, the patients who've committed the most serious crimes are almost never the patients I fear the most on my unit; they're almost never the ones who are aggressive or who attack other patients or my staff. I have learned that it is naïve to base my own sense of safety on my patients' criminal records.

And yet in prison the visceral calculus shifts, even if the reality of risk does not. The location changes how we respond to the people held within it, and it also changes what a person is capable of. If people commit violence in our communities, we lock them away in prisons and jails. If they commit violence in prisons and jails, we lock them away in administrative segregation, in solitary confinement, in places like Northern or places that are far worse. A Northern CO who was attacked by an inmate says of the detainees there, "Of course they're animals and they're monsters. If they weren't, they wouldn't be there." How not to feel afraid of a man in a cage? How not to fear a man shackled at his wrists and ankles? If he were not a monster, why would he be treated as one? But here's the thing.

These same men—even within the prison's confines—I don't fear them once they're sitting in the interview room with me. As I talk to them, look them in their eyes, listen to their symptoms and their stories, they're men again. In a chair beside me, in conversation, they don't spit or masturbate or smear feces on the wall. These are things men do when caged. These are animal behaviors. These are the desperate actions of captivity.

But we are all animals. And perhaps, then, it's useful to think of animal responses to stress. When an organism is under attack, it tries to survive. We know the mechanisms that beings employ in the moment when a threat is posed. The impala runs. The octopus eludes with its cloud of ink. The snake bites. The fire ant stings. If two scared dogs are suddenly placed in the same cage, one will attack the other. Flight or fight. Camouflage. Poison. The drive is the same—to stay alive.

Psychiatry offers us a clear context within which we can understand the devastating effects of segregation and the damage we inflict on imprisoned people more broadly when we dehumanize them, particularly in isolating them from others. My clinical work offers daily examples of how critical meaningful human interaction is to mental well-being. But studies *across* disciplines—biology, anthropology, sociology, psychology— consistently affirm that humans thrive in connection with others, that the deep interpersonal relationships of family and close friends, more than any number of other factors, provide stability, happiness, and purpose in our lives. These same realms of understanding, in addition to a robust body of literature in my own field, consistently expose that ruptures in these relationships and separation from these connections yield predictably devastating results.

In the late 1960s and early 1970s, psychoanalyst Heinz Kohut developed the theory of self-psychology. Kohut and his followers questioned—and eventually upended—the idea that the fundamental human need for connection to others is limited to childhood. Instead they demonstrated that human connection is a critical need that must be met at every stage of life in order to maintain the health and stability of the self. In doing so, self-psychology established and deepened our understanding of the crucial importance of interpersonal relationships as a requirement of mental wellness that is both immutable and lifelong.

The essence of self-psychology is the idea that we exist only in relation to others. Kohut's school of thought lays out three critical pillars of human experience, all provided by relationships with people who offer reliable empathetic connection. There is no way for these foundational frameworks to be built and maintained without healthy human interaction. There is no mechanism by which a person can attain psychological well-being by going it alone.

The first of these pillars is *mirroring*, and as the name suggests, it has to do with a person's being seen and reflected in another. In mirroring, one's strengths and vulnerabilities are seen and appreciated in equal measure. The phrase that has emerged to describe this reciprocal interconnectedness is "the gleam in the mother's eye." Though the experience need not—and does not—transpire only between mother and child, it is the idea of the loving maternal gleam that translates: a readable gaze that says "I see you and I love you" without demanding perfection.

The second experiential pillar—*idealizing*—is the process by which we identify figures who are powerful in their stability, wisdom, and goodness. These ideal figures provide a port in the storm during turbulent times, and they also model key organizing principles of life: how to maintain purpose and meaning even in the midst of distress. These are our role models and heroes, the people in our lives whose positive traits we aspire to embody. And there is health in this aspiration—the human desire to be solid, strong, and good, to emulate those we perceive as being so.

Twinship is the third and final pillar of self-psychology, and the term describes the ability to relate to and feel *like* another human. Doing so combats alienation and estrangement; it makes us feel connected to another person and thus to humanity, more broadly.

The tenets of self-psychology provide critical and logical insight into the brutalizing neuropsychiatric effects of solitary confinement, a harm that philosopher Lisa Guenther describes as one that "violates the very structure of our relational being. . . . There is something about the exclusion of other living beings from the space that they inhabit, and the absence of even the possibility of touching or being touched by another that threatens to undermine the identity of the subject," Guenther writes. "Every time I hear a sound and see another person look toward the origin of that sound, I receive an implicit confirmation that what I heard was something real, that it was not just my imagination playing tricks on me. Every time someone walks around the table rather than through it, I receive an unspoken, usually unremarkable, confirmation that the table exists, and that my own way of relating to tables is shared by others."

In this way our perceptions of the world are constantly affirmed and buoyed up by others. I see people respond to the world in predictable ways and, to use Guenther's phrase, it "supports the coherence of my own experience." When human beings are isolated, they have no such support and thus no way to affirm the reality of their experience, of the world around them, even of their own existence, their own selves.

The field of psychiatry defines two related phenomena—*derealization* and *depersonalization*. The first term describes a pervasive sense that the things around you are not real. In the throes of derealization, a person feels that objects within the world are not as they appear, that the world itself may be a chimeric façade. The second term—depersonalization—describes a mounting confusion or fear as to whether one actually exists, and if so, whether one is the person one has understood oneself to be. These are disturbing, disorienting symptoms in which people experiencing them cannot trust even the most basic facts about themselves or about the world they inhabit.

The writings of men and women who live within our country's supermax prisons and administrative-segregation units describe an environment that is by turns bleak and devoid of stimulation or, conversely, in which sensation arrives in a ceaseless, unwelcome onslaught. They write of stuffing wet toilet paper into their ears and of tying blankets around their heads trying to block out the relentless cacophony of their surroundings. They write of watching frosted windows for hours in order to appreciate even small variations in color or light.

"After only a short time in solitary, I felt all of my senses start to diminish," writes Five Mualimm-Ak. "To fight the blankness, I counted bricks and measured the walls. I stared obsessively at the bolts on the door to my cell."

Not only are men and women living in isolation deprived of the pleasures of sensation—not only separated from birdsong and changing autumn leaves and rainstorms and the voices and caresses of loved ones. They are also robbed of the affirmation of the self that interaction with the world and with others provides.

Well before I encountered Lisa Guenther's assertions about the damage of solitary confinement, I had been struck by the frequency with which people who'd been incarcerated in isolation spontaneously described symptoms of derealization and depersonalization.

University of California Santa Cruz psychology professor Dr. Craig Haney concurred in his 2012 testimony at the U.S. Senate's first-ever congressional hearing on solitary confinement. Some prisoners in solitary confinement, Haney told the senators, are so adversely affected by the degree of isolation imposed upon them that they "are not sure that they exist, and, if they do, exactly who they are."

Psychiatrists know what helps mitigate the symptoms of depersonalization in a clinical population. When patients are unmoored in this way, we encourage relaxation and offer comforting interpersonal interactions. For many people, intense emotional and physical stimulation can also ground them in their bodies and reorient them to their sense of self. Relaxation, comforting interactions, intense emotional and physical stimulation—these are the very experiences of which detainees in isolation are most deprived. If calm, connection, and stimulation can undo the damages of depersonalization, it stands to reason that chaos, deprivation, and isolation are the corrosive forces of harm.

Depersonalization and derealization are considered *dissociative* symptoms—symptoms that occur when there is some psychological breach between the body and the self. And these symptoms most often have their roots in trauma. When people undergo an experience they cannot tolerate, the self *dissociates*, or separates itself from the body, creating distance from the emotional or physical crisis at hand.

The most familiar examples of this phenomenon are the accounts of survivors of sexual abuse who describe floating over their bodies, witnessing what's happening to them but somehow also feeling removed from it. The phenomenon, in the words of renowned psychoanalytic scholar Glen Gabbard, "allows individuals to retain an illusion of psychological control when they experience a sense of helplessness and loss of control over their bodies."

Of particular interest here is that in nonincarcerated populations, dissociation is closely linked to self-injury. Research on nonsuicidal, intentional self-harm emphasizes that people who hurt themselves on purpose often report doing so in order to pierce the numbness of dissociation. Pain. The sight of blood. The smell of burning flesh. These sensations register in a way that self-injurers describe as breaking through numbness, anchoring the real, reestablishing the ability to connect and feel, integrating psychic suffering with physical pain. Self-injury—though maladaptive and obviously harmful in other ways—provides the intense stimulation needed to break through deadening episodes of depersonalization. Knowing that many people *choose* to cut or burn themselves in order to break out of a dissociative state should give us some understanding of the terror involved in experiencing depersonalization. If self-inflicted wounds provide relief, how painful must the state be that they alleviate?

A study of the jail population in New York City found that prisoners in solitary confinement were seven times more likely to harm themselves than were those in the general jail population. When self-injurious behavior occurs in correctional facilities, it is often interpreted as yet another means of acting out. But our understanding of self-harm as a means of piercing dissociation should further complicate the way self-injury in correctional settings is viewed.

Instead of seeing self-injurious behavior as debased, or as manipulative provocation, we should view self-inflicted pain among prisoners as an anchoring force, a search for stimulation in an otherwise untethered, sensory-deprived existence. We should view it as a response—a resistance—to the harm that solitary confinement enacts. Seeing that your own body bleeds, feeling that your body will respond to a wound with screaming pain—these sensations affirm that you are indeed real and alive.

We must remember that twenty-three-hour-a-day confinement is an environment where the pleas of prisoners are ignored, where the needs of prisoners are ignored, where the voices and the songs and the insults and the hungers and the cries and the passions and the silences of prisoners are all, equally, ignored. *Only* the most dramatic acts evoke responses in this environment. *Only* danger will shift attention, will break monotony, will upend power. If a man in solitary confinement feels himself slipping, feels the reality of the world around him slipping, he seeks a response to reassure him, to anchor him to the real. And only a dramatic act will evoke a response in this environment. Aggression and self-injury, then, are not merely about inflicting damage or garnering attention but are about seeking the most basic affirmations of the continued existence of the self.

Self-harm is a complicated phenomenon in any realm. Intentionally inflicting pain upon oneself feels antithetical to our most primal human instinct for self-protection. Witnessing someone be injured in an accident or by another person tends to reflexively evoke empathy and drives others to help or intervene. But hearing about or seeing people hurt themselves on purpose conjures distinctly different reactions: shock, horror, anger, revulsion.

Patients who intentionally harm themselves in the hospital—who sequester pieces of plastic utensils to cut themselves, who bang their heads against walls, who swallow dangerous objects or insert them into their bodily cavities—seem not only to sabotage their own healing but also to undermine the doctors and nurses who are working hard to provide the patient with good care.

Even in a therapeutic environment, caring for self-injurious patients can engender frustration, fury, and disgust. When the person harming himself is not in a psychiatric hospital—is not a patient understood to be ill in a clinical setting devoted to treating illness—but is rather a person we have deemed to be a criminal in a setting intended to control and punish him, the negative sentiments directed toward him are both amplified and tacitly endorsed. Correctional staff members are charged with carrying out punishment and exerting control. They are trained to seek out and identify breaches in protocol and to enforce discipline in a population that has by definition been designated as problematic and disobedient.

If self-injurious behavior already strikes an innate chord of revulsion, if abiding with and having compassion for the self-injurer is already a challenge for seasoned clinical staff, how can we expect correctional staff to respond to the woman who swallows broken toothbrushes and requires frequent trips to the hospital to remove them from her stomach? Or to the man who cuts deeply into his own leg and repeatedly smears his feces on the wound to cause infection?

The *same* symptoms of self-harm that are seen within psychiatric hospitals as a disturbing sign of mental illness are interpreted in prison as volitional means of acting out and causing a disruption. In prison the actions are seen as a challenge to the central tenet of the institution—its purpose of safety and security, of regimented control. And because the very fact that prisoners are housed in isolation reinforces the idea that they are dangerous people who belong in isolation, inmates who behave in monstrous ways therein are deemed even more repulsive, even more out of control, even more monstrous.

Often when discussing acts of grave self-injury in correctional settings, I'll hear COs and prison clinicians describe the behavior as "pure sociopathy"—a coded phrase for "manipulative bad behavior"—making an intentional and important distinction between the actions of those prisoners and the symptoms of other prisoners who are understood to be "truly" mentally ill.

But it is wrong to view self-harm in prison as merely another flavor of degraded and volitional misbehavior. Manipulation is a consistent, key trait of sociopathy in any realm. But self-injurious behavior is not.

The logic, in fact, points squarely toward self-injurious behavior as arising out of desperation in an environment like punitive segregation. The extremity of the control predictably, if inadvertently, ratchets up the frequency and severity of self-injury. And when we view it within this context, we see why the self-injurious behavior in solitary confinement is more gruesome and severe. It is not an indictment of the character of the men held in this environment but an indictment of the environment itself.

This is a psychiatric phenomenon of our own creation. We confine people who have not previously been self-injurious, and we turn them into people who are. We know the means by which self-injury arises out of trauma and powerlessness in a noncorrectional population. To ascribe it to some different, more nefarious cause in a correctional population is both illogical and unjust.

Consider similar behavior in a dramatically different situation. In October 2016, a warming in U.S.-Cuban relations led to a fear among Cubans hoping for refuge in America that the special immigration status of Cuban immigrants would come to an end. The policy, known as "wet-foot, dry-foot," essentially stipulated that if Cuban migrants were able to make it to land in the United States—to set even one foot ashore—they would not be considered illegal immigrants but rather refugees who could begin a fast-tracked path to U.S. citizenship. As relations between the two countries looked to be normalizing, a flood of Cuban migrants intensified, with people trying to make it to land in America before the Cold War–era policy could come to an end. In makeshift rafts and boats, with paddles and oars or with crudely improvised motors, a surge of migrants attempted to cross the Florida Straits. Many boats capsized or flooded. Many vessels were overcrowded. Many people died.

Among those migrants who survived, marine border patrol agents began to see increasingly drastic acts of desperation in attempts to make it to American soil. Agents reported that as circumstances became more dire, they began to encounter a new kind of rash ruthlessness with greater and greater frequency.

A marine-interdiction agent with U.S. Customs and Border Patrol said of the Cuban migrants, "They're going to do everything to get their vessel to shore. Sometimes they'll have homemade weapons on board—machetes, jagged oars. And they will, you know, swing them at you or threaten you to try to keep you away from them."

A coast guard captain concurred. "You just can't make this stuff up," he said. "It's just—it's amazing to me what they'll do." In the hope that they will be taken ashore in the United States for medical treatment—hence establishing a "dry foot"—the coast guard and Border Patrol were encountering people who, during the crossing, hurt themselves on purpose. "They've cut themselves, they've shot themselves. We've seen them drink bleach. We've seen them drink gasoline."

The argument that only depraved people behave in depraved ways does not hold. Instead the argument here should be that inexorable environments of desperation and helplessness can set in motion a kind of evolution, a reactionary sequence of events that operates within its own—predictable and rational, albeit shocking—system of logic.

Neuroscience tells us what happens to the brains and bodies of human beings who exist in isolation. People who are isolated have been shown to have higher blood pressure and higher vascular resistance—meaning their hearts must work harder to propel blood throughout the body. Their immune systems are more sluggish and regulate inflammation less well than those of people who live and interact with others. Their bodies fail to be restored by sleep in typical ways. And the body's central stress-response system—the hypothalamic pituitary adrenal axis—becomes dysregulated, disrupting the neuroendocrine balance that maintains psychological and physical well-being during periods of stress.

When we isolate a monkey in a vertical chamber out of which he cannot climb or when we put a man into a cage, chain his limbs together, lock him to a ring sunk into the concrete floor, we can expect stupor, mutism, passivity. And we can also expect delirium, paranoia, persecutory delusions, aggressive fantasies. We can expect a kind of evolution over years in which the only way to assert agency, to seize control, to alter the environment, is to cut your own leg down to the fascia, to slash your cellie with a razor, to fight someone over soup.

Punishment, isolation, deprivation, restraint, subjugation. These are our societal responses to violence. But we have the sequence wrong. These are the elements that give rise to violence rather than quell it. And misguided attempts to clamp down on violence to an even greater degree can drive a malignant innovation that distills aggression into a more highly evolved form. We have constructed prisons to eradicate human violence, but we have, in fact, created crucibles that render the human capacity for violence even wilier, even less predictable, even more severe.

We're taking troubled people into places like Northern—people whose individual vulnerabilities and personality traits have been identified as being particularly ill-suited for low-stimulation environments—and we're making them worse. Damaging them further. And we're doing so on purpose. We place people in environments meant to evoke fear—"*There's nothing soft. It's hard, and they wanted that . . . a long road . . . a lasting impression*"—despite the fact that we know that when people are afraid, they're *more* apt to feel threatened and to respond with aggression.

Violations of policy and certain behaviors result in additional restrictions. Acting out in those more restricted environments yields more restrictions still. No rec time. No phone calls. No visits. As restrictions are amplified, so, too, are the methods of resisting those restrictions, eventually leading to a game of whack-a-mole in which the modes of self-expression become increasingly disturbing and primitive—masturbation, self-injury, aggression. *This* is the behavior we are creating and reinforcing. Men who did not do these things prior to their containment are being driven to behave in this way and to do so repeatedly. The conditions in prison—which we have created—reinforce these behaviors as a means of coping—as the only means of coping. We foster the creation of these neural pathways and then foster their reinforcement.

We claim that our interest is reform, but by condemning our nation's prisoners to long-term solitary confinement we render them more afraid, more impulsive, less well adjusted, less healthy, and less able to reintegrate into our communities in safe and meaningful ways.

We are rendering the people we hold in solitary confinement less sane. I recently treated a man in the hospital who had just served a three-month sentence in jail for a petty crime but who spent the last twenty-three days of his sentence in segregation. He left the segregation unit and went to downtown Providence, where he caught a bus to my hospital emergency room, saying that he'd spent the time in solitary planning in detail how to murder the men who'd killed his brother and feared he would do so if he weren't hospitalized.

There is the social cost to our communities of absorbing these people, whom our ruthless practices have damaged. There is also the considerable economic toll of solitary confinement that we as taxpayers absorb, funds that could have real social impact in our communities if put instead toward *ex ante* solutions aimed at combating poverty, addiction, hunger, and homelessness.

And there is an ethical cost. What does it mean for us to walk freely in our lives when other of our fellow citizens pass their decades unable to do so? What does it say about our personal and national values?

A VISIT WITH Deputy Warden Adams at Rhode Island's Adult Correctional Institution forces me to confront firsthand the ethics of cages. When we sit together in his office, he is generous with his time, open about the practices of his facility, and honest about the challenges and difficulties within it.

I do my best to listen closely to what he shares with me. Do my best to focus as he answers the questions I ask him. But I cannot fully do so because behind his desk is a screen showing video from the prison's administrative-segregation unit. The screen is a stack of boxes, each showing a live feed from an individual cell. In one a man is curled in the fetal position on his bunk. In another a man on his knees faces away from the camera and prays. He touches his forehead to the floor and rises back up, touches his forehead to the floor again. In a third a man paces from the front of the cell to the back. Front to back. Front to back. Over and over. The man must shorten his third stride each time. The cell is not large enough for three full paces.

The screen of boxed images is like a honeycomb, or like photographs I've seen of pod-style hotels in Japan. Tiny cubes tightly stacked in rows and columns, just large enough for a human being to occupy. Those efficient worlds meant for temporary passage: a bed for one night for a business traveler or a space for a quick nap in an international airport. But here I watch the screens blink black and white and know I'm seeing months, years of these men's lives. The totality of their existence visible on these small screens.

Who knows how many years the men I see on the deputy warden's screen have spent within these small frames? Who knows what fraction of their lives will play out in these constrained dimensions? "Imagine your bathroom," my friend and colleague Dr. Reena Kapoor once said in a lecture, trying to convey to forensic-psychiatry trainees a relatable way to understand what it would mean to be in solitary confinement. "Now imagine living there twenty-three hours a day for eleven years."

I ask the deputy warden about the screen. He shows me how he can click on one image. Zoom in. The cell of the praying man fills the screen, and I feel an intense discomfort as, unbeknownst to this man I've never met, I watch him kneel, bend, rise again, his every move broadcast to his captors, and now to me.

What does it do to a person to be watched every moment of the day and night? And what, too, does it do to a person charged with watching another human being live his life in a box? There is a desensitization that must occur to normalize this surreal scenario. And in an environment that is constantly reactive, constantly devising new means of control, the larger, more important questions—questions about ethics and humanity—can easily become obscured.

Though I know that sadistic prison workers exist, I haven't observed any of them in my many visits to correctional facilities. The men and women I meet most often describe the incredible difficulty of their jobs and their importance in keeping our communities safe. They try to do their dangerous work with integrity. And still. David Cloud, a senior associate at the Vera Institute of Justice, speaks to any illusions we might have about the power of humanity in inhumane places: "Even if you tried to employ solitary confinement with the most humane intentions, people are still going to lose their minds and hurt themselves."

I DO NOT KNOW what I would be capable of doing if I were sent to solitary confinement for days or weeks or years. I cannot say with any confidence who I would become. Someone who hoards too many pencils? Yes. Someone who eats too much or too little of the apple on my tray? Yes. Someone who, in desperation, hurts herself or hurts another? I hope not. I can't imagine it. But neither can I imagine that degree of desperation, that dark night of the soul in which not the tiniest shred of agency is my own, in which I can find no visible future.

If I were told I could never again hold my children, could not go to Deborah if she was sick, could not tend to my mother if she was dying, might I lash out in violent grief and rage? Might I slice through my own skin? Might I try to slay my captor? I hope I would not. I fear I might.

It is easier to live a free life while others live in cages if we see those who are caged as utterly distinct from ourselves.

"How can I eat and drink if I snatch what I eat / From the starving / And my glass of water belongs to someone dying of thirst?" asks the poet Bertolt Brecht. "And yet I eat and drink."

PART III

Our Choice

11.

NUTRALOAF

nsight into the human experience of a condition can change opinions in a way that no statistics can.

As I've been thinking about our nation's approach to corrections, I've often shared with people particularly striking or poignant cases that I've encountered over the course of my research. I've found that few stories resonate with people as much as that of Angela, a woman whose case Sheriff Dart discussed with me during my visit to the Cook County Jail.

Angela was an impoverished young woman who'd been charged with her first offense: retail theft for shoplifting clothes from a discount department store. At the time of her arrest, she was nine months pregnant. Angela had been told by her obstetrician that when her baby was born, she would not be permitted to take it home from the hospital if she didn't have a car seat. The cost was an insurmountable expense, but without a car seat she faced the devastating prospect of delivering a baby who would then be kept from her. Trapped and desperate, Angela stole clothes that she planned to sell in order to obtain enough money to buy a car seat for her baby. She was caught and arrested.

I pause in this part of the story when I tell it to people and ask, *What do you think should have happened to Angela? What should her punishment be?*

But she just needed a car seat, some people will say. *Couldn't the police just take back the clothes and connect her with an agency that donates car seats?*

She's done something wrong, I say. *Broken the law. If the store wants to press charges, what should happen to her?*

She should be given a warning, some suggest. *Maybe she should get probation. Do community service.*

I tell them what actually happened.

The bail set for Angela's minor retail-theft charge was not intended to be prohibitive. She would have had to come up with less than a hundred dollars to be let out of jail. But Angela had no way of paying it—a lack of money was why she'd landed in jail to begin with. As a first-time offender with a misdemeanor charge, Angela would in all likelihood eventually either have her case dismissed or be sentenced to pay a fine or perform community service—all outcomes that would not include any jail time. But because she couldn't afford her nominal bail fee, Angela remained incarcerated awaiting her court proceedings. Within days of her arrest, Angela delivered her baby in jail.

When people hear this, they are aghast. This is the stark dichotomy I encounter time and again as I try to reconcile our personal ideas about justice with the actuality of our criminal legal system. On the one hand, when people hear individual stories, listen to the circumstances, consider the options available, they're considerate and they think about what would be best for everyone involved. There is fairness, thoughtfulness, compassion, justice. But somehow when we don't see crimes and the individuals who commit them within the context of their specific histories and circumstances, these impulses of humanity get supplanted by illogical policies or, in the case of violent or invasive crimes, get derailed by fear.

As ratings-driven news cycles seek and spew the most horrifying and salacious stories of danger in our communities, crimes that are, in fact, few and far between saturate our news feeds and play in loops on our living-room televisions until we begin to feel that we're at risk of being victims of these very same crimes. The odds seem suddenly to be that we ourselves might be targeted by the lone shooter, the carjacker, the armed robber, the gangbanger. Or our children might be.

Politicians promise to be "tough on crime," and in doing so they perpetuate the falsehood that the more aggressively we punish the crimes committed in our communities, the safer we and our families and our neighborhoods will be. Our fear and their promises combine, and suddenly we have elected leaders who push for—and sometimes mandate—maximally harsh sentencing in all circumstances.

We vote "tough on crime" and think we're keeping ourselves safe. Yet as Joyce Vance writes in the *National Review*, "The excessive reliance on arrests and extended incarceration [has been] unsustainable, it [has] disparately impacted racial minorities and the poor, and it [has] had a negligible impact on public safety. People leaving prison are too often unable to find jobs because of their criminal records, and two-thirds of them re-offend within three years. It has become obvious that we must do more than just incarcerate people to make our communities safer."

Vance's perspective highlights that there has been rare bipartisan consensus on this point. In 2015 a Summit on Criminal Justice Reform aimed at reducing mass incarceration and revising sentencing for nonviolent offenses was co-hosted by unexpected bedfellows: the ACLU and Koch Industries. Cory Booker and Newt Gingrich shared a stage, calling together for criminal justice reform. In 2018 President Trump signed the First Step Act into law, a bipartisan measure that modified federal sentencing laws for nonviolent drug offenders, eased some federal mandatory minimum sentences, and expanded early-release programs. And yet at both the federal and the state levels, many problematic practices of mandatory minimums and harsh sentencing continue.

As a society we don't see through the political rhetoric to acknowledge that tough-on-crime policies have not augmented safety. More important, we don't understand that when we vote for tough-on-crime candidates we ourselves are the ones sending children to MYI or sending women like Angela to deliver their babies behind bars.

We subject people accused of having committed a crime to sentences that are unjust and illogical. And we banish them to facilities like Northern, like ADX, like countless others across the country where their invisibility and distance reduces our fear, restores our sense of security, and makes us feel as though we have regained control of our lives and our communities.

Study after study demonstrates that harsh sentencing does nothing to reduce crime. What research *does* consistently show is that prison is a criminogenic environment. Without educational or rehabilitative programming, as a correctional officer in a maximum security prison once said to me, "The only skill you learn in a place like this is how to be a better criminal when you get out." That counterproductive "skill building" helps establish a cyclical path from prison to crime in the community and back again.

We say we want safety, justice, accountability, but our practices reveal that we actually want revenge. We want people in prison to suffer. Suffering is our *intention*. It is our lone goal.

As I've come to understand more about the lingering effects of incarceration, I make it a practice now to ask my patients who I know have served time behind bars, *How was it for you? Did anything happen to you in prison that continues to have an impact on you now? Were you in the general population the whole time, or did you ever end up in seg? Are you still on probation or parole?*

Nearly all my patients who've been imprisoned report having been assaulted at least once while they were there. Many describe nightmares or flashbacks that plague them and have persisted long after they've left prison. Often the assaults were physical in nature—skirmishes over property, or turf wars, or assertions of status. Just as often my patients describe being sexually victimized. None of these admissions surprise me.

But in every conversation that I have with my patients who've served time, new details about the experience emerge.

A patient named Marcus was admitted recently to my care in the psychiatric hospital. His primary symptoms seemed nearly all to be related to his past incarceration. Nightmares of assaults he endured in prison kept him from sleeping soundly through the night. His status as a felon had made it essentially impossible for him to find a job despite earnest effort on his part since the day he was released. Marcus had struggled with drug addiction for more than a decade prior to his arrest but had gotten clean in prison and was fighting to stay sober. Yet without a job he could afford neither rent nor the medications that kept his chronic auditory hallucinations at bay. He had no family in the area, and the friends he could have stayed with were all still using drugs, so for the last few weeks he'd been sleeping on the streets. The voices had gotten worse, and he was becoming hopeless. Increasingly he found that he was thinking of jumping off a bridge.

As days passed in the hospital, Marcus resumed his medication and the voices that plagued him began to abate. Social workers were helping connect him with sober houses so that he'd have a drug-treatment plan and a safe place to stay after he left the hospital. His suicidal feelings were lifting as he stabilized, but the nightmares that punctured his sleep would not cease. "Are the nightmares different every night," I asked him, "or are the themes recurrent, the territory the same?"

"Always the same," Marcus replied. "I always wake up feeling like I'm back in seg." Without prompting he continued.

"Every few days you'd get a shower," Marcus explained. "They'd take you out of your cell and walk you to the shower, but they'd handcuff your wrist to the showerhead. You'd have one hand free to wash yourself, but the problem was that you couldn't do nothing with the water tempera-ture. Some days it was ice cold. Other days it was burning hot. Since you was handcuffed, wasn't no way to get out of the water. Sometimes I got burned bad. Sometimes I thought maybe the COs shut off the cold or hot water on purpose, just to watch us jump. I don't know whether that was true or not," he said. "But it seemed like it could be.

"So sometimes," he went on, "I wake up thinking my skin is burning and I can't get away. Or sometimes it's my eyes burning."

"The water would get in your eyes?" I asked.

"No—see in seg you're on property restriction. That means the only clothes I got to wear was boxers, and the only thing in the cell was a steel bed. If you get in trouble in seg, like if you won't come out of your cell or if you're fighting them or something, they pepper-spray your cell. Only problem is that sometimes it's you and sometimes they spraying someone else's cell but the spray don't know how to stay in one place, so if one person getting sprayed, we was all getting sprayed. Thing is, on property restriction you got nothing to try to shield your eyes with. No sheet, no towel, no newspaper, no nothing. Sometimes it get so bad that I'd take my boxers off and put them over my eyes"—he shook his head—"but that's shameful, and the COs start laughing, and once the spray gets in your eyes even a little bit, holding something over your eyes don't help much anyway."

"Is that the dream you have the most?" I asked him. "The one when your eyes are burning?"

"The most? Nah," Marcus said quickly. "Most every night I dream of the loaf. No question. Wake up gagging."

I had no idea what he was talking about.

"Management loaf, Doc," he said. "You never heard of it?" I hadn't, but Marcus explained it to me. It turns out that in prisons and jails across America, incarcerated men and women are served food that is mashed together and cooked into a loaf. Ingredients that meet nutritional mandates—or ground-up leftovers of prison meals that do—are combined into an indistinguishable mass and served as a meal, often as a punishment to detainees in solitary confinement or as a disciplinary measure against those who've thrown their food or who've misused their utensils.

The loaf goes by different names—"nutraloaf" is perhaps the most unnerving, though "management loaf" is more honest about its intentions, if not its contents. They call it "food loaf" in the state prisons of Pennsylvania, where ingredients are listed as "milk, rice, potatoes, cabbage, oatmeal, beans and margarine." An Illinois court case was among more than twenty-two that have been brought since 2012 contesting that such loaves constitute cruel and unusual punishment. In that state the loaf's primary ingredients are listed as "mechanically separated poultry" and "dairy blend."

Accounts of the loaf by prisoners who've eaten it describe it as tasteless at best and disgusting at worst. Either way, some detainees are served the loaf three meals a day every day, for weeks on end. Many say they'd rather go hungry than eat it, and many do. Despite all this, not one of the twenty-two court cases has been decided in the inmates' favor.

In the correctional facilities that use the loaf, it is seen as yet another disciplinary tool. "When we started to use this," Milwaukee County sheriff David Clarke explained in a 2014 interview with NPR, ". . . all of a sudden the incidence of fights, disorder, of attacks against our staff started to drop tremendously. The word got around—we knew it would. And we'll often hear from inmates, 'Please, please, I won't do that anymore. Don't put me in the disciplinary pod. I don't want to eat nutraloaf.'"

When we incarcerate people, we separate them from their homes and families. We take away everything that is familiar and replace it with something on the spectrum from neutrally foreign and unknown to intentionally painful and injurious.

Nutraloaf is yet another of these things. Human beings have agency in what they eat. They discriminate between tastes and show preferences. Our food choices—and the partialities and aversions that give rise to them—make us feel human. They represent our individuality and independence. And food, perhaps more than any other sensory experience, has the power to connect us to family, to comfort, to culture, to home.

Eventually my patient Marcus got better and left the hospital. The voices, the hopelessness, the thoughts of jumping from a bridge had all subsided. But at night he still woke up gagging, the sensation of the endless, dry, foul-tasting loaf choking him all the same.

Some people may argue here, what right do prisoners have to anything beyond basic nutrition? But this is the wrong question. The relevant question is, what do we accomplish by serving nutraloaf? We shame the men and women who receive it, certainly. We cause them to suffer. Perhaps Sheriff Clarke is correct that the fear of it improves prison discipline in the short term. If these are our only goals—shame, vengeance, and control—then the loaf may well serve these purposes.

If our goals are to have a safer society and for people who've committed crimes to receive some just punishment for their misdeeds and then to reduce or stop their criminal behavior, measures like nutraloaf are at best ineffective and at worst antithetical to our aims.

PRISON HARMS PEOPLE, and then we multiply that harm by adding penalties onto the ends of sentences that extend tendrils of punishment out from the prison gates into ex-offenders' free lives. Conditions of probation and parole often stipulate that the men and women under such monitoring must remain in the communities where their original crimes were committed, making it easier for them to fall back into problematic friend groups and activities and making it harder to seek out new paths and new opportunities. Several states still enact lifetime bans that prevent men and women who've been convicted of felony drug charges from ever receiving food stamps. Certain convictions render people permanently ineligible for public housing assistance. Nearly half of U.S. states allow employers to inquire about criminal history in the job-application process. All these policies make it more difficult for people returning to the community from prison to build a life that is safe, legal, and productive.

These policies of ongoing punishment, like scarlet letters or excommunications, are unnecessary measures that codify an enduring "less than" status on a person once he or she is convicted of a crime. Herein are echoes of the pillories—punishments that serve primarily to shame.

Revocation of voting rights is one of these policies of shame, and states like Florida, California, New York, and Virginia are beginning to relax or reverse some of the voting restrictions that have been put in place. Nonetheless, in forty-eight of fifty states, people with felony convictions still lose the right to vote at least while they are incarcerated.

Only Vermont and Maine preserve the right to vote at all times for all citizens, regardless of their incarceration status. In the majority of states, voting rights are revoked not only during incarceration but are also withheld during periods of probation and parole. The maliciousness of these practices extends beyond individual voting rights, however, as groups that are disproportionately arrested and imprisoned—African American men serve as the foremost example—are disproportionately silenced and shut out of our country's most fundamental democratic processes. More than one out of every eight Black men in America is ineligible to vote, and that number is increasing rather than decreasing.

We also silence the incarcerated when we allocate government funds to communities based on census data. Prison detainees overwhelmingly represent the country's urban areas. Prisons themselves, in contrast, are constructed in rural areas, often far from the communities from which the inmates have come. When census data is collected, prison inmates are counted not as residents of their hometowns but rather as residents of the rural communities where they're held. The per capita resources, then, go to fund libraries, schools, and infrastructure in the communities where the prisons stand rather than the cities and neighborhoods—often in dire need of financial support—from which the men and women held within the prison have come.

In the name of safety and punishment, prison constraints prevent incarcerated men and women from becoming more educated, more skilled, more whole. In addition, the constraints render people less apt to reintegrate into our communities in productive, law-abiding ways. Detainees who participate in educational classes while incarcerated have a 13 percent higher chance of getting a job once they leave prison. More strikingly, they're half as likely to break the law again. Yet two-thirds of American prisons have no means for detainees to take educational classes beyond the high school level.

If what we truly want when we incarcerate people is solely to enact vengeance, then we ought to state plainly that this is our goal. If that is our aim, then we should abandon all pretense of nobler intentions.

But if suffering is *not* our goal, if in fact we *do* desire safer communities and justice above all else, then we must look at a different uncomfortable truth. There are established methods of reducing crime with fairness, but those methods are not our methods. They are not our ways.

In order to reduce criminal behavior, we must build responsibility and routine as opposed to eliminating it. We must enhance job training and reduce obstacles to employment once prison sentences are done. We must foster connections with family and support networks even during periods of incarceration rather than creating barriers to these connections. These are *ex ante* solutions that reduce crime in the long run.

At present we do the opposite. Our current policies create distance between inmates and their families. Prisoners are often held in facilities that are hours from their communities of origin. We curtail visiting. Detainees who cause behavioral problems in prison are often sent to prisons even farther away, sometimes even in states where they have no connections, where they've never even visited. To what end?

Once at the beginning of a competency evaluation, the young man I was evaluating began to cry. We had barely begun the interview—I'd only introduced myself and explained the structure and purpose of the interview—and yet he struggled to compose himself.

"Are you okay?" I asked him gently.

"Yeah," he answered, sniffling. "I'm real sorry for this, I just . . . I got the pass from the CO to come to visiting, and I thought it meant I had a visitor. This whole time I've been locked up, nobody has come to see me."

Extreme sentencing brings out the worst in us as a society. Our punitive policies—undergirded by injustice and illogic—have resulted in an overcrowded federal prison system in which nearly *half* the people held within are serving time not for violent crimes but for drug offenses.

When we implement sweeping policies that punish with consequences that endure long after sentences have been served; when we reduce punishment to the unthinking algorithms of mandatory minimums that remove any possibility for mitigation or acknowledgment of individual circumstance, let alone compassion; when we develop punishments that ostensibly target criminal behavior but instead devastate lives, families, and communities, we allow anger to reign over reason and we prioritize revenge over safety and justice.

Judge Judith Savage served twenty-one years on the Rhode Island Superior Court and stepped down from the bench in order to devote her energy to gathering diverse perspectives to address criminal justice problems. When I met her, it felt like we'd been walking toward each other from opposite ends of a shared road. I was trained in medicine, had patients who struggled within the criminal legal system, and began researching and teaching myself about the law. Judge Savage was trained legally, saw defendants who struggled with psychiatric illness, and began researching and teaching herself about mental health. I asked her about extreme sentencing.

"Sentencing can be driven by fear," she said. "As a judge, you're thinking, 'What if I let this person go too soon? He might hurt someone else and I would have to live with that.' *That* would also be the article the newspapers write. They're not going to write an article complaining that a judge is *too* tough on crime.

"And when you hand down the four consecutive life sentences, you're done," she continued. "You don't see what happens to the person after that."

WHY IS IT that we want those found guilty of crimes to suffer? We offer different explanations, but none of them hold. We want offenders to feel remorse for their actions. Surely depriving them of their liberty and imprisoning them does this already. We want the threat of suffering to deter them from committing crimes. Decades of data have told us that it does not. We aim to acknowledge the losses that victims of crime endure, but we fail to fully recognize that most criminal losses cannot be restored, or they at least cannot be restored in full. Financial losses can be reversed: money can be repaid, property can be replaced. But a woman who's mugged—even if her purse is returned with all the contents within it—cannot easily undo the fact that she's now afraid of walking alone in her neighborhood at night. There is no calculable recompense for a person who's been raped. A man who's been beaten cannot be unbeaten. No act of redemption or repayment can return a murdered child to his bereft family. In the majority of our crimes against one another, there is no possible eye for an eye.

"Doing something different to the offender does not bring dead people back to life, heal a broken limb, or undo a sexual violation," Martha Nussbaum writes. "So why do people somehow believe that it does?"

The "people" that Nussbaum writes about are, in fact, us, and what we really aim to enact is revenge. We seek suffering for suffering, and we should be honest about both our intentions and about the damaging effects of our policies. We intend to make others suffer, and we choose to do so even though we know empirically that we damage them, their families, and our shared communities and shared economies in doing so. In addition we must acknowledge that because our justice system is biased and imperfect, we ourselves are necessarily invoking suffering—and often disproportionate suffering—on some unquantifiable number of innocent people. And some number of people who've committed crimes as a result of mental illness. And others who are disproportionately punished because of racial bias and injustice. The suffering we administer does not differentiate to account for these variations. How will *we* be held accountable for the harm we have inflicted? What will *our* punishment be?

"If the penalty in its most severe forms no longer addresses itself to the body," asks Foucault, "on what does it lay hold? . . . Since it is no longer the body, it must be the soul."

What does it do to people to lock them away for a decade or more? Men are watched on small screens as they pace and pray. Women labor in cells and have their infants taken from them. Children are sent out into the world on cold nights without winter coats, without places to sleep.

I have come to believe that we want both things: safer, just communities and also revenge. But those desires are mutually exclusive. And so, despite countless studies demonstrating that our current prison practices are inefficient, expensive, ineffective, and inhumane, we are not jolted into action because we're unwilling to relinquish our desire for vengeance.

The desire for vengeance is a primal one. Rooted in the deepest origins of our instincts for survival, fear and fury are the neuro-emotional underpinnings of flight or fight. None of us are immune to bloodthirst in the wake of grievous harm. But human beings differ from our fellow animals in our ability to acknowledge that there are instances when our reflexive urges and impulses must be curbed in service of the greater good. Conflict requires a rational and constructive response. Our justice system is based upon this very fact.

Yet somehow when it comes to imprisonment, we have strayed from this necessary philosophy. We have abandoned the goal of rehabilitation in incarceration; we aim only to punish. Our methods of punishment harm prisoners, serving and satisfying our reflexive fury in the short term. But once these harmed men and women return to our cities, to our port authorities, and to our neighborhoods, our methods of punishment prove in the long run to harm us all.

12.

BETTER NEIGHBORS

Time and again in my conversations with people who work in America's jails and prisons—COs, health-care providers, wardens, psychiatrists, and reformers alike—the eventual message that each person conveyed to me was that they viewed the system as broken, perhaps irrevocably so.

One psychiatrist who has continued to work in a state prison for more than a decade despite low pay, grim facilities, and long hours shrugged in a kind of defeat when I asked him what he would fix about our nation's carceral system if he could. "It's not like there's a broken link in a chain that if it were repaired or replaced would make the chain strong again," he said. "Every single link in the chain is broken, and by that I mean broken beyond repair."

I attended a conference on the theme of detention at Yale Law School at which Nils Öberg, the director general of the Swedish Prison and Probation Service, spoke about his country's system of incarceration. His description of one of the earliest moments in a person's sentence in Sweden struck me as a critical point of difference between our countries' correctional philosophies.

As soon as someone is sentenced in Sweden, a needs assessment is performed. The idea of such an assessment is to identify gaps—to diagnose the deficiencies in a person's life that might have led him to engage in criminal behavior, with a particular focus on how to make him more employable in the labor market once the sentence is finished. Once these gaps are identified, it becomes the charge of the prison service to ensure that the time spent in prison is used to address these gaps in a targeted way. To shore up any deficiencies and to create strength and opportunities where there have been none. If you've been homeless, an emphasis is placed on obtaining affordable, reliable housing. If you've been unemployed, there is an assessment of education and job skills, after which a sequence of educational and vocational programming is specifically designed to prepare you for—and then find you—a job in the community once your sentence is done. If you are addicted to drugs or alcohol, substance-abuse treatment is provided. If you have family conflict, then parenting education is provided and family counseling is arranged. If you have medical needs that have gone unmet, you are connected to clinicians who can address your health needs. If you have debt, then debt counseling will be a component of your programming during your sentence. All this with the intention of disrupting the societal and personal issues that lead people to commit crimes.

As Mattias Andersen of the Swedish Prison and Probation Service later explained to me, "We keep the focus on criminogenic factors again and again. This is not just about getting you a place to live and a TV. But to figure out *why* don't you have a place to live and a TV." In stark opposition to the widespread American reality of "doing time"—where the primary work of a sentence is enduring the monotony of the days and years as they drag on—the Scandinavian perspective asserts that the time provided by a sentence of incarceration is in itself an opportunity. I was inspired to see the systems in Sweden and Norway firsthand.

THE EARLY-MORNING TRAIN from Oslo glides for a while along the coast, with glimpses of fjords flashing through the windows. It takes an hour and a half to travel to Halden Station, where Are Høidal, the prison governor, or warden, of Halden Prison meets me. He is jovial and burly and wears dark sunglasses with his warden's uniform.

"Welcome to Norway!" he greets me, beaming. As he drives me in his car from the station to the maximum-security prison he oversees, he chats excitedly about a rock concert he's going to with a group of friends and about an upcoming national holiday in Norway for which people apparently do a lot of yard work to make their lawns particularly lovely. Despite two attempts at understanding the gist of it, I never quite catch on.

We seem to be driving through a park when Høidal suddenly announces, "Here we are, then," and gestures toward a series of attractive buildings through which he'll walk me later in the day. I ask about the prison's location and the parklike grounds, and he tells me that the architects who designed Halden Prison thought it was very important to keep the men close to nature, to ensure that the inmates did not lose connection with the natural world.

This belief was, ironically enough, a fundamental principle in many American sanitariums. The natural environment was viewed as so critical to promoting mental health in institutionalized patients that the superintendent of the New Jersey State Lunatic Asylum bragged in 1853 that the facility was set amid "the most beautiful scenery in the valley of the Delaware, combining all the influences which human art and skill can command to bless, soothe, and restore the wandering intellects that are gathered in its bosom." I see the power of natural beauty in my hospital practice even today—the dining area of one unit has a broad wall of windows overlooking woods and a river, and every day I will find a patient sitting there peacefully, simply looking out, sometimes for hours at a time.

I mention to Høidal that the buildings at his facility look unlike any prison I've ever seen. "For the architects a reduced feeling of being in a high-security prison was also a priority," he explains. "It should not look like a prison. That was very important."

Before I've even set foot in the prison, there is already this marked difference. *There's nothing soft,* James Kessler, the architect of Northern had said. *It's hard.... They see visually it's a long road....*

The importance of not looking like a prison, the immersion in nature, these things are a part of a larger core philosophy that Høidal refers to as "the principle of normality." This principle is a foundational value of the nation's correctional services.

In the 1980s and 1990s, Norway had many of the same problems that plague American facilities today. Norwegian prisons were pervaded with drugs and also with violence. Several high-profile escapes occurred. A series of riots took place, and two officers were murdered. To top it off, the system wasn't reducing crime. Recidivism rates were high—between 60 and 70 percent of people released from Norway's prisons were re-arrested for subsequent crimes, on a par with our current three-year state prison recidivism rate of 68 percent. The correctional system was both dangerous and ineffective.

"Not too many years ago, things were much worse," Høidal confirms, which led to an edict from the country's highest powers. "The government, the politicians said to the justice department, 'Do something. It cannot go on like this. It has to stop.'" So in 1995 the Norwegian justice department created work groups to develop a plan to address the dysfunction and danger in their system of corrections.

The principle of normality is a core part of the new perspective that emerged, and it requires that life inside the prison should resemble life outside the prison as much as possible. Thus inmates do not lose any rights other than their right to liberty while they're incarcerated. This is not just a tenet of Norwegian law. It is also stipulated in international conventions about imprisonment, including the United Nations Standard Minimum Rules for the Treatment of Prisoners—known as the Mandela Rules in honor of Nelson Mandela—which state that "the prison regimen should seek to minimize any differences between prison life and life at liberty that tend to lessen the responsibility of the prisoners or the respect due to their dignity as human beings."

"So while he is here with us," Høidal explains, "other than the fact that he cannot leave here whenever he wants to, the inmate has all the same rights as all other citizens who live in Norway."

The defining ethos of Halden Prison is that the principle of normality best prepares people to leave prison and return to their communities as functional members of society. A relentless and pragmatic focus on what happens after release drives the philosophy. You can't expect someone who's spent months or years sitting in a cell to then hop up in the morning, make his breakfast, and go to work all day the moment he's released. Just as teenagers are armed with more independence and more responsibility before they move out of the family home, you must prepare a person for the transition out of prison and back into the responsibilities of the community if you want that transition to occur with any measure of success. And in order to do this, you must also be realistic about the significant obstacles that a man released from prison is facing: he's been absent from all his relationships; he'll suddenly have financial obligations like rent and groceries and child support; he'll need to find counseling and likely substance-abuse programs.

Without preparation that adequately acknowledges each of these challenges and their individual and cumulative effects, Høidal concludes, "You don't have to be a genius to see that a significant number of people aren't going to make it."

I see a striking example of the principle very early in my visit when Høidal takes me to visit the prison's art class.

The art teacher is a blond, fit woman in her mid-forties. She has an enormous, easy smile that breaks across her face every few moments as she flits around the prison craft room. She sits in the room alone with four hulking male inmates. The door is closed. The art teacher is not afraid.

"Ah!" she exclaims, brightening when Høidal and I enter. I am introduced as a visiting psychiatrist from America. "We are working on sculptures!" She is any teacher enthused by the project at hand, proud of and excited by her pupils' work. "We are making a tic-tac-toe set," she explains to me, "out of . . . of . . . what do you call it in English? Ah!

Soapstone!" She reaches toward the center of the table, toward a heap of rough, irregular rocks the size of large apples, and takes one in her hand. They are silvery gray and without question could be used as a weapon to throw, to strike. To bludgeon. The men sitting around the table working these stones are capable of this and more.

"They are murderers, rapists, pedophiles," Warden Høidal had said as he'd walked me to the classroom, describing the kind of inmates held at Halden. "They have done some very, very bad things."

It hardly matters, though, that the stones could be used as weapons. There are more traditional tools of harm scattered on the table and in the men's hands. One man saws into the stone's edge with a large serrated knife. Another carves details into a rock surface with a box cutter. One man has finished carving three of the stones into pieces for his game set—he's shaped three heads of hammers from the stones and is now at work on the pieces for the other player—three crooked nails.

I'm gawking at all of it. At the inmates holding stones and wielding knives, at their intent focus on the work, at the teacher's infectious pep, at the beauty of what has emerged from the rough-hewn stone.

Here's the thing: It's not just this room. It's not just this teacher. Not just these four men. Not just one knife, one blade, and a pile of stones. Høidal walks me through room after room at Halden where the men learn trades, build things, go to school. And my gaze—trained toward risk, toward danger—alights on one thing after the next after the next. All the many things that one human being could use to kill another.

Wrenches and cables in the auto-body garage. Table saws and hammers in the workshop. Knives and scissors in the kitchen built to serve the prison's small restaurant (which is open to the public and is frequented by many people in the town). Pipes of all lengths and diameters and welding torches in the metal shop.

These job and educational offerings are integrated parts of a larger philosophy at Halden Prison, designed to reflect the intentional policy decisions about corrections and safety that emerged from the justice department's work groups.

The Norwegian government, Høidal explains, "determined that we cannot just go on with hard [treatment of inmates]. It doesn't work. We have to think in a total new way." A decision was made—which later resulted in legislative change—to "meet hard behavior with soft treatment. To stop meeting hard with hard."

This small moment, mentioned by Warden Høidal in passing during a series of much longer and more detailed conversations, differentiates our system from that of others. *It doesn't work to meet hard with hard. Instead we will meet hard with soft.* The focus is no longer on payback and retribution, on making the criminal suffer. Instead the focus is aligned with what will work, with what will reduce crime and diminish violence, with what will increase the safety of the communities and thus the nation.

The locus of that change lay in what Høidal calls "a paradigm shift" in the role of the prison officer, Norway's term for a CO. In the original model, the officer was a guard whose responsibility, first and foremost, was security. "But the security wasn't very good!" Høidal underscores. He had originally been a prison officer himself, charged with guarding inmates and maintaining control at the peak of the system's time of crisis. He was working in one of the prisons when more than a hundred inmates rioted. "They brought down the [cell]block," he says, making a crashing gesture with his hands. "I was really nervous."

To frame the new model, the work group was explicit about a newly envisioned purpose for prison officers: "They shall contribute to efforts to help the inmates to live a life without crime." In this statement of purpose, "help" might be the most operative word. The prison officer, Høidal explains, was now charged to serve as equal parts guard and social worker. Instead of focusing entirely on security and enforcement, officers would be responsible for helping prisoners use the time of their incarceration to address the areas of weakness in their lives that led them to commit the crimes for which they have been sentenced—so that when inmates were released, they would leave prison for good and not reoffend.

Constructing sentences with an eye on discharge makes good sense. The maximum sentence in Norway—for even the most serious crimes—

is twenty-one years. Mechanisms exist through which the maximum sentence could theoretically be extended. "We can hold people longer than twenty-one years," Høidal tells me, "but we have never done it."

The case of Anders Breivik—the man who in 2011 executed sixty-nine teenage students on an island where they were attending a summer political-leadership camp—will surely test this truth. Nonetheless, according to Høidal, no case has yet challenged this threshold. The contrast is striking when this approach is juxtaposed with an American criminal justice system whose prison ranks swell with people serving "three strikes and you're out" life sentences for drug crimes or countless others whose sentences are so illogical in their extremity as to be laughable. In America, Cesar Francisco Villa is serving "348 years to life" for his third armed-robbery conviction; mother of two Danielle Metz is serving three life sentences plus thirty years after being found guilty of assisting in her husband's cocaine business—a crime that was her first offense. Metz's son, Carl, is now an adult but was seven when his mother was incarcerated. He recounts learning the details of his mother's sentence some years after her arrest. "I didn't even think it was real at the time. I thought she was kidding," he says. "I remember saying, 'You can't do triple life. You only have one.'"

It could be easy to be lulled into the idea—especially in light of so many illogically lengthy sentences among U.S. prisoners—that Norway focuses its efforts on rehabilitation and reentry because 100 percent of its prisoners will leave prison someday. But, in fact, on this point the United States and Norway differ very little. The average sentence in Norway is just under six years—slightly *longer*, in fact, than the average U.S. sentence, which comes in at five and a quarter years.

We, too, routinely send our nation's incarcerated citizens back out into our shared neighborhoods. Warden Høidal's explanation as to why Norway's prison system focuses with such commitment on rehabilitation, programming, community integration, and treatment—as opposed to a lack of programming, separation from family and community, and routine use of punishments ranging from nutraloaf to solitary confinement—should resonate with us.

"Of course people leave prison and come back home when they finish their sentences," Høidal says easily. I'm struck that the "of course" is something that's been very hard for us to grasp in America. "Every inmate is going to a community," Høidal continues. "We want to make them into better neighbors."

In Norway it's working. The recidivism rate systemwide in Norway since the government implemented the work group's suggestions has plummeted and is no longer on par with current U.S. numbers. Now only 20 percent of Norwegian prisoners are arrested in the two years after their release. In contrast, a recent Bureau of Justice Statistics report found that 44 percent of American state prisoners were arrested at least once in the first year after their release.

Høidal attributes the Norwegian turnaround directly to the change in officers' responsibilities. Each officer is designated as the "contact officer" for three inmates. The officer is assigned responsibility for these three inmates for the duration of their incarceration. "They're like a coach, motivator, role model," Høidal says of the contact officers. And "like a nurse when you're in the hospital," they are familiar with your case; they're the person to whom you reach out first when you need something, whether that something is help in beginning a job, or classes in the prison, or finding housing or work in the community for the future.

In order to fulfill these functions, Høidal tells me, the government laid out the expectations for what a prison officer must be able to do. In addition to maintaining safety and security, officers must engage with inmates about the crimes they've committed, to talk frankly about what they've done. In this way, I note, a degree of accountability is built into the process—a kind of honest reckoning that is both an important step in forcing the detainee to acknowledge and confront his actions but also a means of assessing the context of *why* such an act was performed and how repetition of it can be prevented in the future.

Høidal emphasizes this element of prevention in the officers' role. Engaging about the crime allows prison workers to ask, "How can you stop that [behavior]? What can we do to help you stop that?" Officers are also expected to be able to plan and monitor the execution of the sentences. This means, Høidal says, that they ask inmates about the future and guide them toward appropriate programming. "They will ask, 'When you go out of the prison, what shall you do when you go out? Have you a plan for your life?'"

The answers to those questions provide both the inmate and the contact officer with a kind of road map for the period of incarceration.

Unsurprisingly, this expansion of the Norwegian officers' responsibilities could not happen overnight. Just as the government's directive had required a reenvisioning of the role, implementation of the new role required radically different job training. Before working in a prison, Norwegian officers are now required to attend a Staff Academy where they are not only taught security procedures but also take courses in psychology, criminology, law, human rights, and ethics. Completing the required training at the academy takes two years, during which time trainees are paid full salaries. As a measure of comparison, the average training program to become a correctional officer in the United States is nine weeks long.

Here is an approach to crime that is proactive instead of punitive. An approach that provides help but in a collaborative, productive, and hopefully lasting way. This is an *ex ante* solution to recidivism. This is not the forty dollars handed to you at the prison gates as you're put on a bus to be dropped off at the Port Authority.

Scandinavian correctional services view ongoing judgment of the offender to be an inappropriate part of any person's sentence. They have a future-oriented perspective. The duty of the correctional service in Sweden, Nils Öberg stated plainly, is not to judge or to punish but rather "to carry out the courts' decisions. Our role is very different from that of police, prosecution, and the courts. Other authorities put their focus on the history of a person's behavior. We do the opposite. We do not look backwards. We look forward."

"Our role is not to explore the criminal act," he continued. "That is the one static factor that we cannot do anything about. In our view that act has been completed. Instead we try to focus on all of the dynamic factors in a person's life which we know affect whether that person is apt to commit another crime." As he spoke, I was reminded of the dialogue *Protagoras*, in which Plato writes, "He who inflicts punishment rationally does so not on account of the past offense—for he cannot make undone what has been done—but for the sake of the future."

This *rational* focus upon the future and this refusal to devalue people because of their pasts is what drives the policies at Halden Prison that allow the men held therein to cook their dinner with knives. To work in the auto-body shop with the tools they need. To have their own rooms with locks on the inside because, as Høidal says to me, prisoners deserve privacy just like the rest of us.

"Their room, that's their home while they're at Halden Prison," Høidal explains as he goes through the daily routine with me in detail. "They get up, have their breakfast. Then they pack a lunch and take it with them to work or school or whatever programmed activities they have starting at eight thirty each morning. Lunch at eleven. Back to work. They go back to their unit and have dinner, then exercise. They're locked in at eight thirty p.m. That's the difference. They don't go home at night. Otherwise all day they have a normal life. Like outside."

Jan Strømnes, the deputy head of Halden Prison, underscores to me why such a routine is of particular importance. "It doesn't take more than a year or two for people to become institutionalized. Time is different in prison—it moves more slowly. It does something to your ability to take responsibility for your own life. We have to minimize the effects." Having a daily schedule that includes the typical responsibilities of an adult in a community is part of the prison's effort to push against the pernicious force of institutionalization.

In addition to being out of the cell from morning to evening and engaged in activity during those hours, men detained at Halden are kept in the company of others all day.

"Together with others—not isolation—is best," Høidal stresses. "That is easy to see! Many places in the world, the inmates get mad from all this isolation." *The edge of madness,* Supreme Court justice Kennedy wrote of solitary confinement, *perhaps . . . madness itself.*

It's hard to explain exactly how little at any point during my day at Halden I feel as if I'm in a prison. Prior to this point, I've been inside perhaps twenty correctional facilities, each different from the others but with many shared traits, particularly in structure and in feel. Other than the fact that this is a complex in which more than two hundred fifty men live together, some for years, as I walk through it, it's hard to come up with even a single similarity between this place and any other jail or prison I've ever seen.

Warden Høidal and I walk outdoors on a winding path that leads us into a modern building that is one of the living units. It's silent.

During my visits to Northern, I'd made notes, trying to capture the feel of the place. Looking back through those notes, I saw that the noise was a theme to which I'd subconsciously returned over and over again.

> Floors, walls, ceilings all concrete. Doors are metal. Railings
> metal. There is nothing to absorb sound—it reverberates, echoes,
> expands. There is constant slamming. Whenever someone speaks
> to me, I have to strain to understand what they are saying. The
> staff that works here doesn't seem to notice.

From a second visit:

> Doors slam. There is yelling out. The walls are concrete and
> cinder block. It is cold, loud, jarring. Every noise echoes, a harsh
> reverberation.

A third:

> The noise is unbelievable. I'm trying to think of the loudest places
> I've been. Concerts. Sporting events. Airfields. This is loud of a
> different quality. It jars. It obscures and obfuscates. I can't hear

what's being said to me. There is yelling, but the words are indistinguishable. Or there is no yelling but inmates on their work duty from other facilities rumble carts of coffee or trash down the hallways and the echoes slam and bang. I notice I keep cringing.

A fourth:

The noise is such that it always sounds like crisis. Like an emergency on my unit would. I keep expecting people to take off running. I hear a bang and look fast over my shoulder, but no one breaks stride. They carry on.

"It is quiet, yes?" asks Høidal as we enter the Halden quarters. "You are wondering where they are, but they are all at work! You will see more of them when we go back to the school and the workshops."

In the men's absence, we walk through the living unit, which is modular and sleek, with the clean lines that define so much of Norwegian design. There's a central area with chairs and sofas surrounding a large television. Adjacent to that space is a long rectangular dining table encircled by neatly pushed-in chairs and a kitchen that could have come out of an IKEA look book. Not fancy, but simple, clean, functional, and well equipped. A magnetic knife strip is anchored onto the white tile kitchen walls. From it hang a pair of kitchen shears and three kitchen knives ranging in size from a paring knife to a large chef's blade. The knives are the most obvious and dramatic objects that could be used as weapons, but in the cabinets are drinking glasses and ceramic dishes that could be broken into sharp pieces. Metal silverware is arranged neatly in unlocked drawers. On the living-room wall is a dartboard, darts still protruding from some previous night's game.

A man in the hallway is mopping the floor—an inmate, it turns out, although I don't immediately recognize him as such because he's wearing his own clothes: jeans and a red graphic T-shirt that says something in black letters in a language I can't decipher. Warden Høidal approaches the man and shakes his hand, saying a phrase the man repeats back to him—a collection of sounds I recognize as a greeting in Norwegian but whose vowel-laden pronunciation I haven't been able to master.

"Do you speak English?" Høidal asks.

The man nods and replies, "A little."

"It is more polite, then," Høidal says with a smile, gesturing toward me as he continues in English so I can understand what's being said between them.

"This is a doctor from America," Høidal says to the man. "She is writing a book, and maybe she will write about Halden Prison in her book. I would like to show her the spaces for each person. Can I show her your room?"

The man laughs self-consciously, nods. "My room is not the cleanest, so . . . But yes, it's fine. It's right over here."

He leads us down a bright hallway with doors to individual cells on each side. In keeping with the idea that prisoners deserve privacy, the doors have no windows in them. As a result, I can't see into the cell until the man opens the door for me and steps to the side, but when I do see in, I understand why the men have used the term "room" rather than "cell" to describe these spaces.

To the right beyond the door is a small private bathroom with a sink, a shower, and a toilet. The main room is furnished with a twin bed, a desk and chair, a shelving unit, a nightstand, all made of blond wood, neatly angular in their simple design. There's a closet whose doors are made of the same wood. The bed is unmade—the only supporting evidence I can see of the resident's claim that his room was not clean—a rumpled yellow comforter strewn haphazardly across the white sheets. A pair of electric-blue sneakers is tucked under the foot of the bed. In this room, and in all the other cells in Halden Prison, is a mini-refrigerator and, mounted on the wall, a small flat-screen television.

The overall feel of the building, from the kitchen to the living room to the individual rooms, is that of a modern university dormitory or a spartan but clean hostel. Depending on who's writing about them, the prisoners' living conditions are either described as humane and just or lavish and ridiculous. THE SUPER-LUX SUPER MAX, blares one headline in an American magazine, describing Halden as looking "more like a posh sleepaway camp" than like Norway's most secure correctional facility. The flat-screen TVs are one of the most frequently cited details when the prison is critiqued as extravagant or overly indulgent of the serious offenders it houses. The luxury of which *I'm* most aware is manpower. In the average prison in America, there's one guard for every 6.4 detainees. At Halden the guard-to-prisoner ratio is 1:1.4.

It's easy to convince oneself that the facilities and guard-to-prisoner ratio at Halden would pose a financial differential insurmountable for American states. A closer look reveals that the reality is far more nuanced.

The cost to hold one prisoner for a year at Halden is approximately $93,000. American prison costs vary widely from state to state and between state and federal facilities. The average cost of incarcerating one person in a U.S. supermax prison for a year ranges from $60,000 to $75,000. Some high-security prisons operate at a per capita budget far above this average. Pelican Bay lists its annual costs per detainee in 2010–11 as $77,740. In 2013 the annual cost per prisoner at ADX was $78,884. And my home state of Rhode Island lists the annual cost of detaining a single prisoner in high security at the Adult Correctional Institute as a shocking $208,911, more than twice the annual cost per prisoner at Halden.

However, even the annual state correctional costs that initially appear lower than Halden's per-inmate budget belie a larger truth. Norway's recidivism rate is now one of the lowest in the world.

This means that even if short-term costs are greater at a place like Halden, which invests significant funds in staff numbers and training, the long-term costs of our recurrent incarcerations quickly multiply, rendering the American system—with one of the *highest* recidivism rates in the world—a far more expensive one. Nils Öberg, in describing the one-to-one staff-to-prisoner ratio in the Swedish Prison and Probation Service, states plainly that their correctional strategy requires a substantial investment. In fact, the Swedish Prison and Probation Service is the fourth-largest state-run agency in the country. "It is extremely expensive," Öberg acknowledges, "but it is money well spent. The alternative would be even more costly."

Regardless of the comparability of our overall expenditures, the money we spend on corrections goes to far different things. A deeper dive into where, exactly, all the money spent on U.S. corrections is going is beyond the scope of this book, although the fact that our country incarcerates more people in private, for-profit prisons than anywhere else in the world is important to note, particularly since in 2015 the two largest private prison corporations that together hold over half of American prison contracts reported a combined revenue of $3.5 billion. And of course there's no incentive to reduce prison populations for the small group of people who make big money from incarceration. But the fact remains that compared with Norway we're paying an amount per detainee that is in the same ballpark, with far less desirable results. In which case we ought to shift our funding priorities toward staff training and lowering the prisoner-to-staff ratio, as Halden has so intentionally done with such good outcomes.

There are of course marked differences between Nordic countries and the United States. Scandinavian countries in general have a greater tradition of social support for their citizens. They have higher tax rates. They have smaller and more homogeneous populations. But when examined closely, these differences are smaller and less significant than we might imagine.

With a population of approximately 5.3 million people, Norway is just smaller than Colorado and Minnesota, just larger than South Carolina and Alabama. As capital cities go, Oslo has a population roughly the same size as Nashville's, and comparing the cities' demographic patterns reveals more similarities than one might expect. Sixty percent of Nashville's citizens are white. Seventy percent of Oslo's residents are ethnic Norwegians; the other 30 percent are either immigrants themselves or were born to immigrants. Pakistanis and Somalis are two of the largest ethnic minorities, but there are also sizable immigrant communities in Norway from Iraq, Iran, Turkey, Vietnam, Morocco, Sri Lanka, Poland, and the Philippines. Forty percent of the children in Olso's primary schools speak a language other than Norwegian as their first language.

The discrepancy between the taxation rates of our two countries is also overblown. Although it's true that Sweden's average personal income tax rate of nearly 60 percent is among the highest in the world and stands apart as such, Norway's, at 38.52 percent, is barely more than the average U.S. rate of 37 percent.

Naturally there are differences between our countries and our cultures. But there's nothing here that would prevent us from trying some version of the Norwegian prison reform in the laboratory of our states.

As we exit the living unit, Warden Høidal points out the laundry facilities. "Of course the prisoners are responsible for washing their own clothes," he says. Later he shows me the prison grocery store, where inmates buy the food to cook for their meals. On the shelves are avocados, grapefruit, squashes, cucumbers. There's a bin full of gingerroot. A whole fresh pineapple. "You and I, we buy our groceries. We cook dinner. We do the laundry. These are things we have to manage in our lives," Warden Høidal reiterates. "It does not help anyone for these things to be done for them.

"The normality principle," he says, grinning at me as I scan the produce. "You are starting to understand!"

A pineapple versus nutraloaf is a shocking comparison, not just for the radical difference in taste and nutrition but also for all that the food implies, and it serves as a perfect mechanism to underscore what the normality principle offers that a punitive stance does not. The pineapple in the shop must be purchased, cored, and cut. Nutraloaf is shoved through a trapdoor. Nutraloaf is not merely disgusting (though it certainly is that). It is also disempowering and infantilizing, and it enforces both a lack of responsibility and a lack of agency in the people to whom it is served.

Warden Høidal and I walk through the parklike grounds of Halden to the facilities where the men work and study. Unlike the quiet emptiness of the living unit, these areas are bustling with activity. Here is the woodshop, the auto-body shop, the metalworking shop. Inside each one are men working with knowledge and purpose. Many of them share a look common to inmates in American prisons—multiple tattoos, some on hands, necks, and faces. Muscle-bound arms bulging out from the sleeves of T-shirts.

In 2014 James Conway, the former superintendent of Attica, New York's famous supermax prison, visited Halden and commented that the tools in the workshops were the kinds of things visitors might try to sneak into American prisons in order to facilitate escape. "You don't have to bake 'em in a cake," Conway jokes on a film clip from the visit, holding in his hands a long metal file.

Yet there's no way to have these men work, and to teach them these trades, and to educate them in these subjects without the proper materials. If your goal is that people convicted of crimes should be educated and learn job skills so they can go on to live productive, taxpaying, crime-free lives once they're released, then you must trust them enough to offer them the tools of their trades.

Despite easy access to any number of items that could be used as weapons at Halden, aggression between inmates is rare. Violence enacted by prisoners against staff? "It's nonexistent," says Høidal. By which he means that they've not had even one incident in the six years since Halden opened.

I ask Høidal why he thinks this is true, despite easy and near-constant access to potential weapons by men who've committed serious, often violent, crimes. To answer he returns to the intentions behind the relationship established between prison officers and inmates.

"Here we not only use static security but also dynamic security," he tells me. Static security is the traditional methodology of correctional facilities, made up of physical measures (high walls, alarm systems, bars) and also monitoring practices (cameras, observation, supervised visitation, cell and body searches, prisoner counts). Dynamic security, in contrast, is based in the interpersonal relationships and interactions be-tween prisoners and prison employees. Høidal points to a prison officer and an inmate working together on a piece of furniture, the officer hold-ing the base of a chair while the prisoner fits a leg onto it. "The relation-ship between staff and inmates is the most important part.

"The prison officers and the prisoners are together all day," Høidal explains. "Officers are in the workshops and in the living units, but ev-eryone also eats meals together. They take leisure together. They do activities together." In addition, 50 percent of the prison officers at Halden are female. And not one of them—male or female—is armed.

"Knowing the inmates is the best security," he continues. That way officers can be on alert if a man is behaving oddly—if he appears to be agitated or is becoming angry, they notice it, because they know that man. Know what it looks like when he is calm and know what it looks like when he begins to rev up. They also, in getting to know him in mul-tiple realms—from his assessment to his living quarters to his place of employment to the playing fields—have come to know what calms him down and how to help him de-escalate. By intervening in the earliest stages of conflict and frustration, officers can avoid a larger confronta-tion. Just as Bre and Summer did with Heather. Just as John and I did with Abraham.

I treat aggressive patients frequently enough that I have a system through which I try to optimize safety for my patients, my coworkers, and myself. Each morning when I come onto the hospital unit, I grab a census sheet that lists the names and room numbers of all the patients I'll see. During the nursing sign-out, I jot relevant notes beside each name: *afraid to shower, refusing meds, hoarding crackers and juice*, reads one from a recent week. *Visit with mom went well, auditory hallucinations are diminishing, no talking to herself x 24 hours*, reads another. If I learn from the nurses that a patient has been aggressive on the unit or has a history of aggression in the hos-pital, I write a bold capital **A** beside his room number and circle it. Most mornings when I do rounds, it's early enough that many of the patients are still in bed, and often I'll walk into their rooms to talk with them. If I see the **A** on my census sheet, it reminds me not to go in alone; I'll ask one of the larger male mental-health workers to come into the room with me, or at least to stand in the doorway in case I were to need him.

The staff members with whom I work know the patients well and are aware enough of the current state of the unit to do this without my even asking. If they see me headed toward the room of a patient with a tendency toward aggression, they follow along. If they've noticed that a patient is particularly agitated or irritable, they may head me off at the pass and encourage me to give him some time to cool off before I try to talk to him. More times than I can count, when a conversation on the unit has escalated to the point where I've begun to feel uncomfortable and concerned that the patient might become violent, I've looked up with the intention to signal to staff members that I'd like one of them to come closer to me in case I should need them, only to see that two of them have already unobtrusively positioned themselves within arm's reach.

The staff in my hospital have been carefully and systematically trained to de-escalate potentially dangerous situations. And the lesson on the psychiatric ward is the same as the lesson from the prison cell: The person with the least control also has the least to lose. To defuse a tense situation, it's often most effective to give the person who feels powerless some bit of control, some sense of agency. To allow Heather to walk to the QR rather than force her there. To give Abraham the chance to head back to his room to calm down on his own. To align with patients when possible rather than stand in opposition to them.

The concept at Halden of staff "being on the same side" as the inmates is not how most people would describe the dynamics within prisons. But it's exactly what I see as Warden Høidal and I continue our tour of the Halden grounds. We pass the prison's print shop, where staff and men are working together, unfurling the posters they've designed as they emerge from machines, assessing them with admiration and critique. Warden Høidal introduces me to a group of the men. One man asks a question in Norwegian, gesturing at me. Høidal nods, and the man bustles away. I look at the warden quizzically.

"They would like to give you a gift," he explains as the man returns. Smiling, the man hands me an apron and a cookbook, both emblazoned with the name of the prison and a wry image of a magnetic kitchen knife strip from which hang two kitchen knives, a carving fork, and a pair of handcuffs. The name of the cookbook is in Norwegian, but Høidal tells me with a chuckle that it translates as *Honest Food from Halden Prison*. The book was published by the men in the print shop. It contains recipes from the prison restaurant compiled and edited by the men who work in the restaurant and in food processing in the prison. And it also has a CD affixed inside the back cover—music that Halden detainees played, recorded, and produced in the prison's music studio.

From the work area, we pass through the school and pop into a few rooms, including the aforementioned art class where the carefully carved tic-tac-toe pieces are emerging from rough-hewn stone. Then we wind through exercise areas: a room equipped with treadmills and rowing machines. A gymnasium with basketball hoops and a rock-climbing wall.

Like the flat-screen TVs, some of these amenities have come under fire—even among Norwegians—as overly luxurious. Jan Strømnes shrugs off these accusations and meets them with pragmatism. Drum sets? Climbing walls? Treadmills? "You're removing frustration and aggression," he responds. "We believe in positive activity." The idea is to teach these men productive ways to channel the energy and emotions that have previously resulted in conflict and violence. Work, school, and exercise are not indulgences but strategic tools.

"We try to get their aggression out with football, with activities," explains Halden psychologist Natalie Manskar Modh. "It's easier for the prison officers to do their jobs if the inmates have had this healthy release of energy and aggression. And it's teaching the inmates healthier coping skills."

Leaving the prison buildings, we cross over to a soccer field where prisoners and officers are in the midst of a game. The teams are intermixed, so that officers and inmates play alongside one another. As we walk by, an errant kick sends the ball sailing toward us. A woman who's been in the game runs after the ball to fetch it. Warden Høidal calls her by name and asks her to come over for a moment to talk to the American visitor. She is petite and lovely, and she runs over to us, her face flushed from the exertion of the game. "Now my English will be put to the test!" she says, laughing.

Høidal explains that the woman teaches both PE and English at the prison and that she's done so for several years. I ask her a question that has been on my mind, and she answers quickly.

"I've not once been scared," she says. "Not once even been nervous." She goes on to recount that there was one time when an inmate had started to grow agitated. "Right away the other prisoners stood up to him," she said. "They protected me." With a quick wave, she ran back onto the field, kicking the ball ahead of her.

As she runs, I find myself thinking again about self-psychology and how it plays a role in the interactions here. Whatever good is to be found in these men is fostered, encouraged, seen, and appreciated. Whereas in our nation's prisons, the mirroring that prison inmates receive is that they are bad and dangerous, in need of control and repression, and deserving of suffering. And opportunities for modeling behind bars are too often malevolent ones.

I mention this to Warden Høidal, and he concurs. "If you treat the men here with respect, they behave as if they deserve it," he says to me. "If you trust them, they internalize that you believe that they are worthy of your trust." And by that logic the inverse is also true: if you treat men like monsters, they behave like monsters.

Maintaining a focus on the men's strengths has a practical purpose for the prison as well—it diminishes conflict and thus makes the job of running the prison easier for those who work within it. "The tougher the prison, the more problems you get," says Jan Strømnes. "It's not rocket science."

It's harder on the prisoners if the relationship between inmates and officers is an adversarial one, but it's harder on the officers if that's the case as well.

"A working environment where you feel danger is not good for the staff," Høidal stresses to me. "If you don't know the inmates, you feel danger. And if you feel danger, it's unhealthy." *We decided to stop meeting hard with hard.*

Of course Halden is not a utopia. There are times when the men held within misbehave or break the rules. "If they are damaging property or if they are violent, we can say that they need to take time away from the company of other prisoners. They can be locked in their cell," Høidal explains. "The cell is not bad, as you've seen. So it's just removal from the community. Like a time-out for a child. We can send them there sometimes for a couple of hours or a couple of days. Not longer than that." The response is more analogous to the two-hour limits on restraint and seclusion in my hospital, or asking Abraham and Heather to take space to calm down, than it is to administrative segregation in the American prisons.

And if that doesn't work? I ask. If they start to destroy things in their cells, or if they're banging on doors or walls, disturbing the environment, or if they were to try to hurt themselves? What then?

"We do have a security cell," Høidal says. "I will show it to you. We use it as little as possible." He walks me inside one of the units and opens the door to a room that looks very much like our hospital QR. "We only use this in very serious circumstances," he stresses. "To prevent serious attack or injury or riots or escape. We record whenever we use it, and since the prison opened, we have used it on average once a month. Actually a little less. Eleven times a year on average.

"And they stay here one to three days," he continues. "Not more. To [have them] stay more, I would have to make a petition to the superintendent. I have never done that and would never want to."

The contrasts between the Norwegian approach toward corrections and the American perspective are so great in number that it begins to feel redundant to delineate them all. It's more accurate to conceptualize the different practices as components of vastly different philosophies. On the one hand, there's the philosophy of vengeance, of punishment, of payback, of suffering. On the other hand is the philosophy of pragmatism, of objective analysis and implementation, of improvement of the individual and strengthening of the community.

There are countries in the world where it's considered inhumane and counterproductive to isolate a man for more than three days. And yet our justice system will isolate children for up to a year. We have built entire prisons with the sole purpose of holding men in seclusion for months, years, even decades.

Warden Høidal shows me that Halden Prison also has a second seclusion room with a restraint bed in the center. A thin mattress rests on a simple metal frame, anchored to the floor. Straps lie buckled across the mattress where they would be needed to hold a man's shoulders. His waist. His wrists. His ankles. "We would use this only if someone was cutting himself or seriously trying to take his life," Høidal explains. "But we have never used it," he says emphatically. "Not once."

The men here have committed crimes of the same severity as have the men in the maximum and supermax prisons in America. *Of course they're animals and monsters*, the CO at Northern had said. *If they weren't, they wouldn't be here.* But the men here at Halden do not injure themselves. They do not attack one another. They do not use the knives and tools to which they have ready access to stab an officer in the neck. They do not throw their bodily fluids at the walls. And this is because they are not treated like monsters. They have jobs that give them meaning. They're forming relationships with staff members and with one another. They're treated like human beings. *It's not rocket science.*

We also know that extreme, maladaptive behaviors are more likely to occur when there is no hope. As Dr. Frayne said of men housed at Northern, aggression and homicidality can increase when people face life imprisonment or death sentences—when they have nothing left to lose. If you're at Northern on death row and another inmate threatens or even annoys you, what do you lose by beating or even killing him? Such an extraordinary action could occur and the trajectory of your life would be absolutely unchanged. The same may be true for detainees who will be released but have no hope on the outside. No housing. No employment prospects. Few social supports. No money. With finite sentences that have a release date in sight, there is the possibility of some hope. Something to work toward. And when the time spent incarcerated is spent addressing the obstacles on the outside, hope for the future grows there, too.

Halden anticipates its residents' return to their communities with something Høidal and Jan Strømnes call the "import model."

"The community is responsible for the inmate, even if he is in prison," Høidal tells me. "The community cannot forget that person." The practical translation of this is that a number of critical services are supplied to the prison by community providers. Unlike prisons in America, prisons in Norway do not have dedicated medical providers, or teachers, or vocational counselors, or librarians, or even clerical workers. In Norwegian prisons these services are *imported* from the community.

This arrangement serves two critical purposes, one social and one financial. From a financial perspective, the arrangement spares the prison from shouldering the economic burden of furnishing such services. The rationale behind this is that other than security, the services that need to be provided in the prison are the same services that are provided to any citizen. As a result, teachers, counselors, doctors, and other professionals are funded by the same government agencies that fund those positions in the community. "These are the rights of every Norwegian citizen," Jan Strømnes explains.

From a social standpoint, bringing community providers into the prisons means that people who are incarcerated will form personal and professional connections during their sentences that will persist after they're freed. So, for example, when a man leaves Halden Prison and returns to the community, he can see the same substance-abuse counselor with whom he formed a relationship during his time of incarceration. He can see the same doctor. The same dentist. Even the same librarian. These longitudinal relationships ease the reentry process and remove some of the obstacles to reintegration.

So the import model serves a constructive purpose for offenders. It also, says Warden Høidal, serves a purpose for people outside the prison walls. "Involvement from the community within the prison system improves the image in the community of prisons and prisoners," he explains. This is the manifestation of what lawyer, author, and civil rights leader Bryan Stevenson means when he implores people to "get proximate" to our carceral facilities and the people within them. Høidal and Stevenson are both tapping into a fundamental human truth: that it's harder to judge and hate people we talk to and come to know.

The import model foresees a progression in an inmate's sentence toward reintegration. The goal of the sentence, from its earliest days, is to return an improved citizen into the community from which he's been removed.

"In Norway we say, 'better out than in,'" Høidal stresses. "It is better for everyone—better for prisoners and better for our communities—if we can have people at home instead of in jail." Movement toward that end is built into the way prison sentences are carried out. Over the course of a sentence, detainees progress from higher-security to lower-security facilities, eventually to halfway houses and then parole. It's not uncommon for the last third of a sentence to be served in the community. Sweden actually has this plan formalized in its sentencing guidelines, stipulating that one-third of *every* person's sentence will be served under observation outside prison.

"Our basic concept," Maria Lindström of the Swedish Prison and Probation Service tells me, "is to *avoid* confinement whenever possible."

Her colleague Mattias Andersen adds, "There's no way to imprison someone without doing some damage. We want to minimize that damage."

The aim, then, is for the sentence to move from the most restrictive, most controlled, highest-security environment to less and less restrictive correctional environments. A gradual transition from captivity to freedom. Høidal points across Halden's campus to a stand-alone building along the property's periphery but outside the wall that encircles the other prison structures. "That's the halfway house," he tells me. Twenty-four men live inside the building. "They leave the prison grounds during the day and go to their jobs," he explains. "Then they come back and sleep in the halfway house at night."

These kinds of models are familiar to me, as a similar step-down trajectory is used when I discharge people from their inpatient hospitalizations to day hospital programs and on to an outpatient level of care. In medicine we also recognize the need for a gradual model of reacclimation.

The seriousness of this Scandinavian commitment yields circumstances that are unimaginable in the realm of American criminal justice. For example, as detainees progress in their sentences, they may go on passes from prison into town to have a cup of coffee in a café or go to a medical appointment or to run a short errand. They may be given permission to go home for a day or even for a night.

In Oslo I met with Dr. Randi Rosenqvist, a whip-smart, no-nonsense forensic psychiatrist who has served as an expert in the country's highest-profile criminal cases. She drove me around on a tour of the city in her tiny car and recounted to me how even men at Stockholm's Ila Prison, which holds the country's most dangerous criminals, go on these kinds of outings.

"Everyone comes back," she says. "Well . . ." she reconsiders. "Maybe twice not. Once a man took off from his pass but then got so scared that he eventually came back to the prison. The other time a man went out the back of the prison, and there's only woods that way, so we found him soon enough."

I asked whether they wore any kind of electronic monitoring when out on passes, picturing the ankle bracelets that are worn in Rhode Island by people on house arrest.

"We have looked into that," Dr. Rosenqvist says. "The kind that beeps if they go beyond certain boundaries or parameters in the community. The problem was that sometimes they go off at the wrong time. We didn't like the idea of exposing them."

She means that they don't want to run the risk of the detainee being publicly shamed. It's a protective instinct. A custodial one. Humane.

Warden Høidal agrees that such measures are not used at Halden and are not even necessary. "Everyone comes back," he tells me. "And ninety-nine percent of them come back on time."

The premise of taking action to avoid unnecessary shame and suffering has its roots in the Mandela Rules, which state emphatically that "imprisonment and other measures that result in cutting off persons from the outside world are afflictive by the very fact of taking from these persons the right of self-determination by depriving them of their liberty. Therefore the prison system shall not, except as incidental to justifiable separation or the maintenance of discipline, aggravate the suffering inherent in such a situation."

The Norwegian government's corresponding edict has important implications for the preservation of relationships and family life during periods of incarceration.

Occasional passes home are part of this effort. But even when men are kept on the grounds of Halden Prison, formal efforts are made to foster and maintain the men's connections with their families, to try to keep them as integrated as possible into the lives of their spouses and children that go on without them during their sentences. There is a "visiting house" on the prison grounds. Høidal apologizes that he cannot take me in to show me because a family is using it right now and he does not want to interrupt their time together.

Prisoners who complete a child-development education program can reserve the house to stay in with their family for an overnight visit. Inside, there are two bedrooms—one with bunk beds and brightly colored comforters, a kitchen, a bathroom, and a living room. Outside is a play area with climbing toys for children. Prison officers check in regularly during the course of the visit, but Høidal tells me that misbehavior in the house is rare. "It is such a privilege for them to have time with their spouse and their children. They know that if they mess up, they will not have that privilege anymore, and they don't want to risk that."

As we walk by, I look at the play equipment on the patio and think of

Danielle Metz's son, who said that every year during his childhood Christmas visits to his mother's prison he would climb onto the lap of the prison Santa, and every year he would say that all he wanted for Christmas was for his mother to be brought back home.

FAMILY CONTACT IS neither preserved nor prioritized by the American criminal justice system. The obstacles to visitation are many, ranging from geographical distance often nowhere near public transportation routes to narrow visiting hours incompatible with many work schedules to the unpredictability of prison lockdowns. Prisoners' families may not even be notified when their incarcerated loved ones are transferred to different facilities or even moved into prisons in faraway states. The data on the tangible damage that this practice causes is unequivocal. People who are able to maintain family relationships during their prison sentences are consistently shown to have better behavior in prison and reduced recidivism rates once they return to society. The preservation of relationships also preserves and fosters a sense of hope.

In the visiting rooms of American prisons, where I often meet with men and women to perform their competency assessments, there are strict rules and boundaries between prisoners and visitors that are impenetrable—sometimes literally, sometimes figuratively.

A sign in the waiting room of Rhode Island's high-security prison:

ITEMS ALLOWED
IN VISITING ROOM

wedding ring
1 diaper
1 clear baby bottle
eyeglasses
life saving meds
medical tag

The handbook of York Correctional Institution, a women's prison where I frequently work, delineates rules for visits:

"Non-Contact Visiting provides for the inmate and her visitor to be separated by a glass partition and to communicate by phone, which may be monitored," it reads.

"Contact Visiting provides for the inmate and the visitor(s) to be in the physical presence of each other. A greeting and parting kiss and embrace may be exchanged. During the visit, physical contact is limited to hand-holding across the table. You are permitted to hold a small child."

Imagine my surprise, then, to see the visiting area in Halden Prison, made up of small rooms with doors that close in which visits take place. "Physical contact is allowed," Warden Høidal says to me, smiling in a way that reveals he knows what he's about to say will stun me. "And we provide condoms in the rooms should they be necessary." *You lose your freedom, but you don't lose anything else.*

When Attica superintendent James Conway visited Halden, he said that if he'd asked his prisoners to "design the prison of their dreams," it would look like Halden Prison. "I don't think you can go any more liberal," he quipped, "other than giving the inmates the keys. If you're going to give them that much freedom and that much of a luxurious environment . . . why have them in prison anyway?"

Conway's question first struck me as draconian. Angry, even. But on further reflection I've come to view it as the essential question facing our country about the intentions of our criminal legal system. Revenge—the practice of hurting someone because that person has hurt you—by definition inflicts harm. If the purpose of incarceration is revenge, then harm is an essential element in the punishment. Any measures that reduce or alleviate that suffering run contrary to our aims. Conway's question acknowledges more honestly that our stated goals for incarceration—increasing safety, reducing recidivism, rehabilitating people who commit crimes—are in truth immaterial. If prison is not a place that serves to compound suffering, if the environment is not harsh, if there isn't some measure of degradation, then *why have them in prison anyway?*

American prisons focus entirely on attempting to eliminate any and all security risks and to deprive our detainees of even the most basic human comforts if we feel it is necessary to do so. Halden operates under an opposite logic: that it's impossible to reduce all risk—undesirable, even. And that the goal of imprisonment is not to achieve ultimate control and enact payback. The stated goal is to utilize the period of the prison sentence constructively and well so that offenders will choose a life free of crime after completing their sentences.

This kind of programming is not a luxury—it's an approximation of real life. Detainees in Norway are paid a modest wage for the work they do in prison, and this money goes toward securing fundamental needs—like housing—in the community when they are released. "Sometimes what people need," Dr. Rosenqvist remarked to me dryly in describing how incarceration can be a constructive period of time, "is experience in keeping a boring job five days a week."

The alternative—releasing men who've been caged and whose norms may have come to include isolation, aggression, self-injury—is an indefensible prospect. And yet in America it is exactly what we do.

Once I understand this clear divergence in philosophies, I begin to try to understand *why* it is that our correctional intentions differ so. *Why* we, as societies, have ended up with such markedly different outlooks on the "right" way to address criminality in our countries. Why, when its prisons were plagued by the problems that currently infest our nation's prisons, did Norway choose this more humane path?

In Stockholm, Mattias Andersen begins by discussing the differences in the ways that our countries' citizens view their governments and the ways our governments define their roles.

"In Sweden," Andersen begins, "there is a long bond of trust between the government and the citizens. In America it seems that there is a great deal of mistrust of the government by the citizens, and that's not how it is here. We believe our elected officials serve us well."

At Halden Prison psychologist Lars Fredrik Skahjem raises the same point. "In Nordic countries we're raised with an emphasis on being good citizens," he explains. "We give away nearly half our income in taxes. But this doesn't upset us, because we think the government is doing a good job with our money!"

"The other thing that strikes me as different," Mattias Andersen continues, "is that we don't have the same kind of conflicts between politics and science as you do. In America perhaps there will be a scientific report on climate change or gun violence or crime or poverty. The scientists report their findings, and then some politicians will dispute those findings because they don't align with their party's moral positions. That kind of conflict does not happen here. Our government asks a question to researchers. Like, 'What methods will be most effective at reducing poverty in our communities?' or 'What kinds of measures have been most reliably shown to reduce urban crime?' The scientists come back with answers. When the government receives those expert opinions, they implement them, and for the most part we see positive outcomes. There's no conflict here between morality and intellect—the good ideas should prevail."

Dr. Lars Stefan Østerholm is a psychiatrist at Dikemark Hospital in Oslo, a specialized psychiatric unit that treats mentally ill people who are convicted by the courts and sentenced to inpatient psychiatric treatment rather than to prison.

"The patients who come here to Dikemark have done very bad things," he tells me when I visit his hospital. "Sometimes they arrive here literally with the blood from the crimes they've committed still dried on their clothes, their hands. It doesn't happen often. Maybe twice a year. But even so I would like to think that every person who came here to Dikemark could be my brother, my sister, or my child. So as I go about my work, even if it's someone who has done something very bad, I am thinking, what can I do to make my brother's life easier to live?"

Dr. Østerholm is thinking this, and I am thinking about the difference between the Scandinavian commitment to protect and rehabilitate those who've been convicted of a crime and the American willingness to disproportionately incarcerate our African American citizens, our poor, our addicted, our mentally ill—whom we've often failed in myriad ways before they became entangled in the criminal legal system. And I'm seeing firsthand the divergences between our systems, with humanity and constructive results on one side and cruelty and madness on the other. America's mass incarceration happened in parallel with the shuttering of state mental-health facilities. Those two realities, combined with our distinct historical posture toward crime and punishment in the West, set the scene for our current prison disaster. Prison has surely always been maddening in some capacity, and the mentally ill have likely long been overrepresented in its confines, but this American epidemic, this madhouse, is a modern creation.

"To wish to punish people," Natalie Manskar Modh said to me at Halden, "you have to have the perspective that those people are not 'us.' They are 'them.' We don't see it that way. We all are people who live in this country. It is all 'us.' So our work is not to punish people we see as 'them.' Our work is to help create good neighbors."

13.

I AM HELPING YOU

Some years ago I was driving my young children through a rural area, and we passed a sign that said PRISON AREA—DO NOT PICK UP HITCHHIKERS.

My daughter, six or seven at the time, read the sign aloud as we passed.

"Why does it say that?" my son asked her, looking, as he still does, to his older sister as the most reliable source of information.

"Because people in prison are bad," she said, "and so you wouldn't want them in your car."

"Not everyone in prison is bad," I said quickly, glancing at my children's bright faces in the car's rearview mirror.

"Then why are they in prison if they're not bad?" my daughter asked.

"Well, for the most part, to get into prison you have to have done bad things," I replied. "But doing bad things doesn't always mean you're a bad person," I continued. Years later, as we sat together at Halden Prison, Jan Strømnes would say something similar. *Do we look at him as a criminal or as a person who has* done *something criminal?* he asked me. *It's not playing with words. It's an important distinction.*

"What do you mean?" my son asked.

"Well," I replied, "if our family didn't have enough money for food . . ."

"We would ask Mimi and Poppa to send us food!" my daughter piped up, ever the problem solver.

"Yes," I continued. "But imagine for a minute that we didn't have family who could help us, that we didn't have friends who had enough to share. We're very lucky that we have people we could turn to for help, but not everybody does. So if our family didn't have enough money to buy food to eat, I would try everything I possibly could to get some food to feed you both. I would ask people to help. I would try any way I could to earn or borrow money. But if none of those things worked and we were out of food and the two of you were starving," I went on, "I can imagine situations where I might steal some food so that you would survive."

The kids sat and listened quietly, cogitating and aghast.

"I would never want to do something bad, and I would try everything else first, but I know I might do something bad if I were desperate to protect you," I said. "And some of the people in prison have done bad things not because they're bad people but because they were desperate."

"If they're not bad people," my daughter asked slowly, thinking through her question as she put it into words, "then why do we put them in a bad place?" A genuine question. A good question. Perhaps what's come to be the central question of this book.

I ask Dr. Rosenqvist on our driving tour why she thinks the Nordic countries have been able to adhere to these ideas of humanism in corrections when the United States has not, especially when it comes to people with mental illness.

"Ah," she says. "We are a country that has evolved over a thousand years. A thousand years ago, we had Viking laws. If you killed someone, you had to be killed or else you became an outlaw." Though she keeps both hands on the wheel navigating the turns of the road, she looks at me out of the corner of her eye for a moment, smiling. Then says, "We consider the U.S. to be a very immature country."

Dr. Rosenqvist is asked to evaluate the country's most dangerous criminals and assess their level of risk to the community, should they be released. I tell her that the Scandinavian approach as I've seen it makes so much sense to me; that it seems to me to be pragmatic, humane.

"When I look at people, I try to see what stresses them and how they cope," she responds. "I try to see the human in everyone."

I tell her that Maria Lindström told me that the tendency at the Swedish Prison and Probation Service is to view criminals as people who haven't had the same opportunities as others. And that the Norwegian sociologist Nils Christie has written that there are no dangerous people, just ordinary people in dangerous situations.

"I agree," she tells me, "but some persons come into dangerous situations more often than others, and that's not by chance!"

"Do you believe that some people are evil?" I ask directly, thinking of the small minority of people in prison who've committed crimes that are truly sadistic.

"I think there are people who are devoid of empathy," she responds.

"Is that different?" I ask.

"I think evil is the intention to hurt and harm," she says. "Without empathy you might not even distinguish between evil and not evil."

In my work I've seen men who've done the worst things I can imagine. The worst acts of violence. The things I fear the most. I've seen men who've killed for pleasure. Who've delighted in another's pain.

A psychologist colleague tells me of a man he saw who killed for sport. On his eyelids he had words tattooed. On the right it read GAME. On the left it read OVER. "What are the tattoos for?" my colleague had asked him during an evaluation.

"It's the last thing you're gonna see," the man replied.

It is this kind of evil that troubles me. The Anders Breiviks of the world. The Jeffrey Dahmers. Of course there are others. Lesser-known people who sexually abuse scores of children, or who delight in cruelly inflicting pain. People who commit evil crimes that are so frigid and calculating, so inhuman, that before we hear of the acts, we could never have even imagined them. These are the cases that cause me to pull up short from those prison abolitionists who say that prisons should not exist in any form, at all. There are people, I believe, who cannot safely remain in society. And whether they innately hold the capacity to commit unimaginable acts of harm or whether they've acquired the capacity through abuse, or trauma, or any other number of combined factors matters little once the crime has been committed. Acts like these compel us to keep a person from repeating them, and imprisonment is at present the best way for us to do that. Our best means of incapacitation.

This is a small number of people—a minuscule fraction of the 2.2 million people incarcerated in America today. Veteran Los Angeles Police Department detective Tim Marcia said as much when describing his interactions with serial killer Samuel Little, who admitted to killing more than ninety women. "Looking into his eyes, I would say that was pure evil," Marcia said. "Believe it or not, you only see evil a few times in your career."

But in order for even this tiny percentage of our nation's currently incarcerated population to be imprisoned for prolonged periods, the people we hold must continue to meet specific criteria for this removal from society. Psychiatrists know perhaps better than anyone how difficult it is to accurately assess risk. We cannot know with certainty which of our suicidal patients will kill themselves, which of our homicidal patients will harm another. Nonetheless, I cannot keep my patients hospitalized indeterminately, so I must use the tools I have to try to predict as best I can.

Our strategy in corrections should be the same. Patients who are found not guilty by reason of insanity undergo periodic evaluations to determine when—or whether—they're likely to be safe to be released. We ought to mandate that men and women who are sentenced to prison in our country undergo these same kinds of evaluations. And rather than the opaque and often arbitrary nature of the nation's parole process, risk assessments should be conducted in a targeted, evidence-based manner by forensic experts. And the evaluations should focus entirely on the risk that, if released, a person will commit acts of violence in the community.

Instead of mandatory minimums, we ought to have sentencing maximums after which point a person must be assessed and deemed to pose a real, continued risk in order to justify his continued incarceration.

It's impossible to know when a person is convicted of a crime whether he will continue to be a danger to others twenty, forty, sixty years from the time of sentencing. How can we possibly purport to know who is irrevocable?

"I've been in debates on TV," Dr. Rosenqvist tells me, "where a politician would say, 'If a man commits murder and walks down the streets of Oslo a few years later, that's not long enough.' To which I say, 'Aren't you happy he received such good treatment that he got well enough to walk down the streets of Oslo?'" We cannot know that because someone is capable of enacting atrocious harm, he will remain a risk for the entirety of his life.

"But there are also times," Dr. Rosenqvist continues, "when prison won't reduce dangerousness. Sadistic traits won't change. In which case the pertinent question is simply, how long does the court think it's reasonable for a person to be here for the crime he's done? The pertinent question is whether the *structure of outpatient treatment is enough* to provide some reassurance that he likely would not pose a risk, or whether he's someone who likely wouldn't cope with the combination of stressors and risk factors outside of prison. The question is not, does he *deserve* to be released?"

Her answer no longer startles me, now that I've become accustomed to the fact that these issues in Scandinavia are guided at all times by a fierce pragmatism. It's not that evil isn't an intellectually interesting question, she seems to be saying, but it's actually not relevant as she goes about her job assessing which of these people—all of whom have done terrible things—remain dangerous enough that they require continued detention.

And Anders Breivik? I asked her.

She nodded. "I met Breivik a few times and talked with him. I said he struck me as very ordinary. There was nothing extraordinary about him. I feel quite sure he did not like that I said this. It made him angry."

"What do you mean he was ordinary?" I asked her, incredulous. "He carried out a mass murder."

"There are many young men who have killed many people they perceive to be the enemy," she responded.

"Yes," I say, "but don't you think he differs from soldiers in a way in that he shows absolutely no remorse? No 'I hate that I had to do it, and it was awful to do, but I had to do it because of the war'?"

Dr. Rosenqvist considers my point, shrugs. "It's true that no war was going on. If it *had* been an act of war, if it had been ISIS that killed those children, we could have been angry. That would have been easier. Because he was Norwegian?" She pauses. "Because he was Norwegian, instead of making us angry, it makes us feel afraid. It's easier to be angry than to be afraid."

Oft have I heard that grief softens the mind, and makes it fearful and degenerate, writes Shakespeare in *Henry VI*. *Think therefore on revenge and cease to weep.*

Vengeance has its roots in anger. But the real issue is the loss, and how the loss makes us afraid and aware of our vulnerability. We worry that the depravity of these actions will touch us. We fear that the people who've committed them can reach us, that we're vulnerable to their crimes, and also to their criminality.

By locking them away, by exiling them, by putting them out of sight, we feel less vulnerable. We feel less mortal. Once they're in the system, locked away, we don't want to think about them. Don't want to examine what the conditions are like for them. Don't want to analyze whether the sentences they receive are fair or effective. We want them to go away, and we want the solution to be a simple one.

Nietzsche says, "Beware that, when fighting monsters, you yourself do not become a monster. For when you gaze long into the abyss, the abyss gazes also into you." That proximity terrifies us.

A friend and colleague of mine who is an excellent, devoted physician worked as a prison psychiatrist for more than a year. She described this proximity as part of the reason she eventually left the position to work in a noncorrectional setting.

"I had this patient who was wonderful," she recounted. "He was not seeking drugs. He was really sad, had real symptoms of depression. And more than anything else, he seemed more mature, more connected, actually open to talking in a real way about his situation.

"I prescribed an antidepressant, and he came back six or eight weeks later saying, 'I feel better, my sleep's better, I feel more motivation for groups.' This was rare—so many of the men were a string of complaints, wanting more medication, dissatisfied with what they perceived to be the fact that I wasn't helping them or wasn't helping them enough.

"One day he left his appointment, and I turned to the nurse that was working with me and said to him, 'That guy is a great guy. What the hell is he in here for?' I operated under the assumption that I didn't ask about the crimes the men had committed and they usually didn't tell me, but I felt like this guy was different—that he somehow didn't belong.

"'He's in for multiple murders,' the nurse said to me. 'He would take women into the woods and split their heads open because he wanted to see what would happen.' I was stunned.

"And so my idea that people did bad things only because bad things had happened to them, because life was unfair—that idea was shifting. Not only could I not predict who was good or bad, but here was this smart, articulate person—if he'd come up to my car at a gas station asking for help, I probably would have . . ." She trailed off, then continued.

"I think I have good intuition. Right? We're trained in our field to assess people, and I think I have good intuition, and I never would have guessed that this guy was capable of doing what he'd done, what he'd wanted to do. It was so disconcerting and scary. And also just knowing that these kinds of people are in the world. That evil exists. It's not necessarily preventable. So I started to ask, why put myself around it more?

"It confronts you with the sadness and unfairness of the world. That's the crux of it for me. Of course things are awful and unfair and tragedies happen that you can't prevent—but I didn't need to be reminded of that every Tuesday and Thursday."

I have had this same feeling during my own work in prisons. I felt it when visiting the unit at Northern that holds the perpetrators of the infamous Cheshire, Connecticut, home invasion in which a local physician was brutally injured and his forty-eight-year-old wife and eleven- and eighteen-year-old daughters were all raped and murdered.

Often my gut response afterward is the same as my colleague's: *I wish I didn't know that people like this existed. That violence like this occurs.* It is Deb saying to me, "Don't tell me when a plane crashes. I don't want to know about it." It is when, in our early forties, I've heard about the deaths of four people our age—sudden cardiac death, vastly metastatic cancer, a ruptured aneurysm, a freak accident—I ask her to stop talking with me about the details of Paul Kalanithi's memoir, *When Breath Becomes Air.* Ask her not to tell me any more stories she reads or hears about forty-something parents of young children who die. I cannot take the proximity of engaging with this idea, uppermost in my list of fears. It's the mounting sense of panic I feel, however irrational, when staring into space, contemplating stars and galaxies and distances I cannot comprehend and the idea of the sun burning itself out. *What then?* My heart seems to beat these syllables as it quickens. Though I know I'll be long dead by then, my children long dead by then, their children long dead, there's still a dreadful horror behind the idea. *What then?* beats my heart. *What then? What then?* There is only gaping uncertainty. Or perhaps that isn't true. There is absolute certainty. A blackness and silence that I cannot bring myself to fathom. Better to push the thought of it away.

Revenge is a response to our inherent and inescapable vulnerability. We cannot know which plane will crash, cannot banish cancer, cannot keep the sun from its inevitable cosmic demise. But identifying a person who has done violence, who embodies risk, and locking him up in a small dank cell for "348 years" provides an opportunity, however illusory, for us to feel as though there is some measurable thing that can be done to protect ourselves from the capricious dangers of human life.

The language of punishment and incarceration is a language of maximizing security and minimizing risk, but the true meaning behind the words is really an attempt to reduce our vulnerability. To guard our own children from the home invasion. To stave off the man with a stockpile of weapons in his apartment. To protect ourselves from the existential threat. Even if we're told it's ineffective, even if there are tragedies and violence that we cannot predict and prevent, action and punishment make us feel otherwise. *It's easier,* says Dr. Rosenqvist, *to be angry than to be afraid.*

Norway's reenvisioned system of justice, and similar philosophies in Sweden and elsewhere, have demonstrated that if our goals for our society are truly to have less crime and safer societies, then we must let go of our drive for vengeance to achieve them. There is no tenable way to hold fast to both desires.

WAITING TO BOARD the train from Halden Station back to Oslo after my visit at Halden Prison, I notice how high the sun is in the sky. Light shimmers on the still surface of the fjord. It is 3:00 p.m., and the sun has been up for more than ten hours already. It will not set for nearly seven more.

The dark of winter in Scandinavia's arctic regions is much, much harder than the perpetual light of summer, one of the people I met in Norway had told me. For the obvious reasons, I imagined. But no. You go months—November to February—without ever being able to determine what time of day it is, he explained. In the summer at least you can see far enough to see whether people are out. If so, you can deduce it is daytime. In the darkness you can see so little. You have no idea whether people are walking through the town, whether cars pass beyond the trees. The disorientation is horrible, he said.

In the northernmost parts of the country, when the first rays break over the horizon in spring—there are only a few, and they last just a few moments—the children are let out of school for the day, and the townspeople set off cannons in celebration.

At Halden Station I board the wrong train car for the hour-and-forty-five-minute ride back to Oslo. I am turning in circles, unable to find my designated seat number when the conductor comes up behind me.

"You have to leave this car and go into the next one down," he says. "You are not supposed to be here."

"Oh, I'm sorry," I say, feeling the instant discomfort of a tourist who missteps in a foreign land.

"It's okay," he says with a smile. "It's okay. I am helping you."

14.

GOOD NEWS

In the winter I go to a cottage in the north woods of Michigan to write. Each day I sit in front of a window that looks out across a frozen lake. I watch the snow blow in. The dark tree line of the lake's opposite shore appears, disappears in snow or fog, reappears. I sit for hours. I stand and stretch, brew a cup of tea, forage around the pantry, sit back down again. It's not polar Norwegian darkness, but the winter sun stays low enough in this northern latitude that much of the daylight is a kind of dusk, and even midday feels reticent.

Temperatures are in the single digits, but at this moment there is only the lightest dusting of snow, so walking out on the lake is quite literally walking across a sheet of ice. After one near wipeout, I clamp on metal-toothed snowshoes to trudge across the lake and have a look around. I stay near the shore as I walk, venturing out thirty or forty feet at most from the lake's perimeter. Bolder souls than I drive snowmobiles from shore to their fishing huts. Still, every fifteen steps or so the ice beneath me cracks with a disconcertingly loud bang. My foot breaks through a layer and lands on another sheet two or three inches below. I keep walking, trusting each time that those lower layers exist. It's hard to trust—the sound and the quick downward pull of gravity register as shock every time.

When I make it back to the cottage, more than an hour has gone by. It's still afternoon, but the sun is already beginning to set. Suddenly, just before I turn to go inside, a quiet shift in the wind, almost imperceptible, and a few moments of one of the most beautiful things I've ever seen in my near half century of coming to this lake. The snow dust on the ice is being blown toward me, not in a cloud or mass but in thin rivulets, coursing and undulating across the frozen surface. Like small streams of water, or of sand, the strands of snow snake across the lake, merge, divide as far as I can see. They're hit by the low light of the setting sun. They glisten. A diaphanous veil stretched across the ice like some Buddhist weaving meant to show impermanence, the strands plait and twist, becoming glorious patterns that are gone as soon as they form—beauty and loss breaking into each other, the two states simultaneous.

When the rivulets reach my snowshoes, they branch and rejoin behind me as if I'm a boulder in a stream. My stillness an unimportant obstacle amid all this collective motion.

That night I dream that my veins rearrange themselves each time my heart beats.

When I wake, I go back to the window to write. Mug of tea in my hand, a table beside me on which my papers are strewn, covering a jigsaw puzzle of vegetables canned in Mason jars. My mother had left the puzzle unfinished when she last was here. Between pages or paragraphs, I'd futz with the pieces, fitting rings of peppers or halves of beets into place until the whole thing was finished. It was a way of thinking, and it somehow felt like talking to her, which always pulls me closer to what I really want to say.

With the puzzle done, I sit and stare out the window more, waiting for ideas to take shape. Suddenly there's movement far out on the ice, a dark, loping animal that can only be a coyote. At first I'm delighted—what a spotting! Rarely, here, I'd hear coyote howls in the woods, the sound cutting across the summer night into my open windows, but not as often as the eerie calls of loons or of the great horned owl. And though I've seen the displaced city versions a time or two in Providence, which feed on urban chicken coops and unfortunate pet cats, I'd never seen a coyote in its true habitat. Now here one was, large, lean frame gracefully making its way across the frozen lake, all shaggy beauty and wildness.

Until something begins to seem wrong. I had eagerly grabbed a set of binoculars and fixed its circle of magnified light on the coyote. He'd trot a ways across the ice, losing his footing occasionally on a slick spot only to regain it. But then he'd turn around and with the same pace run back in the direction whence he'd come. Pause. Another turn. A long run. A turn again. I look more closely. I crane and squint. I see no injury, no limp. No person or thing anywhere around but for the ice-fishing huts more than a hundred yards away. Could he be catching the scent of caught fish and moving toward them, only to be spooked off by the sound of people? But there is no persistence to his movement. It is an aimless rambling. There's no other source of food out there. What's he doing, then, so purposeless and exposed?

I watch and watch. It's easy to train my eyes on him, a lone dark shape in the vastness of white. It's when he lies down on the ice that my heart starts to pound a little. I send a text query to my brother, who hunts deer and turkeys and knows about coyotes from his time in the field.

Call the Department of Natural Resources, he writes back. *Not normal behavior.*

So I do, and they tell me to call Ruth at ARK—the Association to Rescue Kritters.

"Sounds like distemper," Ruth tells me. "Coyotes are pack animals," she continues. "It'd be odd in the first place to see one alone in daylight, let alone out on the ice, let alone lying down out on the ice. They would never choose such an open place that leaves them so vulnerable. But we see this a lot with distemper. The pack somehow understands that one member is sick, and they seem to know that it's dangerous for the whole group. They send the sick one away. We've seen packs chase a sick coyote out onto ice floes. Then when we get the animal, they test positive for distemper."

The picture fits, Ruth explains. Because the later stage of distemper has neurologic involvement, wild animals with the disease behave oddly.

Being out in the open in the middle of the day is a common sign, she tells me. Sometimes the animals look disoriented or confused. Often they're unafraid of people.

"Problem is," she says, "I can't bring a coyote with distemper back here around my other animals. It's so contagious. And if he's lying down on the ice, he's likely too far gone to be helped anyway. What needs to happen is he needs to be euthanized so that he doesn't infect more animals and so that somebody doesn't think he's a pet dog that needs rescuing. You'd be surprised how often that kind of thing happens. Wild coyote. Distemper. Frozen lake. That's a dangerous combination when a well-meaning person gets involved."

"I'll call the DNR back," she tells me. "They need to handle this, and they know me. And anyways, I turn seventy in two weeks. I'm not chancing it and riding a snowmobile out on that lake. I'm done with that crazy stuff."

"I think it's frozen pretty solid," I tell her. "I've seen lots of people riding snowmobiles out to their ice-fishing huts."

"Lots of people are stupid," she tells me. "I'll call the DNR. They'll send someone out."

I hang up. Look back through the binoculars out to the ice. Every few minutes the coyote raises its head. Points its nose in a different direction. Sniffs. Lies back down. I hadn't bargained for the fact that my intervention in this situation was going to get him killed.

I text my brother back, looking for a way out.

Nobody wants an animal around that could spread disease, he writes. *I mean, unknown what the natural course here would be, but right now it sounds like it is going to freeze to death out there, in which case putting an end to it would be merciful.*

Thirty minutes later a man named Jeff shows up at my door wearing Levi's, a hooded sweatshirt, and a camouflage baseball cap with DNR embroidered on the front. He's carrying an enormous shotgun. I hand him my binoculars. Point his gaze to the dark spot of coyote on the ice. "Okay," he says. "You understand I'm going out there to dispatch it." It's a statement, not a question, but I gather from it that he's had other people in my same state of befuddlement. Other people who thought they'd help an animal and instead they help it die. *Dispatch*, I think. *Euthanize.* The way we use language to distance ourselves from our unpleasant actions.

He starts across the lake on foot, gun slung over his shoulder. I see his steps break through patches of ice as mine have done. He stops abruptly when they do, and his gait changes into a slow, cautious shuffle. Step-by-step he makes his way. His large figure grows smaller the closer he gets to the coyote. When he's maybe a hundred yards away, the coyote sits up. Jeff pauses. Slowly lifts his gun to his shoulder. He is standing ramrod straight, utterly still. He peers through the gunsight. I think I've never in my life seen a man so still. He is a statue of a hunter. These things we do that make us good at our jobs that other people can't quite fathom. I keep my cool when patients call me awful names. I sit and talk calmly with them as they rave about poisonings and medical experimentation and the presence of spies. Jeff stands more still than a human can stand and aims his gun.

And then the animal bolts. Jeff keeps his gun trained on the running coyote, but he does not shoot. After a moment or two he lowers his gun and starts back to shore.

"I don't know," Jeff tells me before he leaves. "He really took off running when he got wind of me. Maybe he wasn't sick after all."

I feel giddy with relief at the getaway but remain unsettled. Of course it's still possible that the coyote is sick and now will just find another place to die, comfortably—for me—out of my field of vision. But now what swirls around me is the certainty we all had—Ruth, Jeff, my brother, me—that there was something wrong with this animal, that the situation was potentially dangerous, and that the only thing to be done was to *dispatch.* To *euthanize.* To get rid of this one erratically behaving animal in the name of safety.

Maybe he wasn't sick after all, Jeff had said, but what if the wind had not shifted and the coyote hadn't caught the scent, hadn't sat up and run before Jeff raised his gun and fired a shot aimed true?

I think, too, about how easily I'd been convinced that killing the animal was a necessary measure when the concept of risk was introduced. I would have been sickened at the idea of someone shooting the coyote for sport. Would have felt uneasy at the idea of killing this animal to prevent him from freezing to death. On the one hand, it might spare the coyote some misery. On the other hand, the natural world is full of brutal moments of cruelty. To intervene in this lone instance—when every minute across the globe weaker chicks are pushed out of nests by stronger siblings or baby seals are tossed between orcas as playthings before they're consumed—would very clearly have been more about assuaging our human distress at having to watch an animal suffer than about alleviating suffering in the animal world in any measurable way.

It was when Ruth invoked danger that the argument shifted for me, quickly and completely. A well-meaning soul might venture out on the ice. A compassionate person. A child, even. Someone who mistook the coyote for a beloved pet, wayward and disoriented on the ice, in need of rescue. Sick wild animal. Cracking ice. The risk suddenly became too great. The necessary action became clear, bolstered by the rationalization of certainty. He's clearly sick anyway. Dying, to be sure. He won't survive out there, exposed and vulnerable. There's nothing for him to eat. He's been abandoned by his pack, who had no choice but to protect themselves. There's only one possible outcome, and it's the best thing for all involved.

When the specter of risk was raised, I easily justified the necessity of an action that one hour earlier would have sickened me to see.

The lesson here is an important one. I'm no monster. Just as most judges who invoke harsh sentences and most citizens who call for them must not be. Fear is as powerful a force in driving human action as any that exists. And the sense of being able to reduce risk, to protect, to assert control over chaos and catastrophe, is one of the most alluring of promises, no matter how false and illusory it may be.

We say with certainty that the drastic measures we take in the name of safety are justified, but there are inevitable moments when even the experts among us are wrong. *It's easy to do this job*, Cara Smith had said of her work at the Cook County Jail, *if you presume everyone's guilty.* How can we undertake the severe measures that we do if we don't know for sure? Sacrificing to protect the pack is one thing when we know we've diagnosed the situation correctly, when we know that the measures we take will, in fact, protect the larger group.

Had the coyote been shot, I would have been comfortable with the story we'd all told ourselves. The story of necessity and safety. I would never have allowed myself to think for a minute that the animal might not be sick, not sick at all. That it might have been behaving oddly for some reason we can't understand, as there are many moments in the lives of wild animals we don't understand. But since I'd made the call, since I'd put in motion Jeff with his shotgun, if I'd caused the coyote to die, I would have settled comfortably into the certainty that it had been the right thing to do.

If we're wrong about the way we enact corrections, if we've locked up our sick and most vulnerable, have punished people not because they're bad but because they're ill, if we've caged and manacled our children, if we've treated our fellow citizens with brutality, if solitary confinement is, in fact, torture and we've enacted it on 80,000 of our fellow men and women every year, if we've taken people capable of doing horrible things and instead of attempting to repair their damaged selves have turned them into people capable of doing far worse, if we've had women in childbirth labor in shackles and have taken their babies from them, have separated parents from their children for years on end, if we've done all these things and they turn out to have been the *wrong* things to do for the *wrong* reasons with the *wrong* outcomes, the truth would ravage us.

So better not to look. Better not to consider. Better not to acknowledge. Better not to rectify. Better simply to trust and believe. This has happened throughout human history, of course. The lengths that human beings will go to in order to convince themselves that their ill treatment of others is justified—necessary, even. There are such moments in our country's own history that we now look back upon in shame. Extreme measures of oppression taken in the name of safety.

We do not wish to look closely at how our policies affect the lives of those who are affected by them, other than to look with vengeance and from the comfort of our certitude. Other than to absolve ourselves in the name of safety. The behavior is not normal. The coyote is sick. Safer for everyone if he's shot.

In medicine we aim to manage risk in a more strategic way. One means of decision making we rely upon is a premise called "number needed to treat." Number needed to treat is a statistical analysis that computes how many people would need to be treated in order for one person to benefit from a medical intervention or for one negative outcome to be avoided. For example, current screening-mammography guidelines are heavily influenced by number-needed-to-treat assessments. How many women do we need to screen with mammography before we prevent one death from breast cancer?

In a 2014 summary, the U.S. Preventive Services Task Force calculated that if women ages 39 to 49 were routinely screened, nearly 2,000 of them would need to receive mammograms in order to prevent one breast-cancer death. In women ages 60 to 69, that number is less than 400. The national task force's recommendation, therefore, was that younger women should get screening mammograms only if they "place a higher value on the potential benefit than the potential harms"—harms that include a high rate of false positives leading to further screening, potentially invasive procedures, increased health-care costs, and a whole lot of worry. The goal is to put fewer people through unnecessary measures in order to provide protection to those whom the intervention will help.

It may seem that saving even one life is worth it, no matter how high the number needed to treat. That the benefit of one saved life outweighs any cost. This is, in fact, the stance we take in corrections. Better to err on the side of safety. Better to lock up more people for longer than to let one potentially dangerous person go free.

But in medicine we make hard choices in weighing these kinds of odds as a matter of routine. We recognize that resources are finite and that there need to be limits to the lengths to which we'll go in order to chase down and prevent small numbers of negative outcomes. Being sensible about those limits allows us to direct our resources toward interventions that are proven to be the most effective for the largest numbers of people. The emotional stakes in these decisions are high; the stories involved can be heartbreaking. Herein, for example, is the terminally ill young father whose cancer has not responded to any standard treatments and whose last-ditch appeal to try an experimental therapy that costs hundreds of thousands of dollars is denied. But medicine aims to acknowledge that in gambling on a treatment whose odds of success are terribly low, the money we ante up is pulled from funds that could otherwise provide less expensive, proven, high-impact treatments to large numbers of other people who need them (including, inevitably, other young parents whose deaths would be just as keenly mourned).

In medicine we also acknowledge that we're willing to accept a small amount of risk. This is something that I feel acutely each time I must make the decision to discharge someone from the hospital who came in with thoughts of wanting to harm himself or someone else. There is no proven way for me to be 100 percent sure that the patients I send home will be safe. In fact, in one of the more painful moments of my career, I once discharged a patient who, that very same day, got into an argument with his wife and leaped out of their thirteenth-floor apartment window to his death. *There are two kinds of psychiatrists,* Robert I. Simon said of his own profession. *Those who have had patients commit suicide and those who will.* In the wake of my patient's death, I reviewed my decisions. I had a supervisor read the patient's chart. I discussed the case with other doctors. No one could find anything that would have indicated to me that my patient was not safe to be discharged. So I take solace in the scores of people I've treated who've stayed safe after leaving the hospital, even as I know that working with the sickest patients means that some measure of risk always remains. Yet I cannot keep them safely locked on my hospital ward forever. It would not be right to do so.

For many years Dr. Kevin Baill was the chief psychiatrist on one of the units in the psychiatric hospital where I work. Because our patients have the capacity to be dangerous—whether suicidal, homicidal, aggressive, or self-injurious—he has spent a great deal of time making decisions as to how best to mitigate risk on the unit.

"There are always rare but bad events that happen in any hospital," he tells me. "Some of them are very serious—severe assaults, overdoses, suicide attempts, self-injury. The question we wrestle with is, given how rare these are and how few people are actually involved in these serious events, does it make sense to put *all* patients through additional searches or additional restrictions in order to prevent these very few events? They *are* very serious. And yet they are also very rare."

And there is a cost to all patients when additional restrictions are imposed. As a recent example, one of the hospital units on which I practice is a beautiful new wing. It was designed with incredible care to keep patients safe, given the risks associated with a highly psychiatrically ill population. This means that measures were intentionally taken to prevent patients from harming themselves—the stream of water in the showers, for example, emerges from a special fitting sunk into the wall so that people cannot hang themselves from showerheads. For the same reason, door handles flip down when any weight is put upon them. Furniture is designed to be heavy and shaped in a way that would be too awkward to lift and throw, and on the off chance someone succeeded in doing so, chairs and sofas are rounded, without sharp edges, and are made out of a dense foam material that gives under pressure so that if someone were struck by it, no serious injuries would result. In another suicide-prevention measure, if anything—a sheet or towel or item of clothing—is put over the top of a door, an alarm sounds to notify the staff.

Then one day, more than three years after the unit opened, a patient found a way to wedge a sheet into an open window and attempted to hang himself. Fortunately, he did not succeed. The windows had already been specially designed to open only a few inches to prevent people from trying to jump—either as a means of escape or as a suicide attempt—but the incident highlighted a potential vulnerability in the design (and, I suppose, a potential liability for the hospital). In the weeks that followed, all windows were summarily sealed shut so that no patient could any longer crack a window to get a bit of fresh air.

"If you picture a bell curve," Dr. Baill says to me, "most of the risk falls in the center. So we can aim our restrictions and interventions to prevent as best we can the most common dangers, the most common bad events. And we do a good job of that. But like any curve, it trails off for a ways in either direction." In other words, there are a small number of cases on the edges of the bell curve. On one side it means a small number of our most seriously ill patients would be safe with essentially no special precautions. No locks on the unit doors, no fifteen-minute checks, no special fixtures, no restrictions on property or visitation. On the other side, it means that there are people who will remain a risk even as more and more restrictions are applied. If no visitors were allowed. If patients were not able to wear their own clothing but instead had to dress in hospital garb. If walks on the grounds with staff were discontinued. If no one were allowed to bring in any personal belongings. The environment would be less therapeutic for the vast majority of our patients, and nonetheless some "bad events" would still occur.

"So," Dr. Baill continues, "the question we are always asking ourselves is, how far do we chase the long tail of risk?" And at what cost?

In corrections up to now, our answer has been that we're willing to chase the tail of risk however far it goes. That a nearly infinite number of incarcerations—or years of incarceration—can be justified if one act of violence is prevented.

So, too, in the justification for the use of solitary confinement. In a conversation I had with A. T. Wall, the former director of the Rhode

Island Department of Corrections, he raised the fact that any policy changes he would want to make to reduce the use of solitary confinement would have to go up against the Brotherhood of Correctional Officers. That union consistently cites the safety of their officers as their primary concern and on that basis has refused to implement any such changes. "Institutional memory is long," he told me. "And Rhode Island is small. So even if it's been fifteen years since a correctional officer was killed by an inmate, there are still workers in our state's prisons who were friends with the officer who was killed."

Yet just as we cannot offer the dying father an expensive experimental treatment that could instead pay for thousands of vaccines that could save many lives, we cannot subject people to torture due to institutional memory, especially when we know that science doesn't even support the claim that solitary confinement reduces violence.

In countless realms of our society—medicine, speed limits, alcohol consumption, junk-food intake, scuba diving, the stock market—we're willing to accept a modicum of risk without substantially curtailing our behavior. Except when it comes to curtailing the freedoms of others whom we perceive to be a danger. Whom we perceive to be less than us. Whom we perceive to be bad.

"Does it weigh on you," I ask Randi Rosenqvist in the middle of her driving tour, "that you're the one saying whether or not these men who've proved themselves to be terrifically dangerous are fit to leave prison? Whether or not they'll be a threat to society? Do you worry about what if you're wrong and something horrible happens?"

Dr. Rosenqvist whizzes us around a curve of the famed Oslo ski-jump hill and across a small bridge. Her response is matter of fact. "Of course I'll sometimes get it wrong. I'm human. But I'm the best in Norway at risk assessment. So no one can get it right all the time, but at least I'll know they'll have had the best possible evaluation.

"Ah! There's the river!" she says proudly. "Don't you find that it's very beautiful here?"

WHEN I WAS in my residency training, I worked for a month on the psychiatric consultation service of the local children's hospital. This meant that our team of clinicians provided psychiatric care to children who were hospitalized for medical or surgical reasons. Sometimes the patients fell squarely in both medical and psychiatric camps—critically malnourished eating-disorder patients, for instance, or kids who'd survived suicide attempts—in which case mental-health care was an obvious and crucial component of the treatment plan. Other patients were kids with serious illnesses—cancer or diabetes, for example—who were struggling to cope with the emotional strain that accompanies chronic childhood disease.

But there was also an equally prominent third group of children we'd see: those with medically unexplained symptoms. Herein were kids—typically with gastrointestinal or neurologic complaints—whose tests came back normal and yet whose symptoms persisted. A fifth-grade boy with debilitating bouts of abdominal cramping, for instance, who'd undergone a dizzying range of dietary changes and blood tests and imaging studies and medication trials, none of which had revealed any abnormality or explanatory cause. And an eighth-grade girl who developed a sudden and complete weakness in one leg but whose neurological examination was entirely normal.

In these cases, after medical causes had been exhaustively explored and ruled out one by one, we were likely to be called in to perform a full psychiatric assessment of the patient. Often this ended with an explanation that the symptoms the child was experiencing were psychiatric in their origins.

These patients were not feigning their symptoms. But their conditions were physical manifestations of psychological distress. Which meant they would not improve—and often had not improved—with non-psychiatric medical treatment.

Delivering this news to patients and family members is a delicate task. It can feel as if you're saying to the patient, "Your suffering is all in your head." It can feel like a failure to appreciate that the child is really in pain, really unable to muster the strength or balance to walk. For parents it can feel like danger—as if something gravely serious is being overlooked. Or it can evoke fury—and a belief that the inability to locate a medical cause must be the result of the medical staff's incompetence. To everyone it can feel like an accusation.

The attending psychiatrist from whom I was learning during this monthlong rotation was the head of the consultation service, Dr. Emily Katz. Dr. Katz is unassuming but blindingly smart. Board-certified in both pediatrics and child psychiatry, she brings a deep knowledge of both medical and psychiatric illness to each of her cases, which makes her particularly well suited for children whose unexplained symptoms sit at this very nexus.

Watching Dr. Katz deftly deliver information about the psychiatric etiology of these children's symptoms taught me an enormous amount about honoring our patients' experiences and suffering while being unafraid to steer them away from ineffectual treatments and toward proven and helpful ones, no matter how difficult such a shift in thinking might be to accept. Her method has relevance here, in considering how our nation must move forward to rectify the current injustices and inefficiencies of our criminal justice system.

"We have good news," Dr. Katz would often begin in talking to patients and their families. "We can now say for sure that your child does not have a brain tumor," or epilepsy, or Crohn's disease, or, or, or . . . She would then segue into a respectful explanation of the symptoms' origins as psychiatric rather than medical, stressing that the pain and distress the child was experiencing were real. She would then seamlessly continue, stressing again the good news that there was no evidence of a life-threatening medical illness, and then begin to talk about how we were also fortunate to have proven and effective ways of treating symptoms that presented in this way. That with psychotherapy and sometimes also with psychiatric medications, the symptoms would ameliorate. In many instances they might go away altogether. There would be hard work ahead, to be sure. The symptoms wouldn't disappear on their own. But we've identified the problem, and we know the treatment we need to begin to address it, and we can get started on that together now. *Good news.*

The honesty of this practice always moved me just as much if not more than its effectiveness. In the big picture, all parents want their children to be healthy. Are desperate for it, even. It *is* astonishingly good news to learn that your child does not have a gravely dangerous infirmity or disease. And yet parents often argue against this finding, sometimes out of umbrage but mostly out of fear. *That's impossible,* they say. *Surely there are other tests to be done.* Or, *If you can't figure out what's wrong with him, we'll go to someone who can.* Dr. Katz gently but firmly underscores the illogic—and the potential damage—in this response. This news should come as a relief. You can let go of the fear. You can stop putting your child through endless needle sticks and scopes. You can stop doing the litany of medical interventions that were having no effect, and now we can move on to something that will actually address what's going on and has a good chance of making the situation better. Gradually even resistant parents begin to see that they're pushing for the opposite of what they actually want. They want more than anything for their child to be healthy but somehow have gotten to a position where they're pressing for the doctors to declare the child to be unwell.

This is where we are with our current prison system in America. We know that the system is broken. *Every single link in the chain is broken,* my colleague said to me, *and by that I mean broken beyond repair.*

To which I say, *Good news.*

We know now that there are proven solutions to this problem. People view prisons as a necessary evil. They may well be necessary, but they need not be evil. They need not imprison so many vulnerable people whose real offense is not having any power or agency in our system. They need not employ practices like solitary confinement, like nutraloaf, like youth detention, like family separation. Our prisons need not ruin the mental health—and the futures—of so many. Other countries have transformed dysfunctional prisons into effective, humane systems that render people far less likely to reoffend. This problem is not an impossible one without a solution. It only remains impossible to fix if we insist upon continuing to meet violence with vengeance, if we cannot give up our drive to harm those who've done harm. If we continue on this path, we're like the parents who relentlessly continue to seek out gastrointestinal medications and procedures for their child's abdominal pain when the answer lies not in treating his stomach but in treating his mind.

We should not allow our fear to let us lose sight of our big-picture desires. We desperately want less risk and more safety. Countries like Norway and Sweden offer us another choice. *Good news.*

To avail ourselves of that choice, we must first be honest. "Not everything that is faced can be changed," wrote James Baldwin, "but nothing can be changed until it is faced." We must face the fact that our current practices of incarceration in America are ineffectual and inhumane. We must face the truth that we have endorsed policies that mean our fellow human beings live their lives in cages. We must face that there are children, even as I write these words, who stand on toilets, calling out to other voices in the darkness and waiting for an answer.

ACKNOWLEDGMENTS

The world of prisons was a foreign land to me when I began this project. I owe thanks to the many people who welcomed me into it with trust, among them: A. T. Wall, Dr. Lou Cerbo, Deputy Warden John Adams, Deputy Warden Jack Vicino, Sheriff Thomas Dart, Elli Montgomery, Cara Smith, Annie Fitzgerald, Hanke Gratteau, Dena Williams, Bradley Brockmann, Sarah Martino, Dr. Barry Wall, Dr. Gerard Gagné, and Dr. Pedro Tactacan.

The Yale Department of Law and Psychiatry was my intellectual home as I first began grappling with the issues at the center of this book. I am grateful in particular to Dr. Howard Zonana, Dr. Alexander Westphal, Dr. Reena Kapoor, and Hope Metcalf for including me in their rigorous and vibrant discussions about the confluence of mental illness and the criminal legal system.

Critical enthusiasm and support for this project came to me from the John Simon Guggenheim Foundation and the Cogut Institute for the Humanities at Brown University, as well as from Mary Cappello, Sienna Craig, Linda Gregerson, Dr. Jerome Groopman, Scott and Janice Montross, Mike Smith, and Arnold Weinstein. My dear and brilliant friend Kathleen Hughes was a generous and sharp reader in addition to having been my childhood idol and an absolutely stupendous Little League shortstop.

Seeing firsthand the Scandinavian perspective on corrections was a transformational experience. I owe great thanks to Niklas Åhman, Mattias Andersen, Are Høidal, Maria Lindström, Dr. Lars Håkan Nilsson, Helene Nyman, Dr. Lars Stefan Østerholm, Dr. Randi Rosenqvist, Don Specter, Jan Strømnes, and Dr. Brie Williams for sharing their work and their philosophies with me.

Conversations with Drs. Jennifer Friedman, Sheetal Ghiardi, Jake Kurtis, Curt LaFrance, Elizabeth Loewenhaupt, Rendueles Villalba, Laura Whiteley, and Diana Lidofsky offered invaluable medical and psychological insights into the overlapping territories of medicine and justice.

My coworkers shared their personal observations and experiences with me, among them Dave Boyan, Chris Boxx, Kim Brunelle, Kelly Granada, Jo-Ann Holmes, Ariel Webb, and Dr. Martin Furman.

I could not have been luckier than to have Christianne Cejas, Anna Medina, Maryll Toufanian, and Nader John Toufanian as my team of legal experts.

I am deeply grateful to my wonderful agent and friend Kris Dahl, and to Janie Fleming and Maureen Sugden, whose various editorial perspectives made this book far better than it might have been. Caroline Sydney deserves special recognition for her deep attention to these pages, and for diligently answering years of various far-flung questions. Working with my editor, Virginia Smith Younce, was one of the greatest pleasures I've had as a writer. This manuscript benefited at every stage from her astuteness, her rigor, and her devotion. Thank you, Ginny.

Dr. Stuart Grassian and Jean Casella are both forces of good, shining lights into the most isolated corners of our nation's jails and prisons. I learned much from their crucial work and appreciate their openness in talking and corresponding with me.

My most profound gratitude is reserved for Deborah Salem Smith, who read every word of this book many times as well as heaps of others that landed on the cutting room floor. The great Annie Dillard maintained that it was discourteous for writers to convey to readers the struggles borne in bringing a book to fruition, but I feel that rule does not apply here, where honest acknowledgment is the intent. In the many years of researching and writing this book, I often found myself *within a dark wood where the straight way was lost*. At every turn, Deborah, with her exceptionally keen editorial eye, diagnosed various stumbling blocks to which I was blind and asked essential questions that helped me forge a clearer path forward. Throughout the process she offered me patience, wisdom, generosity, lucidity, and encouragement in equal measure. *I love, to-night—love you . . . and "time and sense"—and fading things, and things that do not fade.*

NOTES

Epigraph

ix **"I would hurl"**: Richard Wright, *American Hunger* (New York: HarperCollins, 1982), introduction.

Introduction

4 not the case: President Donald Trump set off a firestorm of protest from mental-health professionals when, in the wake of two episodes of gun violence in twenty-four hours, he attributed their cause to mentally ill "monsters."

Research confirms that mental illness is not to blame for America's mass shootings. In a 2018 report of active shooters, the FBI "found that 25 percent of active shooters had been diagnosed with a mental illness. And of those diagnosed, only three shooters had been diagnosed with a psychotic disorder." Similarly, "in a 2015 study that examined 235 people who committed or tried to commit mass killings, only 22 percent could be considered" as having a mental illness. William Wan and Lindsey Bever, "Are Video Games or Mental Illness Causing America's Mass Shootings? No, Research Shows," *Washington Post*, August 5, 2019, washingtonpost.com/health/2019/08/05/is-mental-illness-causing-americas-mass-shootings-no-research-shows/.

A report in the Associated Press concurred, stating that mental-health experts "repeated what they have said after previous mass shootings: Most people with mental illness are not violent, they are far more likely to be victims of violent crime than perpetrators, and access to firearms is a big part of the problem." The report went on to say that "the U.S. Secret Service released a report on mass public attacks in 2018, finding that 'no single profile' can be used 'to predict who will engage in targeted violence' and 'mental illness, alone, is not a risk factor.'" Carla K. Johnson, "Experts: Mental Illness Not Main Driver of Mass Shootings," AP News, August 5, 2019, apnews.com/b8ce29d88543479bbd4894f5a39cc686.

7 **known to exacerbate:** J. L. Metzner and J. Fellner, "Solitary Confinement and Mental Illness in U.S. Prisons: A Challenge for Medical Ethics," *Journal of the American Academy of Psychiatry and the Law* 38, no. 1 (2010): 104–8, jaapl.org/content/38/1/104.full.

11 **"You're getting out":** Five Mualimm-Ak, "Invisible," in *Hell Is a Very Small Place: Voices from Solitary Confinement*, ed. Jean Casella, James Ridgeway, and Sarah Shourd (New York: New Press, 2016), 150.

13 **"psychiatrists know more":** Matt Ford, "Invoking Kalief Browder, Justice Kennedy Denounces Solitary Confinement," *Atlantic*, June 18, 2015, theatlantic.com/politics/archive/2015/06/kalief-browder-justice-kennedy-solitary-confinement/396320/.

Chapter One: Three Hots and a Cot

19 **a *rational* understanding:** A rational understanding is a nuanced assessment and aims to establish whether a person accused of a crime possesses the ability to weigh options and make lucid decisions about his case. Here I am asked to assess, for instance, whether the defendant can logically discuss what it means to plead guilty versus not guilty and what would happen in a case after either of those pleas was entered. I must gauge whether he understands the potential consequences of his charges, what entering into a plea bargain means, and whether he can logically weigh the risks and benefits involved in doing so.

25 **now well understood:** "Deinstitutionalization: A Psychiatric 'Titanic,'" *Frontline*, May 10, 2005, pbs.org/wgbh/pages/frontline/shows/asylums/special/excerpt.html.

25 **Today our jails:** Treatment Advocacy Center, "How Many Individuals with Serious Mental Illness Are in Jails and Prisons?," updated November 2014, treatmentadvocacycenter.org/storage/documents/backgrounders/how%20many%20individuals%20with%20serious%20mental%20illness%20are%20in%20jails%20and%20prisons%20final.pdf.

27 **cost per detainee:** Rhode Island Department of Corrections: Institutions & Operations: Facilities: John J. Moran Medium Security Facility, n.d., accessed August 14, 2019, doc.ri.gov/institutions/facilities/moran.php.

27 **nearly five times:** Rhode Island Department of Corrections: Institutions & Operations: Facilities: High Security Center, n.d., accessed August 14, 2019, doc.ri.gov/institutions/facilities/hsc.php.

28 **through the cracks:** Overextended psychiatrists and/or inadequate mental-health services are a problem in countless facilities across the country, not just in Rhode Island. Some states have been mandated to improve their services after lawsuits were brought against them. Others are trying novel approaches. But the problem of ill inmates slipping through the cracks is widespread. Christine Herman, "Most

Inmates with Mental Illness Still Wait for Decent Care," NPR.org, February 3, 2019, npr.org/sections/health-shots/2019/02/03/690872394/most-inmates-with-mental -illness-still-wait-for-decent-care.

30 earn their way: There are often obstacles for inmates attempting to "earn their way" out of seg. A 2018 lawsuit filed on behalf of Nicolas Reyes asserted that Red Onion State Prison in Virginia held Mr. Reyes in solitary confinement for more than twelve years because he did not complete the required programming to return to general population. The programming, called "Step Down," requires reading and writing in English. Mr. Reyes is a native Spanish speaker who can neither read nor write. Michael Sainato, "Mentally Ill US Prisoner Held in Solitary Lost Ability to Speak, Lawsuit Alleges," *Guardian,* September 4, 2019, theguardian.com/us-news /2019/sep/04/virginia-prisons-solitary-confinement-tyquine-lee.

33 "as a toy": Dr. Stuart Grassian told me a story of being involved in monitoring Attica Prison for a class-action lawsuit and touring the Solitary Housing Unit (SHU). He said, "At some point I growled at the prison officer who was leading me through the SHU, 'Do you see what you're looking at here? These are the patients of a state psychiatric hospital! These aren't the worst of the worst. They're the sickest of the sick."

36 We would never: Forensic psychiatrist Dr. Debra Pinals has spoken convincingly and at length about this topic.

Chapter Two: How Are You on the Fourth of July?

56 have post-traumatic stress disorder: Frank Valentino Ferdik and Hayden P. Smith, "Correctional Officer Safety and Wellness Literature Synthesis," National Institute of Justice, July 2017, ncjrs.gov/pdffiles1/nij/250484.pdf.

56 what renders officers: Ariana Nesbit, M.D., and Hal S. Wortzel, M.D., "Correctional Officer Suicide: An Overlooked Problem," *American Academy of Psychiatry and the Law Newsletter* 43, no. 2 (April 2018): 19, 24.

56 risk factors identified: Don Thompson, "California Examines Prison Guards' High Suicide Rate," Associated Press, January 9, 2018, apnews.com/96fdc27aea0c401 ea590b1c74162c43a.

56 officer Scott Jones: Thompson, "California Examines Prison Guards' High Suicide Rate."

Chapter Three: Since Eleven

66 *Ex ante* methods: Martha Craven Nussbaum, *Anger and Forgiveness: Resentment, Generosity, Justice* (New York: Oxford University Press, 2016), 179–83.

67 "Let us consider elevators": Nussbaum, *Anger and Forgiveness*, 180.

67 **U.S. recidivism rate:** Mariel Alper, Matthew R. Durose, and Joshua Markman, "2018 Update on Prisoner Recidivism: A 9-Year Follow-up Period (2005–2014)," Bureau of Justice Statistics, May 23, 2018, bjs.gov/index.cfm?ty=pbdetail&iid=6266.

Chapter Four: You Got Kids?

69 **draconian drug laws:** Dave Collins, "Connecticut Eases Penalties for Most Drug Possession Crimes," Associated Press, June 30, 2015, apnews.com/0216054dc 6cd453f8d83de8bbc84caeb.

69 **heroin or crack:** Few pieces of legislation criminalized drug use more severely and with more racial prejudice than the Anti-Drug Abuse Act (ADAA) of 1986. The ADAA established mandatory minimum sentences for crack cocaine that were a hundred times more severe than the sentences set for equivalent amounts of powder cocaine. Crack was more readily accessible in poor, predominantly African American communities, whereas powder cocaine was more often used by affluent white Americans. These harsh sentencing disparities produced an additive effect when combined with the fact that white Americans are far less likely to be arrested, prosecuted, convicted, or imprisoned for drug offenses. The ACLU highlighted this troubling imbalance in a 2006 report, noting that twenty years after the implementation of the ADAA, African Americans made up "15% of the country's drug users" but constituted "37% of those arrested for drug violations, 59% of those convicted, and 74% of those sentenced to prison for a drug offense." When sentences related to crack were isolated, it was found that "more than 80% of the defendants sentenced for crack offenses [were] African American, despite the fact that more than 66% of crack users [were] white or Hispanic." The impact of the ADAA was devastating and profound. In 1986, before the ADAA's mandatory minimum sentencing for crack cocaine offenses began, "the average federal drug sentence for African Americans was 11% higher than for whites." A mere four years later, "the average federal drug sentence for African Americans was 49% higher" than for whites. "Cracks in the System: 20 Years of the Unjust Federal Crack Cocaine Law," ACLU, October 2006, aclu.org /other/cracks-system-20-years-unjust-federal-crack-cocaine-law.

70 **"unintended detrimental outcomes":** University of Texas at Austin, "Risks of Harm from Spanking Confirmed by Analysis of 5 Decades of Research," *ScienceDaily*, April 25, 2016, sciencedaily.com/releases/2016/04/160425143106.htm.

71 **bail-for-profit is denounced:** Adam Liptak, "Illegal Globally, Bail for Profit Remains in U.S.," *New York Times*, January 29, 2008, nytimes.com/2008/01/29/us /29bail.html.

72 **an annual cost:** Bernadette Rabuy, "Pretrial Detention Costs $13.6 Billion Each Year," Prison Policy Initiative, February 7, 2017, prisonpolicy.org/blog/2017/02/07 /pretrial_cost/.

72 mothers who are: Lauren Glaze and Laura Maruschak, "Parents in Prison and Their Minor Children," Bureau of Justice Statistics Special Report, March 30, 2010, bjs.gov/content/pub/pdf/pptmc.pdf.

72 caregiver in jail: Shaila Dewan, "Family Separation: It's a Problem for U.S. Citizens, Too," *New York Times*, June 22, 2018, nytimes.com/2018/06/22/us/family -separation-americans-prison-jail.html.

73 mothers are locked: The National Bail Out collective has been so concerned about the devastating ripple effects of the pretrial detention of parents that it sponsors National Bail Out Days on Mother's Day and Father's Day, in which community donations are raised to free incarcerated parents who have remained locked up simply due to poverty. In its mission statement, the collective cites not only the social and emotional costs of separating detainees from their families but also the financial burden of incarcerating people who have not been convicted of anything—an estimated $14 billion per year. Cherise Fanno Burdeen, "How Money Bail Traps the Poor," *Atlantic*, April 12, 2016, theatlantic.com/politics/archive/2016/04/the-dangerous -domino-effect-of-not-making-bail/477906/.

74 face increased odds: Elizabeth J. Gifford et al., "Association of Parental Incarceration with Psychiatric and Functional Outcomes of Young Adults," JAMA Network Open, August 23, 2019, jamanetwork.com/journals/jamanetworkopen/fullarticle /2748665.

74 downstream consequences that: Nia Heard-Garris et al., "Health Care Use and Health Behaviors Among Young Adults with History of Parental Incarceration," *Pediatrics* 142, no. 3 (September 1, 2018): e20174314, doi.org/10.1542/peds.2017-4314.

74 wasted time and: Because pretrial detention is by definition temporary, many jails do not feel compelled to provide educational and occupational programming. The health care available may also be minimal, aimed at crisis management only, because jail clinicians may deem the management of chronic medical conditions as outside their purview during this stopgap time.

74 fare far worse: "Presumption of Guilt: The Global Overuse of Pretrial Detention," Open Society Justice Initiative, 2014, justiceinitiative.org/uploads/de4c18f8 -ccc1-4eba-9374-e5c850a07efd/presumption-guilt-09032014.pdf.

75 only nineteen did: "The Troubling Spread of Plea-Bargaining from America to the World," *Economist*, November 9, 2017, economist.com/international/2017/11/09 /the-troubling-spread-of-plea-bargaining-from-america-to-the-world.

79 ravaging one's body: I'm grateful to the writer and teacher Kaia Stern, discussions with whom first led me to consider the relative cruelties of corporal punishment versus incarceration.

82 "world without prisons": Rachel Kushner, "Is Prison Necessary? Ruth Wilson Gilmore Might Change Your Mind," *New York Times Magazine*, April 17, 2019, nytimes .com/2019/04/17/magazine/prison-abolition-ruth-wilson-gilmore.html.

83 another violent crime: Keith Wattley, "Trump's Criminal Justice Reform Is a Step in the Wrong Direction," *New York Times*, December 4, 2018, nytimes.com/2018 /12/04/opinion/trump-criminal-justice-reform.html.

83 *least* likely group: Robert Weisberg, Debbie A. Mukamal, and Jordan D. Segall, "Life in Limbo: An Examination of Parole Release for Prisoners Serving Life Sentences with the Possibility of Parole in California," Stanford Law School, Stanford Criminal Justice Center, September 2011, law.stanford.edu/wp-content/uploads /sites/default/files/publication/259833/doc/slspublic/SCJC%20Lifer%20Parole %20Release%20Sept%202011.pdf.

Chapter Five: Jail, Not Yale

88 fundamental, structural changes: Charles A. Nelson, Charles H. Zeanah, and Nathan A. Fox, "How Early Experience Shapes Human Development: The Case of Psychosocial Deprivation," *Neural Plasticity* 2019 (January 15, 2019), doi.org/10.1155 /2019/1676285.

88 brains that differ: Nelson et al., "How Early Experience Shapes Human Development."

89 "brain awaits instructions": Nelson et al., "How Early Experience Shapes Human Development."

89 "their developmental vulnerability": "Solitary Confinement of Juvenile Offenders," Juvenile Justice Reform Committee, American Academy of Child and Adolescent Psychiatry, April 2012, aacap.org/aacap/Policy_Statements/2012/Solitary_Confine ment_of_Juvenile_Offenders.aspx.

90 "majority of suicides": Even jailed teenagers who are in the general population, not in segregation, have a markedly elevated risk of suicide. Between 2000 and 2014, jailed adolescents were two to three times more likely to kill themselves than unincarcerated young people were. Steven Reinberg, "Teens' Odds for Suicide May Triple While in Jail: Study," accessed August 14, 2019, consumer.healthday.com/gen eral-health-information-16/suicide-health-news-646/teens-odds-for-suicide-may -triple-while-in-jail-study-741928.html.

90 addicted more quickly: Linda Patia Spear, "Consequences of Adolescent Use of Alcohol and Other Drugs: Studies Using Rodent Models," *Neuroscience and Biobehavioral Reviews* 70 (November 2016): 228–43, doi.org/10.1016/j.neubiorev.2016.07.026.

90 compared with adults: Spear, "Consequences of Adolescent Use of Alcohol and Other Drugs."

90 circuitry to mature: S. B. Johnson, R. W. Blum, and J. N. Giedd, "Adolescent Maturity and the Brain: The Promise and Pitfalls of Neuroscience Research in Adolescent Health Policy," *Journal of Adolescent Health* 45, no. 3 (2009): 216–21, doi:10.1016/j.jadohealth.2009.05.016.

91 episode of problematic: Linda Patia Spear, "The Adolescent Brain and Age-Related Behavioral Manifestations," *Neuroscience & Biobehavioral Reviews* 24, no. 4 (June 1, 2000): 417–63, doi.org/10.1016/S0149-7634(00)00014-2.

91 "participation in delinquency": Spear, "The Adolescent Brain and Age-Related Behavioral Manifestations."

92 Many contract STDs: "Young people aged 15–24 years acquire half of all new STDs and . . . one in four sexually active adolescent females has an STD, such as chlamydia or human papillomavirus (HPV)." "STDs in Adolescents and Young Adults," Sexually Transmitted Diseases Surveillance 2017, Centers for Disease Control and Prevention, January 11, 2019, cdc.gov/std/stats17/adolescents.htm.

92 "surviving the lottery": Spear, "The Adolescent Brain and Age-Related Behavioral Manifestations."

93 two landmark decisions: *New York Times* Editorial Board, "Justice at Last for the Youngest Inmates?," *New York Times*, November 20, 2017, nytimes.com/2017/11/20/opinion/life-sentence-youth-parole.html.

93 In the first, *Graham v. Florida*: *Graham v. Florida*, 560 U.S. 48 (2010).

93 In the second, *Miller v. Alabama*: *Miller v. Alabama,* 567 U.S. 460 (2012).

93 a "safety valve": "Fact Sheet: Sentencing Legislation," dcor.state.ga.us/sites/default/files/Sentencing%20Legislation.pdf.

94 racial prejudice influences: Josh Rovner, "Racial Disparities in Youth Commitments and Arrests," Sentencing Project, April 1, 2016, sentencingproject.org/publications/racial-disparities-in-youth-commitments-and-arrests/.

95 for non-homicide cases: Jennifer L. Eberhardt and Aneeta Rattan, "The Race Factor in Trying Juveniles as Adults," *New York Times*, June 5, 2012, nytimes.com/roomfordebate/2012/06/05/when-to-punish-a-young-offender-and-when-to-rehabilitate/the-race-factor-in-trying-juveniles-as-adults?mcubz=1.

95 the disturbing role: Aneeta Rattan et al., "Race and the Fragility of the Legal Distinction Between Juveniles and Adults," *PLOS One* 7, no. 5 (May 23, 2012): e36680, doi.org/10.1371/journal.pone.0036680.

96 a white offender: This very bias might have been at play in a 2017 incident in Claremont, New Hampshire, in which a group of boys allegedly tied a rope around the neck of an eight-year-old biracial boy, taunted him with racial slurs, and kicked him off a picnic table, leaving him injured and hanging. Rachel Siegel, "8-Year-Old Biracial Boy Was Hanged from Rope by N.H. Teenagers Because of His Race, Family Says," *Washington Post*, September 13, 2017, washingtonpost.com/news/morning-mix /wp/2017/09/13/8-year-old-boy-was-hung-from-rope-by-n-h-teenagers-because -of-his-race-family-says/?outputType=amp.

Mark Chase, the police chief of Claremont—a town whose population is listed as 95.2 percent white—was quoted in the immediate aftermath of the incident as urging leniency for the boys who were the accused perpetrators. "These people need to be protected," Chase said of the suspects. "Mistakes they made as young children should not have to follow them for the rest of their life." Jordan Cuddemi, "Claremont Police Still Mum About Boy's Injuries," *Valley News,* September 12, 2017, vnews.com/Public -Wants-More-Info-From-Claremont-Authorities-12353456.

Compare Chase's response to the case of Travion Blount, an African American teenager. When Blount was fifteen years old, he and two eighteen-year-olds went to a house party and, at gunpoint, robbed the teenagers who were there. They stole cash, cell phones, and marijuana. One of the eighteen-year-olds hit a victim with the butt of his gun, but no shots were fired. Blount was offered a plea bargain in which he would serve a sentence of eighteen years in prison in exchange for pleading guilty. He turned it down and elected to take his case to trial. He lost and was found guilty. The court deemed that everyone in the group committed two felonies— armed robbery and abduction—each time that any of them held a gun to one of the twelve people who were robbed. Blount received a mandatory sentence of 118 years in prison without parole for the twenty-four firearms counts. In addition, the court added six life sentences to the 118 years. At age fifteen, for robbing a party with two older kids, Travion Blount has been sentenced to live the rest of his life in prison. Alex Stamm, "15-Year-Old Gets Six Life Sentences?," ACLU, November 22, 2013, aclu.org/blog/criminal-law-reform/15-year-old-gets-six-life-sentences.

96 solitary, Macy writes: Enceno Macy, "Scarred by Solitary," in *Hell Is a Very Small Place: Voices from Solitary Confinement*, ed. Jean Casella, James Ridgeway, and Sarah Shourd (New York: New Press, 2016), 121–24.

99 "about missing people": The separation of children from their parents is not merely a poignant detail. There is quite a bit of psychiatric literature on the neurodevelop- mental and psychiatric sequellae of parental presence versus absence, specifically during periods of stress. In examining the disruption of the hypothalamic-pituitary- adrenocortical system and the autonomic nervous system—the systems that govern stress responses and the stress hormone cortisol—"responsive caregiving seem[s] to buffer the young infant's cortisol responses and enhance recovery during stressful situ- ations." Rodent studies show that the presence of the rat mother "'regulated' the physi- ology of the rat pup. . . . Maternal proximity during a critical period of the rat pup's development operated to downregulate the rat pup's physiological functioning." In other words, in rodent experiments the mere presence of the mother calmed the biological stress response of the child. Nelson, Zeanah, and Fox, "How Early Experience Shapes Human Development."

Chapter Six: Born on Third Base

100 posted a tweet: Malcolm Jenkins (@malcolmjenkins), "Before we enjoy this game let's take some time to ponder that more than 60% of the prison population are people of color. The NFL is made up of 70% African Americans. What you witness on the field does not represent the reality of everyday America. We are the anomalies." Twitter, August 9, 2018, twitter.com/malcolmjenkins/status/1027667736095322113?lang=en.

Chapter Seven: The Architecture of Control

110 fully functional guillotines: Evan Andrews, "8 Things You May Not Know About the Guillotine," History.com, September 15, 2014, updated August 30, 2018, history.com/news/8-things-you-may-not-know-about-the-guillotine.

110 "hung in chains": "Letter from Paul Revere to Jeremy Belknap, circa 1798." Massachusetts Historical Society Collections Online, n.d., accessed August 14, 2019, masshist.org/database/99.

111 carnival-like spectacles where: "History of Racial Injustice: Public Spectacle Lynchings," Equal Justice Initiative, February 14, 2018, eji.org/history-racial-injustice -public-spectacle-lynchings.

111 "reproduce[d] the crime": Michel Foucault, *Discipline and Punish: The Birth of the Prison* (New York: Vintage Books, 1995), 55.

112 failed nineteenth-century: "Pennsylvania System: Penology." *Encyclopaedia Britannica*, n.d., accessed August 14, 2019, britannica.com/topic/Pennsylvania-system.

112 cell was illuminated: David Brown, "Tourists Make Time for a Philadelphia Museum Where Felons Did Theirs," *Washington Post,* January 14, 2016, washington post.com/lifestyle/travel/this-philly-museum-offers-a-chilling-look-at-how -we-used-to-punish-inmates/2016/01/14/a0c0360e-9880-11e5-8917-653b65c809eb _story.html?utm_term=.88c62e1bec4c.

112 in vermin-infested conditions: Norman Bruce Johnston, Kenneth Finkel, and Jeffrey A. Cohen, *Eastern State Penitentiary: Crucible of Good Intentions* (Philadelphia: Philadelphia Museum of Art for the Eastern State Penitentiary Task Force of the Preservation Coalition of Greater Philadelphia, 1994).

113 "man buried alive": Charles Dickens, *American Notes for General Circulation* (London: Chapman and Hall, 1913), gutenberg.org/files/675/675-h/675-h.htm.

113 as "maniac-making": *Times* (London) editorial, November 25, 1843.

113 **recognized as inhumane:** Stuart Grassian, "Psychiatric Effects of Solitary Confinement," *Washington University Journal of Law & Policy* 22 (January 2006): 60.

114 **issue at hand:** In the case of *In re Medley,* James Medley had been sentenced to death for murder and was sent to the state penitentiary to be kept in solitary confinement until his execution. Medley's case was reviewed, and he argued that he should not be kept in solitary confinement because that particular punishment had not been authorized by the statute under which he was sentenced. The Court agreed, finding that the previous statute did not authorize solitary confinement. The state argued that this change in the law was unimportant; the Court disagreed, stating that solitary confinement was awful, and thus a severe—not unimportant—punishment. Because of this position, they found that Medley's constitutional rights were violated by his being kept in solitary. The constitutionality of solitary confinement was not addressed more broadly because that had not been the issue before the Court.

114 **When Alcatraz opened:** Laura Sullivan, "Timeline: Solitary Confinement in U.S. Prisons," NPR.org, July 26, 2006, npr.org/templates/story/story.php?storyId= 5579901.

114 **an Illinois prison:** Sullivan, "Timeline."

114 **facilities followed suit:** Sullivan, "Timeline."

114 **in forty-four states:** Jean Casella, "Solitary 101," Solitary Watch, 2012, 63, solitarywatch.org/wp-content/uploads/2012/11/Solitary-Watch-Solitary-101.pdf.

116 **assessment of rehabilitation:** Joan Petersilia, "Beyond the Prison Bubble," National Institute of Justice, November 2, 2011, nij.gov:443/journals/268/pages/prison-bubble.aspx.

116 **grim new management:** Private prison corporations saw an opportunity in prisons that were over capacity and began building facilities and securing government contracts. The for-profit nature of these prisons—in addition to the jobs that the facilities infused into the communities where they were built—created a system in which the incentive was to fill the prison beds and keep them full, not to keep people out of prison and rehabilitate them to return to the community as quickly as possible. Seminal writings on this topic include Eric Schlosser's 1998 *Atlantic* article, "The Prison-Industrial Complex," *Atlantic,* December 1, 1998, theatlantic.com/magazine /archive/1998/12/the-prison-industrial-complex/304669/, Shane Bauer's *American Prison: A Reporter's Undercover Journey into the Business of Punishment*, and prison abolitionist Ruth Wilson Gilmore's searing book *Golden Gulag.*

117 **80,000 and 100,000:** Sarah Baumgartel et al., "Time-In-Cell: The ASCA-Liman 2014 National Survey of Administrative Segregation in Prison," Yale Law School, Public Law Research Paper No. 552, September 9, 2015, doi.org/10.2139 /ssrn.2655627.

117 **time in segregation:** Allen J. Beck, "Use of Restrictive Housing in U.S. Prisons and Jails, 2011–12," Bureau of Justice Statistics, October 23, 2015, bjs.gov/index.cfm ?ty=pbdetail&iid=5434.

117 **"serious psychological distress":** Beck, "Use of Restrictive Housing in U.S. Prisons and Jails, 2011–12," bjs.gov/index.cfm?ty=pbdetail&iid=5433.

117 **punishments for nonviolent:** Five Mualimm-Ak, "Invisible," in *Hell Is a Very Small Place: Voices from Solitary Confinement*, ed. Jean Casella, James Ridgeway, and Sarah Shourd (New York: New Press, 2016), 8.

117 **too many envelopes:** Nancy Bilyeau, "Solitary Confinement Policies at 'Tipping Point' in U.S., Say Reformers," Crime Report, April 27, 2018, thecrimereport .org/2018/04/27/solitary-confinement-policies-at-a-tipping-point-in-us-say -advocates/.

117 **cash without permission:** Casella, "Solitary 101."

118 **"too many pencils":** Mualimm-Ak, "Invisible," 149.

118 **"apple seeds contain arsenic":** Apple seeds do not in fact contain arsenic but rather amygdalin, a compound of cyanide and sugar that converts to hydrogen cyanide in the digestive system.

119 **rationale behind this:** Emily Bazelon, "The Shame of Solitary Confinement," *New York Times Magazine*, February 19, 2015, nytimes.com/2015/02/19/magazine /the-shame-of-solitary-confinement.html.

119 *years* **in solitary:** Bazelon, "The Shame of Solitary Confinement."

120 **forced to forfeit:** Dave Maass, "Hundreds of South Carolina Inmates Sent to Solitary Confinement Over Facebook," Electronic Frontier Foundation, February 12, 2015, eff.org/deeplinks/2015/02/hundreds-south-carolina-inmates-sent-solitary -confinement-over-facebook.

120 **Level 1 offense:** Correspondence relating to South Carolina Department of Corrections Social Media Policy/Procedure, various dates, eff.org/files/2015/02/12 /scdc_social_media_discipline_policies.pdf.

121 **"architecture of control":** Mark Binelli, "Inside America's Toughest Federal Prison," *New York Times Magazine*, March 26, 2015, nytimes.com/2015/03/29/magazine /inside-americas-toughest-federal-prison.html.

121 **"very stark environment":** Binelli, "Inside America's Toughest Federal Prison."

121 **"UN special rapporteurs":** Jean Theoharis, "Torture of a Student," in *Hell Is a Very Small Place: Voices from Solitary Confinement*, ed. Jean Casella, James Ridgeway, and Sarah Shourd (New York: New Press, 2016), 196.

121 Mississippi's notorious Parchman: Parchman is an institution with a grisly and complicated history that began in 1905. William Faulkner described the prison as "destination doom." It was designed as a self-sufficient plantation whose profits benefited the state. The convicts held in Parchman worked six days a week, were subjected to brutal whippings, and were monitored in the cotton fields by so-called trusty-shooters, the prison's most violent inmates, who were given guns and told to keep the other prisoners in line. "Inside Mississippi's Notorious Parchman Prison," *PBS NewsHour,* January 29, 2018, pbs.org/newshour/arts/inside-mississippis -notorious-parchman-prison.

Until a landmark case in 1971 brought an end to the practice, forced labor at Parchman continued. The state justified the slavelike status of its convict workers by the fact that the Thirteenth Amendment specifically outlaws slavery and involuntary servitude "except as a punishment for crime whereof the party shall have been duly convicted." Forced labor may have ended at Parchman, but there is still good reason to consider the prison farm "destination doom." In her hauntingly beautiful novel, *Sing, Unburied, Sing,* Jesmyn Ward writes of modern-day Parchman that "it's like a snake that sheds its skin. The outside look different when the scales change, but the inside always the same." And the most notorious unit in Parchman was Unit 32.

122 its inhumane conditions: "ACLU Strikes Deal to Shutter Notorious Unit 32 at Mississippi State Penitentiary," ACLU, June 4, 2010, aclu.org/press-releases/aclu -strikes-deal-shutter-notorious-unit-32-mississippi-state-penitentiary.

122 "severely psychotic prisoners": In 2005 the ACLU expanded its efforts and filed a new suit on behalf of all Unit 32 inmates—"more than 1,000 men in permanent lockdown status, many of them for decades, in some of the harshest and most violent conditions in the nation." Challenging the ubiquitous assertion about supermax detainees—that the men held in Unit 32 were "the worst of the worst"—the ACLU asserted that "a significant percentage of Unit 32's prisoners were held there only because they had HIV, were seriously mentally ill or needed protective custody." Despite the range of reasons for which men were housed in Unit 32, all of them "were permanently locked down in solitary confinement with no possibility of earning their way to a less restrictive environment through good behavior."

122 the third murder: "Earnest Lee Hargon Murdered in Prison," WLBT News, August 29, 2007, wlbt.com/story/7001300/earnest-lee-hargon-murdered-in-prison.

122 "inmates are voiceless": Jesse Wilson, "Loneliness Is a Destroyer of Humanity," in *Hell Is a Very Small Place: Voices from Solitary Confinement,* ed. Jean Casella, James Ridgeway, and Sarah Shourd (New York: New Press, 2016), 81–82.

122 "non-insane smearing feces": "Inside America's Toughest Federal Prison," the 2015 *New York Times* feature article on ADX, bolsters Wilson's claim, highlighting the work of forensic psychiatrist Dr. Doris Gundersen. Gundersen was permitted to enter ADX as part of a legal team that had filed an Eighth Amendment lawsuit against the federal Bureau of Prisons, asserting that ADX was failing to properly diagnose and treat its prisoners with serious mental illness. "After evaluating 45 prisoners," the *Times* report explains, Gundersen "estimated that 70 percent met the criteria for at least one serious mental illness." This number is absolutely shocking, and one of two conclusions must be drawn from it. Either it's the severely mentally ill population that is being sent to this "end of the line" or "the end of the line" is quite literally maddening. Gundersen reported that she had seen "inmates who swallowed razor blades, inmates who were left for days or weeks shackled to their beds (where they were routinely allowed to soil themselves)," as well as "an inmate who ate his own feces so regularly that staff psychiatrists made a special note only when he did so with unusual 'voracity.'"

Chapter Eight: The Lost People

124 The stated goal of: "Northern Correctional Institution Administrative Segregation Program," n.d., accessed January 2, 2020, law.umich.edu/special/policyclearinghouse /Documents/Description%20of%20Northern%20Program%20ocr.pdf.

125 tether chain runs: Leo Arnone et al., "Northern Correctional Institution Inmate Handbook," n.d., accessed January 2, 2020, law.umich.edu/special/policyclearinghouse /Documents/CT%20-%20Northern%20Handbook.pdf.

125 "make an impression": Yale Visual Law Program, "The Worst of the Worst: Portrait of a Supermax," Yale Visual Law Program, Vimeo, accessed August 15, 2019, vimeo.com/54826024.

126 "a lasting impression": Yale Visual Law Program, "The Worst of the Worst: Portrait of a Supermax."

127 "Abandon all hope": Dante Alighieri, *The Divine Comedy of Dante Alighieri*, 1: *Inferno*, translated by John Donaldson Sinclair (New York: Oxford University Press, 1961).

136 are particularly vulnerable: A 2016 *New Yorker* article described in harrowing detail how inmates in Florida prisons had been tortured, even to the point of death, by correctional officers whose abusive actions were actively and systemically covered up and denied. Eyal Press, "Madness," *New Yorker*, April 25, 2016, newyorker .com/magazine/2016/05/02/the-torturing-of-mentally-ill-prisoners.

137 monkeys as subjects: H. F. Harlow and S. J. Suomi, "Induced Depression in Monkeys," *Behavioral Biology* 12, no. 3 (November 1974): 273–96.

137 destructive and debilitating: H. F. Harlow, R. O. Dodsworth, and M. K. Harlow, "Total Social Isolation in Monkeys," *Proceedings of the National Academy of Sciences of the United States of America* 54, no. 1 (July 1965): 90–97.

137 "demonstrated the effectiveness": William T. McKinney, Stephen J. Suomi, and Harry F. Harlow, "Vertical-Chamber Confinement of Juvenile-Age Rhesus Monkeys: A Study in Experimental Psychopathology," *Archives of General Psychiatry* 26, no. 3 (March 1, 1972): 223–28, doi.org/10.1001/archpsyc.1972.01750210031006.

137 "common sense results": Deborah Blum, *Monkey Wars* (New York: Oxford University Press, 1995).

138 "the limited environment": Yale Visual Law Program, "The Worst of the Worst: Portrait of a Supermax."

144 "that little lacuna": William Blake, "A Sentence Worse than Death," *Hell Is a Very Small Place: Voices from Solitary Confinement*, ed. Jean Casella, James Ridgeway, and Sarah Shourd (New York: New Press, 2016), 28.

148 sentences induce hopelessness: Anasseril E. Daniel, "Preventing Suicide in Prison: A Collaborative Responsibility of Administrative, Custodial, and Clinical Staff," *Journal of the American Academy of Psychiatry and the Law Online* 34, no. 2 (June 1, 2006): 165–75.

150 "evil in return": W. H. Auden, "September 1, 1939," Poets.org. poets.org/poem/september-1-1939.

152 "sun never sets": Jack Henry Abbott, *In the Belly of the Beast: Letters from Prison* (New York: Vintage Books, 1991), 85.

153 allegations at Rikers: James C. McKinley Jr., "In Rape Case at Rikers: Did Guards Turn a Blind Eye?," *New York Times*, September 21, 2017, nytimes.com/2017/09/21/nyregion/rikers-rape-case-guards.html.

Chapter Nine: Minnows and Killer Whales

157 assaulted by fellow: Dave Gilson, "What We Know About Violence in America's Prisons," *Mother Jones*, Crime and Justice, July/August 2016, motherjones.com/politics/2016/06/attacks-and-assaults-behind-bars-cca-private-prisons/.

157 of "rampant violence": Campbell Robertson, "An Alabama Prison's Unrelenting Descent into Violence," *New York Times*, March 28, 2017, nytimes.com/2017/03/28/us/alabama-prison-violence.html.

157 unrelated inmate murders: "Third Inmate Death in 10 Days at ADOC Facilities in Elmore County," WSFA News, February 27, 2017, updated August 12, 2017, wsfa.com/story/34609657/third-inmate-death-in-10-days-at-adoc-facilities-in-elmore-county.

158 a marine ecosystem: "Act V," *This American Life*, August 9, 2002, thisamericanlife.org/218/act-v.

NOTES

158 sentence was extended: *In the Matter of Jehan Abdur-Raheem, Appellant, v. Louis Mann, as Superintendent of Shawangunk Correctional Facility, et al., Respondents,* February 14, 1995, law.cornell.edu/nyctap/I95_0022.htm.

161 brainwash American POWs: Stuart Grassian, "Psychiatric Effects of Solitary Confinement," *Washington University Journal of Law & Policy* 22 (January 2006).

161 "verge of murder": Richard Evelyn Byrd, *Alone: The Classic Polar Adventure* (Washington, DC: Island Press/Shearwater Books, 2003), 16.

162 United States Navy: E. K. Eric Gunderson, "Emotional Symptoms in Extremely Isolated Groups," *Archives of General Psychiatry* 9 (1963): 362–68.

162 "agitated confusional state": Grassian, "Psychiatric Effects of Solitary Confinement."

162 "Specific Psychiatric Syndrome": Grassian, "Psychiatric Effects of Solitary Confinement."

163 "the most traumatic": C. F. Villa, "Living in the SHU," in *Hell Is a Very Small Place: Voices from Solitary Confinement,* ed. Jean Casella, James Ridgeway, and Sarah Shourd (New York: New Press, 2016), 36.

163 "another tailspin and": Prison officials have made observations similar to Grassian's without knowing they were looking at a defined syndrome. The consistency of description is uncanny. Dr. Milton Meltzer, former chief medical officer at Alcatraz in the 1950s, described a spectrum of psychiatric dysfunction in isolated Alcatraz prisoners, despite stating that inmates there were rarely held in administrative segregation for more than a week. Symptoms he observed ranged "from occasional tense pacing, restlessness and sense of inner tension with noise making, yelling, banging and assaultiveness at one extreme, to a kind of regressed, dissociated, withdrawn, hypnoid and reverie-like state at the other." Leo H. Bartemeier and Group for the Advancement of Psychiatry, eds., *Psychiatry and Public Affairs* (New Brunswick, NJ: Aldine Transaction, 2011).

164 "Lack of respect": Grassian, "Psychiatric Effects of Solitary Confinement," referring to C. S. Mullin and H. J. M. Connery, "Psychological Study at an Antarctic IGY Station," *Armed Forces Medical Journal* 10 (1959): 290–96 .

164 "antisocial and psychotic": Grassian, "Psychiatric Effects of Solitary Confinement," referring to M. W. Wright, J. Chylinski, G. C. Sisler, and B. Quarrington, "Personality Factors in the Selection of Civilians for Isolated Northern Stations: A Follow-up Study," *Canadian Psychologist* 8 (1967): 23–31.

164 "aggression toward staff": Grassian, "Psychiatric Effects of Solitary Confinement."

164 "pathologically 'stimulation seeking'": Grassian, "Psychiatric Effects of Solitary Confinement."

165 **prison violence diminishes:** Casella, Ridgeway, and Shourd, *Hell Is a Very Small Place: Voices from Solitary Confinement*, 12.

176 **Prison Writing Contest:** Thomas Bartlett Whitaker, "A Nothing Would Do as Well," PEN America, July 7, 2014.

176 **even polite grievances:** There are numerous well-documented cases of the medical and mental-health needs of prisoners being ignored. Sometimes this results in death. In February 2019, U.S. District Judge Myron H. Thompson ruled that the Alabama Department of Corrections violated the Eighth Amendment and showed "deliberate indifference" in failing to appropriately monitor and treat prisoners in solitary confinement who either were known to be mentally ill or whose mental health deteriorated substantially as a result of being held in segregation. Of note, Judge Thompson wrote in his opinion that "the psychological harms of isolation can affect anyone subjected to segregation, including those who were not previously mentally ill." "SPLC, Victims' Families Demand Comprehensive ADOC Reform as Suicide Toll Increases," Southern Poverty Law Center, February 8, 2019, splcenter.org/news/2019/02/08/splc-victims %E2%80%99-families-demand-comprehensive-adoc-reform-suicide-toll-increases.

Chapter Ten: Imagine Your Bathroom

181 **theory of self-psychology:** Heinz Kohut, *The Analysis of the Self* (New York: International University Press, 1971); Heinz Kohut, *How Does Analysis Cure?* (Chicago: University of Chicago Press, 1984).

182 **philosopher Lisa Guenther:** Lisa Guenther, "The Living Death of Solitary Confinement," *Opinionator* (blog), August 26, 2012, opinionator.blogs.nytimes.com /2012/08/26/the-living-death-of-solitary-confinement/.

183–84 **"I counted bricks":** Five Mualimm-Ak, "Invisible," in *Hell Is a Very Small Place: Voices from Solitary Confinement*, ed. Jean Casella, James Ridgeway, and Sarah Shourd (New York: New Press, 2016), 148.

184 **first-ever congressional hearing:** Mark Binelli, "Inside America's Toughest Federal Prison," *New York Times Magazine*, March 26, 2015, nytimes.com/2015/03/29 /magazine/inside-americas-toughest-federal-prison.html.

184 **mitigate the symptoms:** Daphne Simeon et al., "Feeling Unreal: A Depersonalization Disorder Update of 117 Cases," *Journal of Clinical Psychiatry* 64, no. 9 (September 2003): 990–97.

185 **"sense of helplessness":** Glen O. Gabbard, *Psychodynamic Psychiatry in Clinical Practice*, 4th ed. (Washington, DC: American Psychiatric Publishing, 2005), 284.

185 **likely to harm:** Fatos Kaba et al., "Solitary Confinement and Risk of Self-Harm Among Jail Inmates," *American Journal of Public Health* 104, no. 3 (March 2014): 442–47, doi.org/10.2105/AJPH.2013.301742.

188 fear among Cubans: Melissa Block and Marisa Peñaloza, "Improved U.S.-Cuba Relations Are Creating a Surge of Cuban Migrants," NPR.org, October 24, 2016, npr .org/sections/parallels/2016/10/24/498840762/why-improved-u-s-cuba-relations -are-creating-a-surge-of-cuban-migrants.

189 "machetes, jagged oars": Block and Peñaloza, "Improved U.S.-Cuba Relations Are Creating a Surge of Cuban Migrants."

189 Neuroscience tells us: Stephanie Cacioppo, John P. Capitanio, and John T. Cacioppo, "Toward a Neurology of Loneliness," *Psychological Bulletin* 140, no. 6 (November 2014): 1464–1504, doi.org/10.1037/a0037618.

189 stress-response system: A. H. Mohammed et al., "Environmental Enrichment and the Brain," *Progress in Brain Research* 138 (2002): 109–133, doi.org/10.1016/S0079 -6123(02)38074-9.

191 impulsive, less well adjusted: Elsewhere in the world, the risks of such an approach are recognized and measures are taken to counteract the damages of isolation. Sweden's Sollentuna Remand Prison, for example, holds some of its inmates in "restriction" if they believe that having them in the general prison population has the potential to sabotage an ongoing investigation. Restriction is a form of pretrial detention that is essentially isolation, but the government openly acknowledges the detrimental consequences of isolation and employs specific measures to reduce that damage. In the Sollentuna prison, there are four staff members whose entire job is dedicated to spending time with people in isolation. They spend four hours per day engaging detainees in restriction in conversation and activities including playing games, painting, and cooking.

Niklas Åhman, the assistant governor, or warden, for Sollentuna Remand Prison, tells me that without these mitigating interventions people held in restriction get sleepy, just as Rivers described to Dr. Gagné. "They sleep all day and all night," Åhman underscores. "They are always tired. They are not eating. The joy of life is pouring out of them." The engagement with staff, then, is meant to prevent this type of decompensation.

Helen, a nurse at the prison, puts her role bluntly: "We have to take action to deter the craziness of isolation."

193 "lose their minds": Binelli, "Inside America's Toughest Federal Prison."

193 "From the starving": Bertolt Brecht, "To Those Born Later," translated by Steven Monte, eportfolios.macaulay.cuny.edu/smonte10/files/2010/08/Brecht-Born-Later.pdf.

Chapter Eleven: Nutraloaf

197 can change opinions: One example of the capacity for a rapid, dramatic change in public opinion and simultaneous changes in critical policies would be the gay-rights movement. In 1988 only 11.6 percent of Americans supported marriage equality. Just thirty years later, in 2018, that number had skyrocketed to 68 percent. Visibility of human stories—and empathic connection with gay couples as people with fundamental human rights no different from those of straight people—fueled this shift in perception and in policy. Vedantam Shankar et al., "Radically Normal: How Gay Rights Activists Changed the Minds of Their Opponents," NPR.org, April 3, 2019, npr.org /2019/04/03/709567750/radically-normal-how-gay-rights-activists-changed -the-minds-of-their-opponents.

198 baby in jail: An estimated fourteen hundred babies per year are born to women in correctional custody in our country. Some mothers labor and give birth in shackles. Others do so in solitary confinement. The psychosocial implications for both mothers separated from their babies and children who have incarcerated mothers are immense. Children born to women in prison not only lack the presence of their mothers, they also are likely to wind up in foster care and have an increased risk of becoming incarcerated themselves. Jonathan Lambert, "Pregnant Behind Bars: What We Do and Don't Know About Pregnancy and Incarceration," NPR.org, March 21, 2019, npr.org/sections/health-shots/2019/03/21/705587775/pregnant-behind-bars-what -we-do-and-dont-know-about-pregnancy-and-incarceration.

The 2019 case of Tammy Jackson was a particularly egregious example of labor and delivery in a correctional facility. Seven hours after Ms. Jackson, a mentally ill woman incarcerated in Broward County, Florida, requested medical attention from officers, she delivered her full-term baby by herself in an isolation cell. Ms. Jackson had previously had a cesarean section and thus was at heightened risk for obstetric complications during a vaginal delivery. By the time the on-call physician arrived to treat her, Ms. Jackson was holding her baby in her arms. Deanna Paul, "A Pregnant Inmate Came to Term in Jail. Lawyers Say She Was Forced to Give Birth There— Alone," *Washington Post*, May 4, 2019, washingtonpost.com/nation/2019/05/04/men tally-ill-woman-gives-birth-alone-broward-county-jail-attorney-says/?utm _term=.51fb024338a3. Sandra E. Garcia, "Ordeal of Woman Who Gave Birth in Florida Jail Cell Prompts Internal Investigation," *New York Times*, May 7, 2019, nytimes .com/2019/05/07/us/woman-gives-birth-jail-cell.html.

199 the *National Review*: "On Criminal Justice, Sessions Is Returning DOJ to the Failed Policies of the Past," *National Review* (blog), September 12, 2017, national review.com/2017/09/jeff-sessions-tough-crime-policies-already-tried-failed/.

199 by unexpected bedfellows: "A Bipartisan Summit on Criminal Justice Reform," cut50.org, March 27, 2015, cut50.org/summit1.

199 Booker and Newt: Leon Neyfakh, "Cory Booker and Newt Gingrich Want to Redefine What Is Considered a 'Violent' Crime," *Slate*, March 26, 2015, slate.com /news-and-politics/2015/03/bipartisan-summit-on-criminal-justice-reform-cory -booker-and-newt-gingrich-want-to-redefine-what-is-considered-a-violent-crime .html.

199 First Step Act: Nicholas Fandos, "Senate Passes Bipartisan Criminal Justice Bill," *New York Times,* December 18, 2018, nytimes.com/2018/12/18/us/politics/senate -criminal-justice-bill.html.

201 "you was handcuffed": In 2012 a man named Darren Rainey, who was incarcerated at the Dade Correctional Institution in Florida, collapsed and died after having been locked in a shower stall for approximately two hours with a water temperature of 180 degrees. "Rainey had burns on more than ninety percent of his body, and . . . his skin fell off at the touch." Eyal Press, "The Torturing of Mentally Ill Prisoners," *New Yorker,* April 25, 2016, newyorker.com/magazine/2016/05/02/the-torturing-of -mentally-ill-prisoners.

202 ingredients are listed: "Food as Punishment: Giving U.S. Inmates 'The Loaf' Persists," NPR.org, January 2, 2014, npr.org/sections/thesalt/2014/01/02/256605441 /punishing-inmates-with-the-loaf-persists-in-the-u-s.

203 "mechanically separated poultry": Jeff Ruby, "Dining Critic Tries Nutraloaf, the Prison Food for Misbehaving Inmates," *Chicago Magazine,* September 2010, chicago mag.com/Chicago-Magazine/September-2010/Dining-Critic-Tries-Nutraloaf -the-Prison-Food-for-Misbehaving-Inmates/.

203 another disciplinary tool: "Food as Punishment."

204 receiving food stamps: Eli Hager, "Six States Where Felons Can't Get Food Stamps," Marshall Project, February 4, 2016, themarshallproject.org/2016/02/04 /six-states-where-felons-can-t-get-food-stamps.

204 job-application process: Tammy LaGorce, "As 'Ban the Box' Spreads, Private Employers Still Have Questions," *New York Times,* November 22, 2017, nytimes.com /2017/11/22/business/small-business-criminal-record.html.

204 relax or reverse: Jacey Fortin, "Can Felons Vote? It Depends on the State," *New York Times,* April 21, 2018, nytimes.com/2018/04/21/us/felony-voting-rights -law.html.

205 ineligible to vote: The absence of these voices disempowers communities— particularly communities of color—and changes the political fabric of our country. In 2000 the state of Florida had 620,000 citizens whose right to vote had been rescinded due to felony convictions. That presidential election, which sent George W. Bush to the White House, was decided by the outcome in the state of Florida. Bush won the state by a margin of 537 votes. In the November 2018 election, Florida citizens decided via referendum to restore these voting rights, a monumental reversal. *New York Times* Editorial Board, "Florida's 1.5 Million Missing Voters," *New York Times,* January 2, 2018, nytimes.com/2018/01/02/opinion/florida-missing-voters.html.

205 **Detainees who participate:** Elizabeth Hinton, "Turn Prisons into Colleges," *New York Times*, March 6, 2018, nytimes.com/2018/03/06/opinion/prisons-colleges -education.html.

206 **overcrowded federal prison:** Oliver Roeder, "Releasing Drug Offenders Won't End Mass Incarceration," FiveThirtyEight.com, July 17, 2015, fivethirtyeight.com /features/releasing-drug-offenders-wont-end-mass-incarceration/.

208 **"back to life":** Martha Craven Nussbaum, *Anger and Forgiveness: Resentment, Generosity, Justice* (New York: Oxford University Press, 2016), 21–22.

208 **"be the soul":** Michel Foucault, *Discipline and Punish: The Birth of the Prison* (New York: Vintage Books, 1995), 16.

Chapter Twelve: Better Neighbors

212 **"most beautiful scenery":** Carla Yanni, *The Architecture of Madness: Insane Asylums in the United States* (Minneapolis: University of Minnesota Press, 2007).

212 **a broad wall of windows:** The United Nations Standard Minimum Rules for the Treatment of Prisoners state that "in all places where prisoners are required to live or work, . . . the windows shall be large enough to enable the prisoners to read or work by natural light and shall be so constructed that they can allow the entrance of fresh air whether or not there is artificial ventilation."

In contrast, in researching prison architecture I came across the beautifully named but horrifying concept of "borrowed light," described in a book about prison architecture as "this decade's major correctional breakthrough." The term refers to window-less rooms only receiving light that is reflected into them from adjacent windowed spaces. The book states that borrowed light "now factors into most inner-city proposals precisely because it allows jails to be completely walled off . . . and keeps inmates from seeing and often signaling out to the street."

James Kessler, the architect of Northern, is described as being unconvinced that detainees suffer from a lack of windows. Instead he posits a belief that the lack of natural light serves a beneficial function by pulling inmates "into a commons of directly supervised interaction." Joe Day, *Corrections and Collections: Architectures for Art and Crime* (New York: Routledge, 2013), 259.

Doris Canales, whose son was in solitary confinement for nearly twenty years, might disagree about the effects of living without natural light. She wrote of the eerie fact that her son's face had not aged over the two decades he'd been held in isolation. "Being in solitary, they get almost no sunlight," she wrote. "They're not making a lot of facial expressions either, so they don't get wrinkles. So he looked similar to how he did when he was eighteen at thirty-six." Doris Canales, "Because I Could Laugh," in *Hell Is a Very Small Place: Voices from Solitary Confinement*, ed. Jean Casella, James Ridgeway, and Sarah Shourd (New York: New Press, 2016), 142.

213 **"principle of normality"**: Are Høidal, "Normality Behind the Walls: Examples from Halden Prison," *Federal Sentencing Reporter* 31, no. 1 (October 1, 2018): 58–66, doi .org/10.1525/fsr.2018.31.1.58.

213 **Recidivism rates were high:** Mariel Alper, Matthew R. Durose, and Joshua Markman, "2018 Update on Prisoner Recidivism: A 9-Year Follow-up Period (2005– 2014)," Bureau of Justice Statistics, May 23, 2018, bjs.gov/index.cfm?ty=pbdetail& iid=6266.

213 **United Nations Standard:** "Resolution 70/175. United Nations Standard Mini- mum Rules for the Treatment of Prisoners (the Nelson Mandela Rules)," December 17, 2015, undocs.org/A/RES/70/175. The UN Minimum Standards are not legally binding but are meant to guide international and domestic law and were adopted unanimously in December 2015 by the General Assembly.

217 **theoretically be extended:** A maximum sentence of thirty years exists for crimes of genocide, war crimes, or crimes against humanity. Norway also has a pro- gram called preventive detention in which people deemed dangerous are detained and their continued dangerousness is assessed in five-year increments. "About the Norwegian Correctional Service," Kriminalomsorgen.no, accessed August 16, 2019, kriminalomsorgen.no/information-in-english.265199.no.html.

217 **challenged this threshold:** Preventive detention could theoretically extend be- yond twenty-one years, but the program was introduced in 2002 so has not yet reached the twenty-one-year threshold. Randi Rosenqvist elaborated on this fact, stating that one person currently in preventive detention "will stay here. He served a long sentence previously and was released in 1998 for about three months before committing a new homicide. There are just a few here who I would think will stay for more than twenty-one years. Mr. Breivik is among them."

217 **serving "348 years":** C. F. Villa, "Living in the SHU," in *Hell Is a Very Small Place: Voices from Solitary Confinement.*

217 **"'only have one'":** Nell Bernstein, *All Alone in the World: Children of the Incarcerated* (New York: New Press, 2007), 28.

217 **average U.S. sentence:** Justice Policy Institute, "Finding Direction: Expanding Criminal Justice Options by Considering Policies of Other Nations," April 2011, justice policy.org/uploads/justicepolicy/documents/sentencing.pdf.

218 **current U.S. numbers:** "Recidivism," National Institute of Justice, accessed Au- gust 14, 2019, nij.gov:443/topics/corrections/recidivism/pages/welcome.aspx.

218 **44 percent of American state prisoners:** Alper et al., "2018 Update on Prisoner Recidivism."

221 *edge of madness*: *Davis v. Ayala*, No. 13-1428, 576 U.S. (2015) (Kennedy, J., concurring).

224 "posh sleepaway camp": Matt Johnson, "The Super-Lux Super Max," *Foreign Policy* (blog), July 26, 2011, foreignpolicy.com/slideshow/the-super-lux-super-max/.

224 every 6.4 detainees: Association of State Correctional Administrators, "ASCA Responses: Staff to Inmate Ratio Survey," June 2010, prisonlegalnews.org/media/publications/ASCA%20Responses%20Staff%20to%20Inmate%20Ratio%20Survey%2C%20Association%20of%20State%20Correctional%20Administrators%2C%202010.pdf. The Association of State Correctional Administrators' report of one guard for every 6.4 detainees may be the true average, but the U.S. Government Accountability Office review of the Bureau of Prisons has a small section buried within it with far more dramatic numbers for an unnamed facility. The authors write that "at one high security facility we visited, we estimated there was an average of 41 inmates to one correctional officer in the SHU during a 24-hour period. This contrasts to an inmate-to-correctional-officer ratio of about 124:1 in general population housing units in the same facility during a 24-hour period." United States Government Accountability Office, "Bureau of Prisons: Improvements Needed in Bureau of Prisons' Monitoring and Evaluation of Impact of Segregated Housing," May 2013, gao.gov/assets/660/654349.pdf.

Staffing is often higher for solitary confinement than for general-population units, not because there is a higher degree of interpersonal and rehabilitative support but because of the dependency that comes with twenty-three-hour-per-day confinement. Meals must be delivered to each cell. Officers must escort prisoners to and from the shower, to and from their rec time. Any services provided to men and women held in solitary—from laundry to religious services—must be brought to them individually. Jobs—like cooking and cleaning—performed by prisoners in other facilities must be performed by hired staff in many supermax facilities. In addition, high-security prisons that house detainees in single cells cost two to three times as much to build when compared with lower-security facilities. "Paying the Price for Solitary Confinement," PrisonLegalNews.org, n.d., accessed January 2, 2020, prisonlegalnews.org/media/publications/Paying%20the%20Price%20for%20Solitary%20Confinement%20ACLU%20Factsheet%202015.pdf.

224 At Halden the guard-to-prisoner: "How Norway Turns Criminals into Good Neighbours," BBC News, July 7, 2019, bbc.com/news/stories-48885846. Casey Tolan, "Inside the Most Humane Prison in the World, Where Inmates Have Flatscreen TVs and Cells Are Like Dorms," *Splinter*, September 14, 2016, splinternews.com/inside-the-most-humane-prison-in-the-world-where-inmat-1793861894.

224 cost to hold: Jessica Benko, "The Radical Humaneness of Norway's Halden Prison," *New York Times Magazine*, March 26, 2015, nytimes.com/2015/03/29/magazine/the-radical-humaneness-of-norways-halden-prison.html.

224 cost of incarcerating: Jeffrey Ian Ross, "Supermax Prisons," *Society* 44, no. 3 (March/April 2007), convictcriminology.org/pdf/jiross/SupermaxPrisons.pdf.

224 Pelican Bay lists: "Fact Sheet: The High Cost of Solitary Confinement," Solitary Watch, n.d., accessed January 3, 2020, solitarywatch.org/wp-content/uploads/2011 /06/fact-sheet-the-high-cost-of-solitary-confinement.pdf.

224 ADX was $78,884: United States Government Accountability Office, "Bureau of Prisons: Improvements Needed in Bureau of Prisons' Monitoring and Evaluation of Impact of Segregated Housing."

224 a shocking $208,911: "Rhode Island Department of Corrections: Institutions & Operations: Facilities: High Security Center," n.d., accessed August 14, 2019, doc .ri.gov/institutions/facilities/hsc.php.

224 Norway's recidivism rate: "How Norway Turns Criminals into Good Neighbours"; Seena Fazel and Achim Wolf, "A Systematic Review of Criminal Recidivism Rates Worldwide: Current Difficulties and Recommendations for Best Practice," *PLOS One* 10, no. 6 (June 18, 2015), doi.org/10.1371/journal.pone.0130390.

225 private prison corporations: Private prisons are used by the federal government and twenty-seven states; 8.5 percent of prisoners in state and federal prisons are in private prisons. Kara Gotsch and Vinay Basti, "Capitalizing on Mass Incarceration: U.S. Growth in Private Prisons," Sentencing Project, August 2, 2018, sentencingproject.org /publications/capitalizing-on-mass-incarceration-u-s-growth-in-private-prisons/.

225 Nashville's citizens are: "Nashville, Tennessee, Population 2019," World Population Review, worldpopulationreview.com/us-cities/nashville-population/.

226 sizable immigrant communities: "Oslo Population 2019," World Population Review, worldpopulationreview.com/world-cities/oslo-population/.

226 other than Norwegian: "Oslo Population 2019."

226 personal income tax rate: "List of Countries by Personal Income Tax Rate," Trading Economics, n.d., accessed September 17, 2019, tradingeconomics.com/country -list/personal-income-tax-rate.

227 "in a cake": *The Norden—Nordic Prisons*, YouTube video (excerpt), YouTube video, October 13, 2014. youtube.com/watch?v=2g56susrNQY#t=201.

238 the prison Santa: Bernstein, *All Alone in the World*, 47.

238 reduced recidivism rates: Ryan Shanahan and Sandra Villalobos Agudelo, "The Family and Recidivism," *American Jails*, September/October 2012, prisonpolicy .org/scans/vera/the-family-and-recidivism.pdf.

239 rules for visits: "York Correctional Institution Inmate Handbook," September 30, 2010, law.umich.edu/special/policyclearinghouse/Documents/CT%20-%20Women%27s%20Facility%20Handbook.pdf.

239 "inmates the keys": *The Norden—Nordic Prisons* (excerpt).

240 securing fundamental needs: "I Did It Norway," Marshall Project, November 1, 2017, themarshallproject.org/2017/10/31/i-did-it-norway.

240 "a boring job": It might also be the first and most sustained period of education and support for prisoners who came from chaotic childhoods. Dr. Elizabeth Lowenhaupt describes how the graduation ceremony at the RI Training School, Rhode Island's juvenile detention facility, is highly emotional in that the kids who are honored are sometimes the first in their families to graduate from high school. Some of their peers have died on the streets, victims of gang violence. The Training School (which, incidentally, does not permit segregation of juveniles) has a larger budget than most state juvenile detention facilities do and it can, in certain circumstances, provide the teens held there with safety and structure that they may not have experienced had they not been incarcerated. It is important, however, to recognize this fact as a critique of the lack of opportunity that these children had and the chaotic environments from which they have come, rather than to draw the conclusion that prison is a solution to those social ills.

Chapter Thirteen: I Am Helping You

245 no dangerous people: Lill Scherdin writes of Nils Christie's work that Christie "takes as [his] starting point the fact that most of those committing atrocities [in the Holocaust] were ordinary people who found themselves enmeshed in extraordinary or abnormal social situations." In attempting to assess Norwegian guards who actively took part in death camps looking for individual monstrosity, he found none. "Instead he found the guards to be ordinary people caught in an extraordinary stressful and extreme situation. This situation opened the way for, and even encouraged, violent abuse at the same time as it blocked empathy. In a variety of ways it prevented the guards from seeing the prisoners as fellow human beings. . . . Christie went on to explore social conditions in modern societies that stop us seeing others as people like ourselves, thus creating the conditions for extreme forms of punishment and the use of the death penalty." Lill Scherdin, ed., *Capital Punishment: A Hazard to a Sustainable Criminal Justice System?* (Farnham, Surrey, UK: Ashgate, 2014).

246 "only see evil": Timothy Williams, "He Says He Got Away with 90 Murders. Now He's Confessing to Them All," *New York Times*, November 26, 2018, nytimes.com/2018/11/26/us/samuel-little-serial-killer-murderer.html.

251 no tenable way: There is, however, hope in the darkness. The Prison Law Office in California in partnership with the Vera Institute of Justice has established a program where prison officials and correctional officers from American prisons are taken on organized trips to visit prisons in Norway, Germany, and the Netherlands. The trips have led to small changes in practice in state facilities, and the hope is that the success of these initial changes will lead to larger, more sweeping philosophical changes.

Men in North Dakota prisons who are nearing their release dates can now apply to move into dormitory-style housing units, complete with doors that lock. Dashka Slater, "North Dakota's Norway Experiment," *Mother Jones* (blog), July–August 2017, mother jones.com/crime-justice/2017/07/north-dakota-norway-prisons-experiment/.

Idaho prison officials have organized opportunities for detainees and staff members to socialize together, even introducing their families to one another. They have also added couches and rugs to dayrooms, prompting one man held in an Idaho prison to say, "This is the first soft thing I've had a chance to sit on in five years." "I Did It Norway," Marshall Project.

Chapter Fourteen: Good News

259 we've enacted it: Dan Nolan and Chris Amico, "Solitary by the Numbers," *Frontline*, April 18, 2017, apps.frontline.org/solitary-by-the-numbers/index.html.

260 2,000 of them: "Final Evidence Summary: Breast Cancer: Screening—US Preventive Services Task Force," August 13, 2014, uspreventiveservicestaskforce.org /Page/SupportingDoc/breast-cancer-screening/final-evidence-summary9.

260 task force's recommendation: "Final Update Summary: Breast Cancer: Screening—US Preventive Services Task Force," January 2016, uspreventive servicestaskforce.org/Page/Document/UpdateSummaryFinal/breast-cancer -screening1.

Acknowledgments

270 discourteous for writers: Annie Dillard, *The Writing Life* (New York: Harper & Row, 1989), 7.

270 *a dark wood*: Dante Alighieri, *The Divine Comedy of Dante Alighieri*, 1: *Inferno*, translated by John Donaldson Sinclair (New York: Oxford University Press, 1961), 23.

270 *"time and sense"*: Letter from Emily Dickinson to Mrs. J. G. Holland, early August 1856(?), archive.emilydickinson.org/correspondence/holland/l185.html.

BIBLIOGRAPHY

Abbott, Jack Henry. *In the Belly of the Beast: Letters from Prison*. New York: Vintage Books, 1991.

"About the Norwegian Correctional Service." Kriminalomsorgen.no, n.d. Accessed August 16, 2019. kriminalomsorgen.no/information-in-english.265199.no.html.

"ACLU Strikes Deal to Shutter Notorious Unit 32 at Mississippi State Penitentiary." ACLU, June 4, 2010. aclu.org/press-releases/aclu-strikes-deal-shutter-notorious -unit-32-mississippi-state-penitentiary.

"Act V." *This American Life*, August 9, 2002. thisamericanlife.org/218/act-v.

Ahalt, Cyrus, and Brie Williams. "Reforming Solitary-Confinement Policy— Heeding a Presidential Call to Action." *New England Journal of Medicine* 374, no. 18 (May 5, 2016): 1704–6. doi.org/10.1056/NEJMp1601399.

Alexander, Michelle. *The New Jim Crow: Mass Incarceration in the Age of Colorblindness*. Revised edition. New York: New Press, 2012.

Alighieri, Dante. *The Divine Comedy of Dante Alighieri*, 1: *Inferno*. Translated by John Donaldson Sinclair. New York: Oxford University Press, 1961.

Allen, Danielle S. *Cuz: The Life and Times of Michael A*. New York: Liveright, 2017.

Alper, Mariel, Matthew R. Durose, and Joshua Markman. "2018 Update on Prisoner Recidivism: A 9-Year Follow-up Period (2005–2014)." Bureau of Justice Statistics. May 23, 2018. bjs.gov/index.cfm?ty=pbdetail&iid=6266.

Andrews, Evan. "8 Things You May Not Know About the Guillotine." History.com, September 15, 2014; updated August 30, 2018. history.com/news/8-things-you-may -not-know-about-the-guillotine.

Appelbaum, Kenneth L. "American Psychiatry Should Join the Call to Abolish Solitary Confinement." *Journal of the American Academy of Psychiatry and the Law Online* 43, no. 4 (December 1, 2015): 406–15.

Appelbaum, Paul S. *Almost a Revolution: Mental Health Law and the Limits of Change.* New York: Oxford University Press, 1994.

Arnone, Leo, James Dzurenda, Cheryl Cepelak, Monica Rinaldi, and Kimberly Weir. "Northern Correctional Institution Inmate Handbook," n.d. Accessed January 3, 2020. law.umich.edu/special/policyclearinghouse/Documents/CT%20 -%20Northern%20Handbook.pdf.

Associated Press. "A State-by-State Look at Juvenile Life Without Parole." July 31, 2017. apnews.com/9debc3bdc7034ad2a68e62911fba0d85.

Association of State Correctional Administrators. "ASCA Responses: Staff to Inmate Ratio Survey," June 2010. prisonlegalnews.org/media/publications/ASCA %20Responses%20Staff%20to%20Inmate%20Ratio%20Survey%2C%20Association %20of%20State%20Correctional%20Administrators%2C%202010.pdf.

Auden, W. H. "September 1, 1939." Poets.org. poets.org/poem/september-1-1939.

Barnes, T. C. "Isolation Stress in Rats and Mice as a Neuropharmacological Test." *Federation Proceedings* 18 (1959): 365.

Bartemeier, Leo H., and Group for the Advancement of Psychiatry, eds. *Psychiatry and Public Affairs.* New Brunswick, NJ: Aldine Transaction, 2011.

Bath, Eraka, Kayla Pope, Roya Ijadi-Maghsoodi, and Christopher Thomas. "Juvenile Life Without Parole: Updates on Legislative and Judicial Trends and on Facilitating Fair Sentencing." *Journal of the American Academy of Child & Adolescent Psychiatry* 54, no. 5 (May 1, 2015): 343–47. https://doi.org/10.1016/j.jaac.2015.02.011.

Bauer, Shane. *American Prison: A Reporter's Undercover Journey into the Business of Punishment.* New York: Penguin Press, 2019.

———. "My Four Months as a Private Prison Guard." *Mother Jones* (blog). July–August 2016. motherjones.com/politics/2016/06/cca-private-prisons-corrections -corporation-inmates-investigation-bauer/.

Baum, K. "'To Comfort Always': Physician Participation in Executions." *New York University Journal of Legislation and Public Policy* 5, no. 1 (2001): 47–82.

Baumgartel, Sarah, Corey Guilmette, Johanna Kalb, Diana Li, Josh Nuni, Devon E. Porter, Judith Resnik, Camille Camp, and George Camp. "Time-In-Cell: The ASCA-Liman 2014 National Survey of Administrative Segregation in Prison." Yale Law School, Public Law Research Paper No. 552, September 9, 2015. doi.org/10.2139 /ssrn.2655627.

Bazelon, Emily. "The Shame of Solitary Confinement." *New York Times Magazine*, February 19, 2015. nytimes.com/2015/02/19/magazine/the-shame-of-solitary -confinement.html.

Beck, Allen J. "Use of Restrictive Housing in U.S. Prisons and Jails, 2011–12." Bureau of Justice Statistics, October 23, 2015. bjs.gov/index.cfm?ty=pbdetail&iid= 5433.

———. "Use of Restrictive Housing in U.S. Prisons and Jails, 2011–12." Bureau of Justice Statistics, October 23, 2015. bjs.gov/index.cfm?ty=pbdetail&iid=5434.

Bernstein, Nell. *All Alone in the World: Children of the Incarcerated*. New York: New Press, 2007.

Biderman, Albert D., and Herbert Zimmer. *The Manipulation of Human Behavior*. New York: Wiley, 1961.

Bilyeau, Nancy. "Solitary Confinement Policies at 'Tipping Point' in U.S., Say Reformers." Crime Report, April 27, 2018. thecrimereport.org/2018/04/27 /solitary-confinement-policies-at-a-tipping-point-in-us-say-advocates/.

Binelli, Mark. "Inside America's Toughest Federal Prison." *New York Times Magazine*, March 26, 2015. nytimes.com/2015/03/29/magazine/inside-americas -toughest-federal-prison.html.

———. "Super Max Story of Desperate Conditions for Everyone in ADX." *People's Advocacy Council* (blog), March 31, 2015. peoplesadvocacycouncil.wordpress.com /2015/03/31/super-max-story-of-desperate-conditions-for-everyone-in-adx/.

"A Bipartisan Summit on Criminal Justice Reform." cut50.org, March 27, 2015. cut50.org/summit1.

Block, Melissa, and Marisa Peñaloza. "Improved U.S.-Cuba Relations Are Creating a Surge of Cuban Migrants." NPR.org, October 24, 2016. npr.org/sections/parallels /2016/10/24/498840762/why-improved-u-s-cuba-relations-are-creating-a-surge -of-cuban-migrants.

Blum, Deborah. *Monkey Wars*. New York: Oxford University Press, 1995.

Brecht, Bertolt. "To Those Born Later." Translated by Steven Monte. eportfolios .macaulay.cuny.edu/smonte10/files/2010/08/Brecht-Born-Later.pdf.

Breslow, Jason M. "What Does Solitary Confinement Do to Your Mind?" *Frontline*, April 22, 2014. pbs.org/wgbh/frontline/article/what-does-solitary-confinement-do -to-your-mind/.

Briggs, Jean L. *Never in Anger: Portrait of an Eskimo Family*. Cambridge, MA: Harvard University Press, 1975.

Brooks, Megan. "Brain Lesions May Explain Criminal Behavior." Medscape, December 20, 2017. medscape.com/viewarticle/890413.

Brown, David. "Tourists Make Time for a Philadelphia Museum Where Felons Did Theirs." *Washington Post*, January 14, 2016. washingtonpost.com/lifestyle/travel /this-philly-museum-offers-a-chilling-look-at-how-we-used-to-punish-inmates /2016/01/14/a0c0360e-9880-11e5-8917-653b65c809eb_story.html?utm _term=.88c62e1bec4c.

Brownfield, Charles A. *Isolation: Effects of Restricted Sensory and Social Environments on Human Beings*. New York: Random House, 2010.

Burdeen, Cherise Fanno. "How Money Bail Traps the Poor." *Atlantic*, April 12, 2016. theatlantic.com/politics/archive/2016/04/the-dangerous-domino-effect-of-not -making-bail/477906/.

Byrd, Richard Evelyn. *Alone: The Classic Polar Adventure*. Washington, DC: Island Press/Shearwater Books, 2003.

Cacioppo, Stephanie, John P. Capitanio, and John T. Cacioppo. "Toward a Neurology of Loneliness." *Psychological Bulletin* 140, no. 6 (November 2014): 1464–1504. doi.org/10.1037/a0037618.

Carter, Stephen. "Plans Are Useless but Planning Is Essential." International Corrections & Prison Association, n.d. Accessed August 24, 2019. icpa.org/plans -are-useless-but-planning-is-essential/.

Casella, Jean. "Solitary 101," Solitary Watch, 2012. solitarywatch.org/wp-content /uploads/2012/11/Solitary-Watch-Solitary-101.pdf.

Casella, Jean, James Ridgeway, and Sarah Shourd, eds. *Hell Is a Very Small Place: Voices from Solitary Confinement*. New York: New Press, 2016.

Chen, Daniel, Tobias Moskowitz, and Kelly Shue. "Decision Making Under the Gambler's Fallacy: Evidence from Asylum Judges, Loan Officers, and Baseball Umpires." *Quarterly Journal of Economics* 131, no. 3 (August 2016). academic.oup.com /qje/article/131/3/1181/2590011.

Childress, Sarah. "Trapped in the Hole: America's Solitary Problem." *Frontline*, June 14, 2013. pbs.org/wgbh/frontline/article/trapped-in-the-hole-america-solitary -problem/.

Christie, Nils, and Howard Zehr. *Limits to Pain*. Eugene, OR: Wipf & Stock, 2007.

Clark, Andrew B. "Juvenile Solitary Confinement as a Form of Child Abuse." *Journal of the American Academy of Psychiatry and the Law Online* 45, no. 3 (September 1, 2017): 350–57.

Clark, Brant, and Captain Ashton Graybiel. "The Break-Off Phenomenon: A Feeling of Separation from the Earth Experienced by Pilots at High Altitude." *Journal of Aviation Medicine* 28 (April 1957): 6.

Cochrane, J. J., and S. J. Freeman. "Working in Arctic and Sub-Arctic Conditions: Mental Health Issues." *Canadian Journal of Psychiatry. Revue Canadienne De Psychiatrie* 34, no. 9 (December 1989): 884–90. org/10.1177/070674378903400908.

Cohen, Ronnie. "People with Brain Injuries More Likely to Go to Prison." *Huffington Post,* December 9, 2016. huffpost.com/entry/people-with-traumatic -brain-injuries-more-likely-to-go-to-prison_n_584adb00e4b04c8e2baf7559.

Coll, Steve. "The Jail Health-Care Crisis." *New Yorker,* March 4, 2019. newyorker .com/magazine/2019/03/04/the-jail-health-care-crisis.

Collins, Dave. "Connecticut Eases Penalties for Most Drug Possession Crimes." Associated Press, June 30, 2015. apnews.com/0216054dc6cd453f8d83de8bbc84caeb.

CR10 Publications Collective, ed. *Abolition Now! Ten Years of Strategy and Struggle Against the Prison Industrial Complex.* Oakland, CA: AK Press, 2008.

"Cracks in the System: 20 Years of the Unjust Federal Crack Cocaine Law." ACLU, October 2006. aclu.org/other/cracks-system-20-years-unjust-federal-crack -cocaine-law.

Crist, Carolyn. "Suicide-Risk Screening Might Cut Deaths Among Incarcerated Youth." Reuters, January 31, 2019. reuters.com/article/us-health-youth-prison -suicide/suicide-risk-screening-might-cut-deaths-among-incarcerated-youth -idUSKCN1PP2LH.

Cuddemi, Jordan. "Claremont Police Still Mum About Boy's Injuries." *Valley News,* September 12, 2017. vnews.csom/Public-Wants-More-Info-From-Claremont -Authorities-12353456.

Daniel, Anasseril E. "Preventing Suicide in Prison: A Collaborative Responsibility of Administrative, Custodial, and Clinical Staff." *Journal of the American Academy of Psychiatry and the Law Online* 34, no. 2 (June 1, 2006): 165–75.

Davis, Angela Y. *Abolition Democracy: Beyond Empire, Prisons, and Torture.* New York: Seven Stories Press, 2005.

———. *Are Prisons Obsolete?* New York: Seven Stories Press, 2003.

Day, Joe. *Corrections and Collections: Architectures for Art and Crime.* New York: Routledge, 2013.

Dayan, Colin. "Prison Hunger Strikes: Barbarous Confinement," *New York Times,* July 18, 2011. nytimes.com/2011/07/18/opinion/18dayan.html.

De Avila, Joseph. "Prison Officials Resist Push to Curb Solitary Confinement." *Wall Street Journal*, April 28, 2017. wsj.com/articles/bid-to-curb-solitary-confinement -faces-pushback-1493384400.

"Deinstitutionalization: A Psychiatric 'Titanic.'" *Frontline*, May 10, 2005. pbs.org /wgbh/pages/frontline/shows/asylums/special/excerpt.html.

Derrida, Jacques. *On Cosmopolitanism and Forgiveness*. New York: Routledge, 2001.

Dewan, Shaila. "Family Separation: It's a Problem for U.S. Citizens, Too." *New York Times*, June 22, 2018. nytimes.com/2018/06/22/us/family-separation-americans -prison-jail.html.

Dickens, Charles. *American Notes for General Circulation*. London: Chapman and Hall, 1913. gutenberg.org/files/675/675-h/675-h.htm.

Dillard, Annie. *The Writing Life*. New York: Harper & Row, 1989.

Dunaif, S. L., and P. H. Hoch. "Pseudopsychopathic Schizophrenia." *Proceedings of the Annual Meeting of the American Psychopathological Association* (January 1955): 169–95.

Durst, R., K. Jabotinsky-Rubin, and M. Fliman. "Pseudopsychopathic Schizophrenia—a Neglected Diagnostic Entity with Legal Implications." *Medicine and Law* 16, no. 3 (1997): 487–98.

"Earnest Lee Hargon Murdered in Prison." WBLT, August 29, 2007. wlbt.com /story/7001300/earnest-lee-hargon-murdered-in-prison.

Eberhardt, Jennifer L., and Aneeta Rattan. "The Race Factor in Trying Juveniles as Adults." *New York Times*, June 5, 2012. nytimes.com/roomfordebate/2012/06/05 /when-to-punish-a-young-offender-and-when-to-rehabilitate/the-race-factor-in -trying-juveniles-as-adults?mcubz=1.

Ewing, Charles Patrick. *Insanity: Murder, Madness, and the Law*. New York: Oxford University Press, 2008.

"Examining the Impact of Race and Ethnicity on the Sentencing of Juveniles in the Adult Court—Kareem L. Jordan, Tina L. Freiburger, 2010." n.d. Accessed August 26, 2019. journals.sagepub.com/doi/abs/10.1177/0887403409354738.

"Fact Sheet: The High Cost of Solitary Confinement." Solitary Watch, n.d. Accessed January 3, 2020. solitarywatch.org/wp-content/uploads/2011/06/fact-sheet-the -high-cost-of-solitary-confinement.pdf.

Fandos, Nicholas. "Senate Passes Bipartisan Criminal Justice Bill." *New York Times*, December 18, 2018. nytimes.com/2018/12/18/us/politics/senate-criminal-justice -bill.html.

Fazel, Seena, and Achim Wolf. "A Systematic Review of Criminal Recidivism Rates Worldwide: Current Difficulties and Recommendations for Best Practice." *PLOS One* 10, no. 6 (June 18, 2015). doi.org/10.1371/journal.pone.0130390.

Ferdik, Frank Valentino, and Hayden P. Smith. "Correctional Officer Safety and Wellness Literature Synthesis." National Institute of Justice, July 2017. ncjrs.gov /pdffiles1/nij/250484.pdf.

Ferguson, Robert A. *Inferno: An Anatomy of American Punishment.* Cambridge, MA: Harvard University Press, 2014.

Feuer, Alan. "Upstate County Jails Are Challenged for Sending Juveniles to Solitary." *New York Times,* July 31, 2017. nytimes.com/2017/07/31/nyregion /upstate-ny-county-jails-juveniles-solitary-confinement.html.

"Final Evidence Summary: Breast Cancer: Screening—US Preventive Services Task Force." August 13, 2014. uspreventiveservicestaskforce.org/Page /SupportingDoc/breast-cancer-screening/final-evidence-summary9.

"Final Update Summary: Breast Cancer: Screening—US Preventive Services Task Force." January 2016. uspreventiveservicestaskforce.org/Page/Document /UpdateSummaryFinal/breast-cancer-screening1.

Fingarette, Herbert. *The Meaning of Criminal Insanity.* Berkeley: University of California Press, 1974.

"Food as Punishment: Giving U.S. Inmates 'The Loaf' Persists." NPR, January 2, 2014. npr.org/sections/thesalt/2014/01/02/256605441/punishing-inmates-with -the-loaf-persists-in-the-u-s.

Ford, Matt. "The Reckoning over Young Prisoners Serving Life Without Parole?" *Atlantic,* July 14, 2017. theatlantic.com/politics/archive/2017/07/juvenile-life -without-parole/533157/.

————. "Invoking Kalief Browder, Justice Kennedy Denounces Solitary Confinement." *Atlantic,* June 18, 2015. theatlantic.com/politics/archive/2015/06 /kalief-browder-justice-kennedy-solitary-confinement/396320/.

Fortin, Jacey. "Can Felons Vote? It Depends on the State." *New York Times,* April 21, 2018. nytimes.com/2018/04/21/us/felony-voting-rights-law.html.

Foucault, Michel. *Discipline and Punish: The Birth of the Prison.* New York: Vintage Books, 1995.

Gabbard, Glen O. *Psychodynamic Psychiatry in Clinical Practice,* 4th ed. Washington, DC: American Psychiatric Publishing, 2005.

Garcia, Sandra E. "Ordeal of Woman Who Gave Birth in Florida Jail Cell Prompts Internal Investigation." *New York Times*, May 7, 2019. nytimes.com/2019/05/07/us /woman-gives-birth-jail-cell.html.

Garcia-Navarro, Lulu, and Carrie Johnson. "This Week on The Call In: Criminal Justice Reform." NPR, May 21, 2017. npr.org/2017/05/21/529364464/this-week -on-the-call-in-criminal-justice-reform.

Gawande, Atul. "Is Long-Term Solitary Confinement Torture?" *New Yorker*, March 30, 2009. newyorker.com/magazine/2009/03/30/hellhole.

Georgia Department of Corrections. "Fact Sheet: Sentencing Legislation 2019. Criminal Justice Reform House Bill 1176." dcor.state.ga.us/sites/default/files /Sentencing%20Legislation.pdf.

Gilmore, Ruth Wilson. *Golden Gulag: Prisons, Surplus, Crisis, and Opposition in Globalizing California*. Berkeley: University of California Press, 2007.

Gilson, Dave. "What We Know About Violence in America's Prisons." *Mother Jones*. Crime and Justice. July/August 2016. motherjones.com/politics/2016/06/attacks -and-assaults-behind-bars-cca-private-prisons/.

Glaze, Lauren, and Laura Maruschak. "Parents in Prison and Their Minor Children." Bureau of Justice Statistics Special Report, March 30, 2010. bjs.gov /content/pub/pdf/pptmc.pdf.

Goffman, Erving. *Asylums: Essays on the Social Situation of Mental Patients and Other Inmates*. New York: Anchor, 1990.

Goode, Erica. "Solitary Confinement: Punished for Life." *New York Times*, August 3, 2015. nytimes.com/2015/08/04/health/solitary-confinement-mental -illness.html.

Gotsch, Kara, and Vinay Basti. "Capitalizing on Mass Incarceration: U.S. Growth in Private Prisons." Sentencing Project. August 2, 2018. sentencingproject .org/publications/capitalizing-on-mass-incarceration-u-s-growth-in-private -prisons/.

Gottschalk, Marie. *Caught: The Prison State and the Lockdown of American Politics*. Princeton, NJ: Princeton University Press, 2015.

Grassian, Stuart. "Psychiatric Effects of Solitary Confinement." *Washington University Journal of Law & Policy* 22 (January 2006): 60.

———. "Psychopathological Effects of Solitary Confinement." *American Journal of Psychiatry* 140, no. 11 (November 1983): 1450–54. doi.org/10.1176/ajp.140.11.1450.

Grassian, Stuart, and Nancy Friedman. "Effects of Sensory Deprivation in Psychiatric Seclusion and Solitary Confinement." *International Journal of Law and Psychiatry* 8, no. 1 (1986): 49–65. doi.org/10.1016/0160-2527(86)90083-X.

Guenther, Lisa. *Solitary Confinement: Social Death and Its Afterlives.* Minneapolis: University of Minnesota Press, 2013.

———. "The Living Death of Solitary Confinement." *Opinionator* (blog), August 26, 2012. opinionator.blogs.nytimes.com/2012/08/26/the-living-death-of-solitary -confinement/.

Gunderson, E. K. Eric. "Emotional Symptoms in Extremely Isolated Groups." *Archives of General Psychiatry* 9 (1963): 362–68.

———. *Human Adaptability to Antarctic Conditions.* Antarctic Research Series, vol. 22. Washington, DC: American Geophysical Union, 1974.

Gunderson, E. K. Eric, and Paul D. Nelson. "Adaptation of Small Groups to Extreme Environments." *Aerospace Medicine* 34, no. 12 (1963): 1111–15.

Hager, Eli. "Six States Where Felons Can't Get Food Stamps." Marshall Project, February 4, 2016. themarshallproject.org/2016/02/04/six-states-where-felons-can -t-get-food-stamps.

Hall, Jerome. *Factors Used to Increase the Susceptibility of Individuals to Forceful Indoctrination.* Hove, UK: Brunner-Routledge, 1967.

Haney, Craig. "Infamous Punishment: The Psychological Consequences of Isolation." *National Prison Project Journal* 8, no. 2 (Spring 1993): 3–7.

Hare, Robert D. "Psychopathy and Antisocial Personality Disorder: A Case of Diagnostic Confusion." *Psychiatric Times*, February 1, 1996. psychiatrictimes.com /psychopathy-and-antisocial-personality-disorder-case-diagnostic-confusion.

Harlow, H. F., R. O. Dodsworth, and M. K. Harlow. "Total Social Isolation in Monkeys." *Proceedings of the National Academy of Sciences of the United States of America* 54, no. 1 (July 1965): 90–97.

Harlow, H. F., and S. J. Suomi. "Induced Depression in Monkeys." *Behavioral Biology* 12, no. 3 (November 1974): 273–96.

Harris, Kamala, and Rand Paul, "To Shrink Jails, Let's Reform Bail." *New York Times*, July 20, 2017. nytimes.com/2017/07/20/opinion/kamala-harris-and-rand -paul-lets-reform-bail.html.

Heard-Garris, Nia, Tyler N. A. Winkelman, Hwajung Choi, Alex K. Miller, Kristin Kan, Rebecca Shlafer, and Matthew M. Davis. "Health Care Use and Health.

Behaviors Among Young Adults with History of Parental Incarceration." *Pediatrics* 142, no. 3 (September 1, 2018). e20174314. doi.org/10.1542/peds.2017–4314.

Herman, Christine. "Most Inmates with Mental Illness Still Wait for Decent Care." NPR, February 3, 2019. npr.org/sections/health-shots/2019/02/03/690872394 /most-inmates-with-mental-illness-still-wait-for-decent-care.

Hinton, Elizabeth. "Turn Prisons into Colleges." *New York Times*, March 6, 2018. nytimes.com/2018/03/06/opinion/prisons-colleges-education.html.

"History of Racial Injustice: Public Spectacle Lynchings." Equal Justice Initiative, February 14, 2018. eji.org/history-racial-injustice-public-spectacle-lynchings.

Høidal, Are. "Normality Behind the Walls: Examples from Halden Prison," *Federal Sentencing Reporter* 31, no. 1 (October 1, 2018): 58–66. doi.org/10.1525/fsr.2018.31.1.58.

Hollis, F., C. Isgor, and M. Kabbaj. "The Consequences of Adolescent Chronic Unpredictable Stress Exposure on Brain and Behavior." *Neuroscience* 249 (September 26, 2013): 232–41. doi.org/10.1016/j.neuroscience.2012.09.018.

"How Norway Turns Criminals into Good Neighbours." BBC News, July 7, 2019. bbc.com/news/stories-48885846.

"I Did It Norway." Marshall Project, November 1, 2017. themarshallproject.org /2017/10/31/i-did-it-norway.

In the Matter of Jehan Abdur-Raheem, Appellant, v. Louis Mann, as Superintendent of Shawangunk Correctional Facility, et al., Respondents. February 14, 1995. law.cornell.edu /nyctap/I95_0022.htm.

Ingraham, Merle R., and David M. Moriarty. "A Contribution to the Understanding of the Ganser Syndrome." *Comprehensive Psychiatry* 8, no. 1 (February 1, 1967): 35–44. doi.org/10.1016/S0010-440X(67)80012-9.

"Inside Mississippi's Notorious Parchman Prison." *PBS NewsHour,* January 29, 2018. pbs.org/newshour/arts/inside-mississippis-notorious-parchman-prison.

Ives, George. *A History of Penal Methods: Criminals, Witches, Lunatics*. Montclair, NJ: Patterson Smith, 1970.

Jenkins, Malcolm (@malcolmjenkins). "Before we enjoy this game let's take some time to ponder that more than 60% of the prison population are people of color. The NFL is made up of 70% African Americans. What you witness on the field does not represent the reality of everyday America. We are the anomalies." Twitter, August 9, 2018. twitter.com/malcolmjenkins/status/1027667736095322113?lang=en.

Johnson, Carla K. "Experts: Mental Illness Not Main Driver of Mass Shootings." AP News, August 5, 2019. apnews.com/b8ce29d88543479bbd4894f5a39cc686.

Johnson, Matt. "The Super-Lux Super Max." *Foreign Policy* (blog), July 26, 2011. foreignpolicy.com/slideshow/the-super-lux-super-max/.

Johnston, Norman Bruce, Kenneth Finkel, and Jeffrey A. Cohen. *Eastern State Penitentiary: Crucible of Good Intentions*. Philadelphia: Philadelphia Museum of Art for the Eastern State Penitentiary Task Force of the Preservation Coalition of Greater Philadelphia, 1994.

"Judge: Alabama's Prison System Violates Eighth Amendment, 'Deliberately Indifferent' to Mental Health of People in Solitary Confinement." Southern Poverty Law Center, February 12, 2019. splcenter.org/news/2019/02/11/judge -alabama%E2%80%99s-prison-system-violates-eighth-amendment-%E2%80 %9Cdeliberately-indifferent%E2%80%9D-mental.

Kaba, Fatos, Andrea Lewis, Sarah Glowa-Kollisch, James Hadler, David Lee, Howard Alper, Daniel Selling, Ross MacDonald, Angela Solimo, Amanda Parsons, and Homer Venters. "Solitary Confinement and Risk of Self-Harm Among Jail Inmates." *American Journal of Public Health* 104, no. 3 (March 2014): 442–47. doi.org /10.2105/AJPH.2013.301742.

Kohut, Heinz. *The Analysis of the Self*. New York: International University Press, 1971.

———. *How Does Analysis Cure?* Chicago: University of Chicago Press, 1984.

Kristof, Nicholas. "Imprisoned for Trying to Save His Son." *New York Times*, May 4, 2019. nytimes.com/2019/05/04/opinion/sunday/prison-mass-incarceration-trump .html.

Kupers, Terry Allen. *Prison Madness: The Mental Health Crisis Behind Bars and What We Must Do About It*. San Francisco: Jossey-Bass, 1999.

Kushner, Rachel. "Is Prison Necessary? Ruth Wilson Gilmore Might Change Your Mind." *New York Times Magazine*, April 17, 2019. nytimes.com/2019/04/17/magazine /prison-abolition-ruth-wilson-gilmore.html.

LaGorce, Tammy. "As 'Ban the Box' Spreads, Private Employers Still Have Questions." *New York Times*, November 22, 2017. nytimes.com/2017/11/22/business /small-business-criminal-record.html.

Lambert, Jonathan. "Pregnant Behind Bars: What We Do and Don't Know About Pregnancy and Incarceration." NPR, March 21, 2019. npr.org/sections/health-shots /2019/03/21/705587775/pregnant-behind-bars-what-we-do-and-dont-know-about -pregnancy-and-incarceration.

Leiderman, P. Herbert. "Man Alone." *Sensory Deprivation and Behavioral Change* 16, no. 1 (1962).

"Letter from Paul Revere to Jeremy Belknap, circa 1798." Massachusetts Historical Society Collections Online. Accessed August 14, 2019. masshist.org /database/99.

Liptak, Adam. "Illegal Globally, Bail for Profit Remains in U.S." *New York Times*, January 29, 2008. nytimes.com/2008/01/29/us/29bail.html.

"List of Countries by Personal Income Tax Rate." Trading Economics, n.d. Accessed September 18, 2019. tradingeconomics.com/country-list/personal -income-tax-rate.

Maass, Dave. "Hundreds of South Carolina Inmates Sent to Solitary Confinement Over Facebook." Electronic Frontier Foundation, February 12, 2015. eff.org /deeplinks/2015/02/hundreds-south-carolina-inmates-sent-solitary-confinement -over-facebook.

Malmquist, Carl P. *Homicide: A Psychiatric Perspective.* Washington, DC: American Psychiatric Publishers, 2006.

Martin, Andrew J. "The Bail System and Its Injustices." Letter to the Editor, *New York Times*, July 30, 2017. nytimes.com/2017/07/30/opinion/the-bail-system-and-its -injustices.html.

Matsumoto, K., B. Cai, T. Satoh, H. Ohta, and H. Watanabe. "Desipramine Enhances Isolation-Induced Aggressive Behavior in Mice." *Pharmacology, Biochemistry, and Behavior* 39, no. 1 (May 1991): 167–70. doi.org/10.1016/0091 -3057(91)90416-y.

McKinley Jr., James C. "In Rape Case at Rikers: Did Guards Turn a Blind Eye?" *New York Times*, September 21, 2017. nytimes.com/2017/09/21/nyregion/rikers-rape -case-guards.html.

McKinney, William T., Stephen J. Suomi, and Harry F. Harlow. "Vertical-Chamber Confinement of Juvenile-Age Rhesus Monkeys: A Study in Experimental Psychopathology." *Archives of General Psychiatry* 26, no. 3 (March 1, 1972): 223–28. doi .org/10.1001/archpsyc.1972.01750210031006.

Mohammed, A. H., S. W. Zhu, S. Darmopil, J. Hjerling-Leffler, P. Ernfors, B. Winblad, M. C. Diamond, P. S. Eriksson, and N. Bogdanovic. "Environmental Enrichment and the Brain." *Progress in Brain Research* 138 (2002): 109–33. doi.org /10.1016/S0079-6123(02)38074-9.

Mullin, C. S., and H. J. Connery. "Psychological Study at an Antarctic IGY Station." *United States Armed Forces Medical Journal* 10, no. 3 (March 1959): 290–96.

Mulvaney, Katie. "Mentally Ill Inmates Face Solitary Confinement in R.I. Prisons." *Providence Journal*, January 5, 2017. providencejournal.com/news/20170105/mentally -ill-inmates-face-solitary-confinement-in-ri-prisons.

———. "R.I. Corrections Officials to Examine Their Use of Solitary Confinement." *Providence Journal*, March 9, 2017. providencejournal.com/news /20170309/ri-corrections-officials-to-examine-their-use-of-solitary-confinement.

"Nashville, Tennessee, Population 2019." World Population Review. worldpopulationreview.com/us-cities/nashville-population/.

National Collaborating Centre for Mental Health (UK). "Interventions for People with Antisocial Personality Disorder and Associated Symptoms and Behaviours." NICE Clinical Guidelines, No. 77. British Psychological Society, 2010. ncbi.nlm .nih.gov/books/NBK55350/.

Nelson, Charles A., Charles H. Zeanah, and Nathan A. Fox. "How Early Experience Shapes Human Development: The Case of Psychosocial Deprivation." *Neural Plasticity* 2019 (January 15, 2019). doi.org/10.1155/2019/1676285.

Nesbit, Ariana, and Hal S. Wortzel. "Correctional Officer Suicide: An Overlooked Problem." *American Academy of Psychiatry and the Law Newsletter* 43, no. 2 (April 2018).

New York Times Editorial Board. "A Bad Idea to Cut Prison Visitations." *New York Times*, March 28, 2017. nytimes.com/2017/03/28/opinion/a-bad-idea-to-cut-prison -visitations.html.

———. "At Long Last, a Measure of Justice for Some Drug Offenders." *New York Times*, August 25, 2019. nytimes.com/2019/06/11/opinion/first-step-act-drug -offenders.html.

———. "Cruel Isolation of Prisoners." *New York Times*, August 1, 2011. nytimes .com/2011/08/02/opinion/cruel-isolation-of-prisoners.html.

———. "Florida's 1.5 Million Missing Voters." *New York Times*, January 2, 2018. nytimes.com/2018/01/02/opinion/florida-missing-voters.html.

———. "Justice at Last for the Youngest Inmates?" *New York Times*, November 20, 2017. nytimes.com/2017/11/20/opinion/life-sentence-youth-parole.html.

Neyfakh, Leon. "Cory Booker and Newt Gingrich Want to Redefine What Is Considered a 'Violent' Crime." *Slate*, March 26, 2015. slate.com/news-and-politics /2015/03/bipartisan-summit-on-criminal-justice-reform-cory-booker-and-newt -gingrich-want-to-redefine-what-is-considered-a-violent-crime.html.

Nietzsche, Friedrich. *Beyond Good and Evil/On the Genealogy of Morality*. In *The Complete Works of Friedrich Nietzsche*, vol. 8. Stanford, CA: Stanford University Press, 2014.

Nitsche, Paul H., Karl Willmanns, Frances Merriman Barnes, and Bernard Glueck. *The History of the Prison Psychoses*. Nervous and Mental Disease Monograph Series, no. 13. New York: Journal of Nervous and Mental Disease Publishing Company, 1912.

Nolan, Dan, and Chris Amico. "Solitary by the Numbers." *Frontline*, April 18, 2017. apps.frontline.org/solitary-by-the-numbers/index.html.

"'No One Feels Safe Here': Life in Alabama's Prisons." *New York Times*, April 29, 2019. nytimes.com/2019/04/29/us/alabama-prison-inmates.html.

Norden—Nordic Prisons, The. YouTube video (excerpt). October 13, 2014. youtube .com/watch?v=2g56susrNQY#t=201.

"Northern Correctional Institution Administrative Segregation Program," n.d. Accessed January 3, 2020. law.umich.edu/special/policyclearinghouse/Documents /Description%20of%20Northern%20Program%20ocr.pdf.

Norwegian Correctional Service. "Operations Strategy 2014–2018." April 8, 2014. webcache.googleusercontent.com/search?q=cache:TdSS5l-y1eYJ:kriminalomsorgen .custompublish.com/getfile.php/2766216.823.fvprryqpxf/Operations%2BStrategy %2B2014-2018.pdf+&cd=1&hl=en&ct=clnk&gl=us&client=safari.

Norwegian Ministry of Justice and the Police. "Punishment That Works—Less Crime—A Safe Society: Report to the Storting on the Norwegian Correctional Services (English Summary)." *Federal Sentencing Reporter* 31, no. 1 (October 1, 2018): 52–57. doi.org/10.1525/fsr.2018.31.1.52.

Nussbaum, Martha Craven. *Anger and Forgiveness: Resentment, Generosity, Justice*. New York: Oxford University Press, 2016.

"On Criminal Justice, Sessions Is Returning DOJ to the Failed Policies of the Past." *National Review* (blog), September 12, 2017. nationalreview.com/2017/09/jeff -sessions-tough-crime-policies-already-tried-failed/.

"Oslo Population 2019." n.d. Accessed August 15, 2019. World Population Review. worldpopulationreview.com/world-cities/oslo-population/.

"Paying the Price for Solitary Confinement." PrisonLegalNews.org, n.d. Accessed January 3, 2020. prisonlegalnews.org/media/publications/Paying%20the%20Price %20for%20Solitary%20Confinement%20ACLU%20Factsheet%202015.pdf.

"Pennsylvania System: Penology." *Encyclopaedia Britannica*, n.d. Accessed August 14, 2019. britannica.com/topic/Pennsylvania-system.

Petersilia, Joan. "Beyond the Prison Bubble." National Institute of Justice, November 2, 2011. nij.ojp.gov/topics/articles/beyond-prison-bubble.

Petterui, Amanda. "Finding Direction: Expanding Criminal Justice Options by Considering Policies of Other Nations." Justice Policy Institute, April 2011. justicepolicy.org/uploads/justicepolicy/documents/sentencing.pdf.

Pompili, Maurizio, and Andrea Fiorillo. "Aggression and Impulsivity in Schizophrenia." *Psychiatric Times*, July 23, 2015. psychiatrictimes.com/trauma-and -violence/aggression-and-impulsivity-schizophrenia.

Press, Eyal. "Madness." *New Yorker*, April 25, 2016. newyorker.com/magazine/2016 /05/02/the-torturing-of-mentally-ill-prisoners.

"Presumption of Guilt: The Global Overuse of Pretrial Detention." Open Society Justice Initiative, 2014. justiceinitiative.org/uploads/de4c18f8-ccc1-4eba-9374 -e5c850a07efd/presumption-guilt-09032014.pdf.

Quay, Herbert C. "Psychopathic Personality as Pathological Stimulation-Seeking." *American Journal of Psychiatry* 122, no. 2 (August 1, 1965): 180–83. doi.org/10.1176 /ajp.122.2.180.

Rabuy, Bernadette. "Pretrial Detention Costs $13.6 Billion Each Year." Prison Policy Initiative, February 7, 2017. prisonpolicy.org/blog/2017/02/07 /pretrial_cost/.

Raemisch, Rick. "My Night in Solitary." *New York Times*, February 21, 2014. nytimes .com/2014/02/21/opinion/my-night-in-solitary.html.

Rathbone, Cristina. *A World Apart: Women, Prison, and Life Behind Bars.* New York: Random House, 2006.

Rattan, Aneeta, Cynthia S. Levine, Carol S. Dweck, and Jennifer L. Eberhardt. "Race and the Fragility of the Legal Distinction Between Juveniles and Adults." *PLOS One* 7, no. 5 (May 23, 2012): e36680. doi.org/10.1371/journal .pone.0036680.

"Recidivism." National Institute of Justice, n.d. Accessed August 14, 2019. nij.gov:443/topics/corrections/recidivism/pages/welcome.aspx.

Reinberg, Steven. "Teens' Odds for Suicide May Triple While in Jail: Study." HealthDay.com, January 24, 2019. consumer.healthday.com/general-health -information-16/suicide-health-news-646/teens-odds-for-suicide-may-triple-while -in-jail-study-741928.html.

Reiter, Keramet. "The Social Cost of Solitary Confinement." *Time*, October 21, 2016. time.com/4540112/the-social-cost-of-solitary-confinement/.

"Resolution 70/175. United Nations Standard Minimum Rules for the Treatment of Prisoners (the Nelson Mandela Rules)." U.N. General Assembly, December 17, 2015. undocs.org/A/RES/70/175.

Rhode Island Department of Corrections: Institutions & Operations: Facilities: High Security Center. n.d. Accessed August 14, 2019. doc.ri.gov/institutions /facilities/hsc.php.

Rhode Island Department of Corrections: Institutions & Operations: Facilities: John J. Moran Medium Security Facility. n.d. Accessed August 14, 2019. doc.ri.gov /institutions/facilities/moran.php.

Robertson, Campbell. "An Alabama Prison's Unrelenting Descent into Violence." *New York Times*, March 28, 2017. nytimes.com/2017/03/28/us/alabama-prison -violence.html.

Robertson, Joe. "Mental Health Crises Land on Specially Trained Officers." *Washington Times*, May 13, 2016. washingtontimes.com/news/2016/may/13 /mental-health-crises-land-on-specially-trained-off/.

Robles-Ramamurthy, Barbara, and Clarence Watson. "Examining Racial Disparities in Juvenile Justice." *Journal of the American Academy of Psychiatry and the Law Online* 47, no. 1 (March 1, 2019): 48–52. doi.org/10.29158/JAAPL.003828-19.

Roeder, Oliver. "Releasing Drug Offenders Won't End Mass Incarceration." FiveThirtyEight.com, July 17, 2015. fivethirtyeight.com/features/releasing-drug -offenders-wont-end-mass-incarceration/.

Ross, Jeffrey Ian. "Supermax Prisons." *Society* 44, no. 3 (March/April 2007): 60–64. convictcriminology.org/pdf/jiross/SupermaxPrisons.pdf.

Ross, Rupert. *Returning to the Teachings: Exploring Aboriginal Justice.* Toronto: Penguin Canada, 2006.

Rovner, Josh. "Juvenile Life Without Parole: An Overview." Sentencing Project, July 23, 2019. sentencingproject.org/publications/juvenile-life-without-parole/.

———. "Racial Disparities in Youth Commitments and Arrests." Sentencing Project, April 1, 2016. sentencingproject.org/publications/racial-disparities-in -youth-commitments-and-arrests/.

Rovner, Laura L. "'Everything Is at Stake if Norway Is Sentenced. In That Case, We Have Failed': Solitary Confinement and the 'Hard' Cases in the United States and Norway." *UCLA Criminal Justice Law Review* 1, no. 1; University of Denver Legal Studies Research Paper No. 17-24 (August 22, 2017). ssrn.com/abstract=3024183.

Ruby, Jeff. "Dining Critic Tries Nutraloaf, the Prison Food for Misbehaving Inmates." *Chicago Magazine*, September 2010. chicagomag.com/Chicago-Magazine

/September-2010/Dining-Critic-Tries-Nutraloaf-the-Prison-Food-for
-Misbehaving-Inmates/.

Sahlin, Hanna, Ralf Kuja-Halkola, Johan Bjureberg, Paul Lichtenstein, Yasmina
Molero, Mina Rydell, Erik Hedman, Bo Runeson, Jussi Jokinen, Brjánn Ljótsson,
and Clara Hellner. "Association Between Deliberate Self-Harm and Violent
Criminality." *JAMA Psychiatry* 74, no. 6 (June 2017): 615–21. doi.org/10.1001
/jamapsychiatry.2017.0338.

Sainato, Michael. "Mentally Ill US Prisoner Held in Solitary Lost Ability to Speak,
Lawsuit Alleges." *Guardian*, September 4, 2019. theguardian.com/us-news/2019/sep
/04/virginia-prisons-solitary-confinement-tyquine-lee.

Scherdin, Lill, ed. *Capital Punishment: A Hazard to a Sustainable Criminal Justice System?*
Farnham, Surrey, UK: Ashgate, 2014.

Schlosser, Eric. "The Prison-Industrial Complex." *Atlantic*, December 1, 1998.
theatlantic.com/magazine/archive/1998/12/the-prison-industrial-complex/304669/.

Seierstad, Åsne, and Sarah Death. *One of Us: The Story of Anders Breivik and the
Massacre in Norway.* New York: Farrar, Straus & Giroux, 2015.

Shanahan, Ryan, and Sandra Villalobos Agudelo. "The Family and Recidivism."
American Jails, September/October 2012. prisonpolicy.org/scans/vera/the-family
-and-recidivism.pdf.

Shankar, Vedantam, Parth Shah, Tara Boyle, and Jennifer Schmidt. "Radically
Normal: How Gay Rights Activists Changed the Minds of Their Opponents." NPR,
April 3, 2019. npr.org/2019/04/03/709567750/radically-normal-how-gay-rights
-activists-changed-the-minds-of-their-opponents.

Siegel, Rachel. "8-Year-Old Biracial Boy Was Hanged from Rope by N.H. Teenagers
Because of His Race, Family Says." *Washington Post*, September 13, 2017.
washingtonpost.com/news/morning-mix/wp/2017/09/13/8-year-old-boy-was-hung
-from-rope-by-n-h-teenagers-because-of-his-race-family-says/?outputType=amp.

Simeon, Daphne, Margaret Knutelska, Dorothy Nelson, and Orna Guralnik.
"Feeling Unreal: A Depersonalization Disorder Update of 117 Cases." *Journal of
Clinical Psychiatry* 64, no. 9 (September 2003): 990–97.

Sivilombudsmannen. "Activity Programme and Measures to Combat Isolation."
Sivilombudsmannen.no, April 15, 2016. sivilombudsmannen.no/en/news/prevention
-torture/activity-programme-and-measures-to-combat-isolation/.

———. "The Role of Health Personnel in Treating People Who Are Deprived of
Their Liberty." Sivilombudsmannen.no, April 14, 2016. sivilombudsmannen.no/en
/news/prevention-torture/the-role-of-health-personnel-in-treating-people-who
-are-deprived-of-their-liberty/.

———. "The Use of Coercive Measures During Deprivation of Liberty." Sivilombudsmannen.no, April 14, 2016. sivilombudsmannen.no/en/news /prevention-torture/the-use-of-coercive-measures-during-deprivation-of -liberty/.

Skeem, Jennifer L., Sarah Manchak, and Lina Montoya. "Comparing Public Safety Outcomes for Traditional Probation vs. Specialty Mental Health Probation." *JAMA Psychiatry* 74, no. 9 (September 2017): 942–48. doi.org/10.1001/jamapsychiatry .2017.1384.

Slater, Dashka. "North Dakota's Norway Experiment." *Mother Jones* (blog), July–August 2017. motherjones.com/crime-justice/2017/07/north-dakota-norway -prisons-experiment/.

"Solitary Confinement." MacArthur Justice Center, n.d. Accessed August 15, 2019. macarthurjustice.org/issue/rights-of-the-incarcerated/solitary-confinement/.

"Solitary Confinement of Juvenile Offenders." Juvenile Justice Reform Committee, American Academy of Child & Adolescent Psychiatry. April 2012. aacap.org/aacap /Policy_Statements/2012/Solitary_Confinement_of_Juvenile_Offenders.aspx.

Solomon, Dave. "Sununu Expected to Call for Secure Psychiatric Hospital in Budget Address." *New Hampshire Union Leader,* February 12, 2019. unionleader.com /news/courts/sununu-expected-to-call-for-secure-psychiatric-hospital-in-budget /article_704ecc83-e9db-5684-8294-17db853ffd86.html.

Solomon, Philip, Philip Kubzansky, P. Herbert Leiderman, Jack H. Mendelson, Richard Trumbull, and Donald Wexler, eds. *Sensory Deprivation: An Investigation of Phenomena Suggesting a Revised Concept of the Individual's Response to His Environment.* A Symposium at Harvard Medical School: The President and Fellows of Harvard College, 1961.

Southall, Ashley, and Jan Ransom. "New York City's Young Inmates Are Held in Isolation Upstate, Despite Ban." *New York Times,* July 22, 2018. nytimes.com/2018 /07/22/nyregion/inmate-solitary-young-nyc.html.

Spear, L. P. "The Adolescent Brain and Age-Related Behavioral Manifestations." *Neuroscience & Biobehavioral Reviews* 24, no. 4 (June 1, 2000): 417–63. doi.org/10.1016 /S0149-7634(00)00014-2.

———. "Consequences of Adolescent Use of Alcohol and Other Drugs: Studies Using Rodent Models." *Neuroscience and Biobehavioral Reviews* 70 (November 2016): 228–43. doi.org/10.1016/j.neubiorev.2016.07.026.

"SPLC, Victims' Families Demand Comprehensive ADOC Reform as Suicide Toll Increases." Southern Poverty Law Center, February 8, 2019. splcenter.org/news

/2019/02/08/splc-victims%E2%80%99-families-demand-comprehensive-adoc
-reform-suicide-toll-increases.

Stamm, Alex. "15-Year-Old Gets Six Life Sentences?" ACLU, November 22, 2013.
aclu.org/blog/criminal-law-reform/15-year-old-gets-six-life-sentences.

"STDs in Adolescents and Young Adults." Sexually Transmitted Diseases
Surveillance 2017. Centers for Disease Control and Prevention, January 11, 2019.
cdc.gov/std/stats17/adolescents.htm.

Steinberg, Laurence. "Adolescent Development and Juvenile Justice." *Annual Review
of Clinical Psychology* 5 (2009): 459–85. doi.org/10.1146/annurev.clinpsy.032408.153603.

Stevenson, Bryan. *Just Mercy: A Story of Justice and Redemption.* New York: Spiegel &
Grau, 2015.

———. "A Presumption of Guilt." *New York Review of Books,* July 13, 2017. nybooks
.com/articles/2017/07/13/presumption-of-guilt/.

Subramanian, Ram, and Alison Shames. "Sentencing and Prison Practices in
Germany and the Netherlands: Implications for the United States (Vera Institute of
Justice, October 2013)." *Federal Sentencing Reporter* 27, no. 1 (October 2014): 33–45. doi
.org/10.1525/fsr.2014.27.1.33.

Sullivan, Laura. "Timeline: Solitary Confinement in U.S. Prisons." NPR, July 26,
2006. npr.org/templates/story/story.php?storyId=5579901.

Sutker, Patricia B., Daniel K. Winstead, Z. Harry Galina, and Albert N. Allain.
"Cognitive Deficits and Psychopathology Among Former Prisoners of War and
Combat Veterans of the Korean Conflict." *American Journal of Psychiatry* 148 (1991):
67–72.

"Third Inmate Death in 10 Days at ADOC Facilities in Elmore County." WSFA
News, February 27, 2017; updated August 12, 2017. wsfa.com/story/34609657
/third-inmate-death-in-10-days-at-adoc-facilities-in-elmore-county.

Thompson, Don. "California Examines Prison Guards' High Suicide Rate."
Associated Press, January 9, 2018. apnews.com/96fdc27aea0c401ea590b1c74162c43a.

Toch, Hans. "Effective Treatment for Disturbed Violent Prisoners?" In *Violence
Among the Mentally Ill: Effective Treatments and Management Strategies,* ed. Sheilagh
Hodgins. NATO Science Series. Dordrecht: Springer Netherlands, 2000, 313–37.
doi.org/10.1007/978-94-011-4130-7_17.

Tolan, Casey. "Inside the Most Humane Prison in the World, Where Inmates Have
Flatscreen TVs and Cells Are Like Dorms." *Splinter,* September 14, 2016.
splinternews.com/inside-the-most-humane-prison-in-the-world-where-inmat
-1793861894.

Torrey, E. Fuller. *American Psychosis: How the Federal Government Destroyed the Mental Illness Treatment System.* New York: Oxford University Press, 2014.

"Troubling Spread of Plea-Bargaining from America to the World, The." *Economist,* November 9, 2017. economist.com/international/2017/11/09/the-troubling-spread -of-plea-bargaining-from-america-to-the-world.

Tyndel, Milo. "Some Aspects of the Ganser State." *Journal of Mental Science* 102, no. 427 (April 1956): 324–29.

United States Government Accountability Office. "Bureau of Prisons: Improvements Needed in Bureau of Prisons' Monitoring and Evaluation of Impact of Segregated Housing." May 2013. gao.gov/assets/660/654349.pdf.

University of Texas at Austin. "Risks of Harm from Spanking Confirmed by Analysis of 5 Decades of Research." ScienceDaily, April 25, 2016. sciencedaily.com /releases/2016/04/160425143106.htm.

Uy, Jessica P., and Adriana Galván. "Acute Stress Increases Risky Decisions and Dampens Prefrontal Activation Among Adolescent Boys." *NeuroImage* 146 (February 1, 2017): 679–89. doi.org/10.1016/j.neuroimage.2016.08.067.

Wacquant, Loic. "From Slavery to Mass Incarceration." *New Left Review* 13 (January– February 2002). newleftreview.org/issues/II13/articles/loic-wacquant-from -slavery-to-mass-incarceration.

Wan, William, and Lindsey Bever. "Are Video Games or Mental Illness Causing America's Mass Shootings? No, Research Shows." *Washington Post,* August 5, 2019. washingtonpost.com/health/2019/08/05/is-mental-illness-causing-americas-mass -shootings-no-research-shows/.

Washburn, D. A., and D. M. Rumbaugh. "Impaired Performance from Brief Social Isolation of Rhesus Monkeys (Macaca Mulatta): A Multiple Video-Task Assessment." *Journal of Comparative Psychology* 105, no. 2 (June 1991): 145–51.

Washington Post Editorial Board. "A Much-Needed Wake-up Call on Solitary Confinement." *Washington Post,* July 1, 2015. washingtonpost.com/opinions /a-wake-up-call-on-solitary-confinement/2015/07/01/86117602-1aa3-11e5-ab92 -c75ae6ab94b5_story.html.

Wattley, Keith. "Trump's Criminal Justice Reform Is a Step in the Wrong Direction." *New York Times,* December 4, 2018. nytimes.com/2018/12/04/opinion /trump-criminal-justice-reform.html.

Weisberg, Robert, Debbie A. Mukamal, and Jordan D. Segall. "Life in Limbo: An Examination of Parole Release for Prisoners Serving Life Sentences with the Possibility of Parole in California." Stanford Law School, Stanford Criminal Justice

Center. September 2011. law.stanford.edu/wp-content/uploads/sites/default/files /publication/259833/doc/slspublic/SCJC%20Lifer%20Parole%20Release %20Sept%202011.pdf.

Whitaker, Thomas Bartlett. "A Nothing Would Do as Well." PEN America, July 7, 2014. pen.org/a-nothing-would-do-as-well/.

Williams, Timothy. "He Says He Got Away with 90 Murders. Now He's Confessing to Them All." *New York Times*, November 26, 2018. nytimes.com/2018/11/26/us /samuel-little-serial-killer-murderer.html.

Wolff, Nancy, and Jing Shi. "Contextualization of Physical and Sexual Assault in Male Prisons: Incidents and Their Aftermath." *Journal of Correctional Health Care: The Official Journal of the National Commission on Correctional Health Care* 15, no. 1 (January 2009): 58–82. doi.org/10.1177/1078345808326622.

Wright, C. D. *One Big Self: An Investigation*. Port Townsend, WA: Copper Canyon Press, 2007.

Wright, Morgan W., George C. Sisler, and Joanne Chylinski. "Personality Factors in the Selection of Civilians for Isolated Northern Stations." *Journal of Applied Psychology* 47, no. 1 (1963): 24–29. doi.org/10.1037/h0042053.

Wright, Richard. *American Hunger*. New York: HarperCollins, 1982.

Yale Visual Law Project. "The Worst of the Worst: Portrait of a Supermax." Vimeo. 2012. vimeo.com/54826024.

"York Correctional Institution Inmate Handbook," September 30, 2010. law.umich .edu/special/policyclearinghouse/Documents/CT%20-%20Women%27s %20Facility%20Handbook.pdf.

Zimbardo, P. G., S. M. Andersen, and L. G. Kabat. "Induced Hearing Deficit Generates Experimental Paranoia." *Science* 212, no. 4502 (June 26, 1981): 1529–31. doi.org/10.1126/science.7233242.

Ziskind, Eugene. "Isolation Stress in Medical and Mental Illness." *JAMA* 168, no. 11 (November 15, 1958): 1427–31. jamanetwork.com/journals/jama/article -abstract/324897.

Zoukis, Christopher. "Report Documents U.S. Recidivism Rates for Federal Prisoners." *Huffington Post*, March 25, 2016. huffpost.com/entry/report-documents -us-recid_b_9542312.

Zubek, John Peter, ed. *Sensory Deprivation: Fifteen Years of Research*. Century Psychology Series. New York: Appleton-Century-Crofts, 1969.

INDEX